Decadent Aesthetics and the Acrobat in Fin-de-Siècle France

In his discussion of clowns in nineteenth-century French painting, from Jean-Léon Gérôme's 1857 *La Sortie du bal masqué* to Georges Rouault, art historian Francis Haskell wondered why they are so sad. The myth of the sad clown as an allegory for the unappreciated artist found echoes in the work of literary counterparts like Charles Baudelaire and his "Vieux saltimbanque," who seeks in vain a responsive public. For some, the attraction of the acrobatic clown for the creative imagination may have been his ability to embody the plight of the artist: these *artistes* generally led an ambulatory and uncertain existence. Other artists and writers, however, particularly the Decadents, perceived in the circus acrobat – including the acrobatic clown – a conceptual and performative tool for liberating their points of view from the prison-house of aesthetic convention. If authors' protagonists were themselves sometimes failures, their aesthetic innovations often produced exhilarating artistic triumphs. Among the works examined in this study are the circus posters of Jules Chéret; Thomas Couture's Pierrot and Harlequin paintings; Honoré Daumier's *saltimbanque* paintings; Edgar Degas's *Miss Lala au Cirque Fernando*; Édouard Manet's *Un bar au Folies-Bergère*; the pantomimes of the Hanlon-Lees troupe; and novels, short stories, and poems by Théodore de Banville, Edmond de Goncourt, J. K. Huysmans, Gustave Kahn, Jules Laforgue, Catulle Mendès, Octave Mirbeau, Jean Richepin, Edouard Rod, and Marcel Schwob.

Jennifer Forrest is Professor of French at Texas State University. She is the editor of *The Legend Returns and Dies Harder Another Day: Essays on Film Series* (McFarland, 2008) and co-editor of *Dead Ringers: The Remake in Theory and Practice* (SUNY, 2002).

Routledge Studies in Nineteenth-Century Literature

47 **Constructions of Agency in American Literature on the War of Independence**
War as Action, 1775–1860
Martin Holtz

48 **Neglected American Women Writers of the Long Nineteenth Century**
Progressive Pioneers
Edited by Verena Laschinger and Sirpa Salenius

49 **W.S. Gilbert and the History of Comedy**
The Progress of Fun
Richard Moore

50 **The Nineteenth-Century French Short Story**
Masterpieces in Miniature
Allan H. Pasco

51 **Incorporation, Authorship, and Anglo-American Literature (1815–1918)**
Jasper Schelstraete

52 **Nineteenth-Century Southern Women Writers**
Grace King and Modernism
Edited by Melissa Walker Heidari and Brigitte Zauggsss

53 **Decadent Aesthetics and the Acrobat in Fin-de-Siècle France**
Jennifer Forrest

For more information about this series, please visit: https://www.routledge.com

Decadent Aesthetics and the Acrobat in Fin-de-Siècle France

Jennifer Forrest

Routledge
Taylor & Francis Group
NEW YORK AND LONDON

First published 2020
by Routledge
52 Vanderbilt Avenue, New York, NY 10017

and by Routledge
2 Park Square, Milton Park, Abingdon, Oxon, OX14 4RN

Routledge is an imprint of the Taylor & Francis Group, an informa business

Library of Congress Cataloging-in-Publication Data
A catalog record for this title has been requested

ISBN: 978-0-367-35814-3 (hbk)
ISBN: 978-0-429-34196-0 (ebk)

Typeset in Sabon
by codeMantra

Contents

List of Figures

Acknowledgments

My sincerest thanks to my wonderful friends and colleagues, who encouraged me to write this book over these many years: Elizabeth Emery, Marc Smeets, Julia Przyboś, Allan Pasco, Dominique Bauer, Rae Beth Gordon, Hélène Marquié, and Michelle Cheyne. If I left Robert Ziegler out of that list, it is to single him out for special recognition: he read each chapter of this work and sent me invaluable comments and revision recommendations.

My education in the nineteenth-century circus in France owes a great deal to a summer spent in Paris archives in 1998. I received immeasurable assistance from André Thill, Elisabeth Peyré, Emmanuel Roy, Jacqueline Christophe, and Aroquiadasse Adéikalam at the Musée des Arts et Traditions Populaires; from Anita Mengozzi and Dominique Bergougnian at the Bibliothèque de l'Arsenal; from Mmes Billaud and Morlet of the Bibliothèque Historique de la Ville de Paris; and from the print department of the Bibliothèque nationale de France.

I would also like to thank those who made obtaining reproductions a pleasant process: Erin Mazzei and Todd Peters, digital librarians at Texas State University, Flore Campestrini of the Musée des Arts Décoratifs, Raven Amiro of the Musée des Beaux-Arts du Canada, Danielle Currie of the Vancouver Art Gallery, Jennifer Camilleri and Susana Vásquéz Fernández of the Royal Academy of Arts, Joyce Faust of Art Resources, Camilla Marking of the National Gallery, Florence Le Bègue of the Oskar Reinhart Collection "Am Römerholz," Jack Glover Gunn of the Victoria & Albert Museum, Michael and Judy Steinhardt, Jacob Daugherty of Bridgeman Images, and Rob Lees of Heritage Digital Ltd.

I also thank the journal *Dix-Neuf* for permission to reprint "Clownesque Poetics in Jules Laforgue's *Moralités légendaires*," *Dix-neuf* 20.1 (2016), 81–96. This article appears as part of Chapter 6.

Introduction

The last half of the nineteenth century represents the height of the circus as an elegant entertainment, doomed to become thereafter associated almost exclusively with the pastimes of the popular classes and children. Patronized assiduously by high society, the bourgeoisie, artists, poets, and novelists, the performance of the circus acrobat offered to creative minds new aesthetic opportunities that challenged conventional concepts of narrative technique, space, time, and identity.

This book explores the practices that some artists, poets, and novelists of late nineteenth century in France adopted in the creation of a modern artistic form as suggested by acrobatic performance. As has persuasively been argued regarding Decadence, what is perhaps most interesting are not the movement's thematic perversions (a privileging of the artificial, a twisted inversion of the values of the dominant narrative mode of Naturalism, overly refined sensibilities), but its aesthetic innovations (semantic instability, narrative fragmentation, *dédoublement*). From literary critic Jean Starobinski, we learn that the space of circus is a threshold separating the possible from the impossible, the real from the unreal, sense from non-sense. On the other side of the threshold lies the world of the paradoxical acrobat, one without constraints on meaning and being, where the inanimate is animate, where gender and race are perceived as their opposites, and where the stupid beast is socially adept. While the acrobats did not specifically recommend themselves to all Decadents, the ambiguities produced by their performance seeped into the movement's imaginary, indicating the threshold through which they, too, must pass in order to expand the boundaries of creativity and transition into the modern era.

Many scholars of French Decadence from the last twenty years have shifted lines of study from an examination of Decadent perversions, excesses, and eccentricities to that of *romanesque* innovation, beginning with *Le Roman célibataire: d'À rebours à Paludes* (1996) by Jean-Pierre Bertrand, Michel Biron, Jacques Dubois, and Jeannine Paque. Despite a staggering number of acrobats and acrobatic references in works from the period, no recent scholar has treated them, however, as anything more than an allegory or theme. While Starobinski's seminal *Portrait de l'artiste en saltimbanque* (1970) does suggest that there is more to the acrobat than analogy in painting, illustration, and literature, and while Louisa E. Jones's invaluable *Sad Clowns and Pale Pierrots: Literature and the Popular Comic Arts in Nineteenth-Century France* (1984) does examine circus and pantomime acrobatic clowns in performance and literature, these studies are at least thirty-five years old. Since then, the general trend has been to confine circus acrobats and pantomime characters to the mediums in which they appear – performance, literature, popular art – or to a specific figure, notably Pierrot.

Jean de Palacio's excellent *Pierrot fin-de-siècle, ou les métamorphoses d'un masque* (1990), for example, deals exclusively with the commedia dell'arte character Pierrot in literature and to a limited degree in illustration. As regards pantomime as a medium whose performers were always clowns (acrobatic to varying degrees), the most significant contributions have been Robert F. Storey's *Pierrot: A Critical History of a Mask* (1978) and his *Pierrots on the Stage of Desire: Nineteenth-Century French Literary Artists and the Comic Pantomime* (1985), both grounded in psychoanalytical methodology, and, again, Jones's *Sad Clowns and Pale Pierrots*. More recently, Gilles Bonnet's *La Pantomime noire, 1836–1896* (2014) and Arnaud Rykner's *Corps obscènes* (2014) have proposed that the medium's effects are at the heart of the major aesthetic considerations that preoccupied nineteenth-century French artists and writers, and are therefore at the forefront of the upheaval that would mark literature in the early twentieth century. While these excellent studies do discuss performance as an effective tool for neutralizing the barriers to creation erected by literary convention (in this case, Realism and Naturalism), they only address in passing the holistic vision at the center of my project: the close family ties of pantomime and circus, the links between the novel, poetry, and art, and most notably the ways in which fin-de-siècle writers and artists found exhilarating liberation in adapting to their practices the paradoxes offered by the acrobatic body in performance. I identify the *funambule* – acrobatic clown *and* pantomimist, tightrope walker, trapezist, equestrienne, and more – as an important performative device for many artists and authors creating during the Decadence.[1] These artists and authors sought to replicate through their work the disruptive, disorienting, and ultimately liberating sensations that one experiences during acrobatic performance.

My book integrates these multiple threads – Decadent stylistic and aesthetic innovation; the pantomimist as a confrère of the acrobatic circus clown; the acrobat as performative device for stylistic and aesthetic change in literature, pantomime, painting, and popular art; and the semiotics of the circus – in order to account for the fin-de-siècle fascination with acrobats. My theoretical approach has been shaped significantly by circus semiotics in the works of Paul Bouissac and Yoram Carmeli.

*

While the title of this book promises to concentrate on the incorporation of *funambulesque* aesthetics into Decadent practices in the fin de siècle, I begin Chapters 1 and 2 in 1857. It was an eventful year for literature with the publication of Théodore de Banville's *Odes funambulesques*, Jules Champfleury's *Réalisme*, Gustave Flaubert's *Madame Bovary*, and Charles Baudelaire's *Les Fleurs du mal*. The public decency trials for the latter two works in particular point to writers pushing aesthetic boundaries. It was a watershed year for art as well. Indeed, while my focus in these chapters is primarily literary, I have chosen to frame my discussion around two paintings representing the same event, a duel in the Bois de Boulogne conducted by participants still wearing their masquerade attire. One painting has enjoyed continued success with the general public for over 150 years, eclipsing the other to this day. Its painter has been largely dismissed until recently as more interested in public accolades and personal affluence than in producing great works of art. The latter's artist is recognized as a much greater artist who absorbed deeply the tensions that emerged in that year, feeling pulled, like Honoré Daumier, between the straitjacket of the Academy and the will to explore and impose a more personal expression. The new conditions that emerged for artists placed them in the market, a situation to which they responded with the derision of the *funambule*. The *funambule* steps literally and figuratively on the stage at this aesthetic turning point.

In 1972, Francis Haskell cited Jean-Léon Gérôme's *La Sortie du bal masqué* (1857) as launching the cycle of representations of the artist as sad clown in art and literature in the last half of the nineteenth century, and his identification and reading of the motif has determined the focus of most subsequent scholarly studies. The allegory of the sad clown, however, did not exhaust the types of engagement that other artists, poets, and novelists established with the figure of the acrobat. The powerful compositional and thematic staging of Gérôme's painting – its mark on much work in the visual and popular arts, theater and literature is palpable for the remainder of the century – could not diminish the perception by other artists of acrobatic performance as an aesthetic model for the modern, one that unraveled the conventions then governing the visual arts and literature. Art history obligingly offered a counter model to the sad clown in the same year as Gérôme's painting in Thomas Couture's *Le Duel après le bal masqué*, a work that literally and figuratively set the stage of nineteenth-century aesthetic movements in a duel.

Couture's and Daumier's literary colleagues were Banville and Baudelaire. Banville set the groundwork for the *funambulesque* aesthetics adopted later by many Decadents. Contemporaries and scholars have generally characterized his use of the figure of the acrobat as representative of an allegorical relationship defined not by the sad clown, but by technical skill and grace. Beginning with the poetry collection *Odes funambulesques* (1857), Banville and his work became irrevocably associated with the acrobat, resulting in him being often dismissed as all style and little substance. In the *Odes* (and in much of his later work, in particular his short stories), however, aesthetic, not metaphysical or psychological concerns, determine the uses to which he put the figure. Banville was the first French writer to propose the acrobat as an analogue of the artist, and his adoption of it worked against Realism by imagining the real as a dual state defined by discomforting desemantization.

For Baudelaire, too, the unsettling yet thrilling duality produced in pantomime performance serves as a vivid illustration of the "comique absolu," an analytical term that the poet proposed as the highest form of the comic, but which offered itself more emphatically as a viable template for modern literary and artistic practice (375). He put that model to appropriate use in "Une mort héroïque," a prose poem in which his clown wields masterfully the sword of disruption, bringing it down heavily on the Prince's social-cultural system in order to reveal the arbitrariness of its "truths." His Fancioulle enjoyed, however momentarily, absolute freedom, a freedom that threatened the Prince's legitimacy to its very core. This is the desemantization that the Decadents would later embrace.

Apart from Gérôme's melodramatic Pierrot, the clown adopted by artists and writers in 1857 is not a pathetically sad clown, but a tool. Indeed, the perceived dolor of Pierrot's face signals this body feature, which has traditionally and reliably cued the viewer not only to an internal emotional state but to identity, as the producer of semantic disturbance. The ambiguity of the clown's facial expression suspends not only his identity but, acting as a reflective screen, that of the viewer or reader as well. Figuratively for Banville and literally for Couture, the *funambule* orchestrates a defacing of powerful figures. Suspended identity paradoxically returns agency to the artist and writer, playfully short-circuiting convention and meaning, and in doing so opening new paths of creative experimentation.

For Chapters 3 and 4, I examine another year, 1879. The celebrated acrobatic pantomime troupe, the Hanlon-Lees, had been performing at the Folies Bergère since July 1878. They bedazzled Paris, in particular its literary and artistic inhabitants, with their mind-bending acrobatics and scenarios. The setting for the first half of their engagement was the 1878 *Exposition universelle*, an event that prepared significantly the topsy-turvy atmosphere that greeted spectators once they entered the cabaret's doors. The brothers introduced discerning Parisians to the principles of pantomime and circus, through which the performer offers the paradox of a real acrobat performing his own body as an object, a phenomenon literally embodied by the mirror routine of *Une soirée en habit noir*. The mirror routine, characterized by alarming semantic rupture, became a recurring theme in the Decadent imaginary. In these tales, mirror images do not reflect back and confirm the identity of the original, but are objects possessing their own, sometimes nefarious, agency.

Paris during an *exposition universelle* became an extension of the apparatuses for which the Hanlon-Lees were famous. The acrobat's apparatus is a tool designed for the limited purpose of a particular action whose implementation is, as a rule, successful, a detail that removes it from the contingency of everyday time and space in which tools do not guarantee certain results. The time of the apparatus reflects a simultaneous process of ideation and execution. As for the space of any of the Hanlon-Lees' tools, ordinary household objects and pieces of furniture, even the myriad structural features of the cityscape, find their textures, angles, and surfaces repurposed into the characteristic traits of the universe of the apparatus. The works that I study in this chapter all offer apparatuses that produce in some fashion the altered time and space of the acrobat: Edmond de Goncourt's *Les Frères Zemganno*, Édouard Manet's *Un bar aux Folies-Bergère*, Catulle Mendès's *La Vie et la mort d'un clown*, Edgar Degas's *Miss Lala au Cirque Fernando*, and J. K. Huysmans's "Les Folies-Bergères en 1879" in his *Croquis parisiens*. To different ends and with exciting results, these men willingly followed the Hanlon-Lees' lead into an unfiltered and porous territory marked by temporal and spatial confusion.

Acrobats' performances inhibit the production of meaning, and because of that, they are necessarily silent. Starobinski reminds us not to "leur assigner un rôle, une fonction, un sens" (141). The lady acrobat's silence is demonstrably more disturbing than her male counterpart's, principally because of the upending of preconceptions about her body, its social function, and its capabilities. She possesses a virility inconsistent with the women associated with the male spectator's social sphere of activity: mothers, sisters, lovers, passers-by. In Chapter 5, I explore how her problematic gender puts in question the fundamental organization of society. She attracts some men who are eager to experience their own gender reversal in their contact with her. Sometimes, she revulses in the way she overturns the worldview that gender assignment is natural: the male spectator struggles to return the signifier of her gender to the body/signified to which it no longer seems attached. These are considerations that do not arise while male spectators watch the evolutions of the male acrobatic body. Some Decadent protagonists are tempted to oblige the lady acrobat to perpetuate through words the extraordinary experience of derealization that she induces. When her speech threatens to be wanting in signification or enlightenment, some characters provide her with a script. The error of these male protagonists is that in forcing the lady acrobat into the realm of speech, they break the acrobat-spectator bond and replace it with the relation woman-man, a connection in which the conditions that lead to momentary liberation do not, indeed cannot, materialize.

Gender enters into the mix in the case of adolescents, too, who, like children and artists, have a more fluid relationship with the social codes into which they are being integrated (Bouissac 8). It is perhaps no wonder that adolescents are attracted in particular to *écuyères*, who leap through paper hoops while on horseback. Visually and for a young boy, metaphorically, "une limite apparente est victorieusement outrepassée" (Starobinski 140). Mixed in with that eruption of the lady acrobat into his space is the boy's still unformed relation to his awakening sexuality.

The artist most in tune with the rich codes of circus acrobatics and most receptive to the social-cultural play of gender in the lady acrobat was Jules Chéret. In his posters from the 1880s and 1890s, the equestrienne or her horse jump into the viewer's realm, clowns tumble, and aerialists fly weightlessly into the space of the viewer. This weightlessness, however, owes a tremendous debt to the lady acrobat, whose body enters the frame with a leap as if emerging impossibly from another world. He captures the pull of her allure as she enters our space, an attraction complicated by the impassable distance of the incongruities of her duality: she moves laterally but is perceived moving diagonally as well; she possesses all the markers of a flesh-and-blood being, but she is enmeshed in the graphic lettering of the poster. She is a paradox, and she is the prototype for Chéret's signature *chérette*.

In Chapter 6, I explore Jules Laforgue's rich engagement with the aesthetics of pantomime and circus. His Pierrot is generally described as a sad clown mask behind which lies the poet's ennui. His word play and penchant for mischievous citation are treated as figurative verbal acrobatics. In his unpublished and incomplete pantomime *Pierrot fumiste*, however, it becomes clear that Pierrot is more than a mask, more than a metaphor. He is above all an aesthetic practice. Laforgue enlists the strategies of pantomime, the circus, and graphic art (particularly the comic strip) in order to maintain as possible the impossible pairing of contradictory words and ideas (*nonsens*) in the production of a new *sens* – perhaps a sixth sense – that exists only in a pantomime, in the circus ring, or in a comic strip.

While associated primarily with the pantomime Pierrot, Laforgue revealed in his *Moralités légendaires* (1887) a deep affinity with the circus. In 1883, he described his literary expression as *clownesque*. While this characterization generally suggests the figure of Pierrot to those familiar with the poet's *Les Complaintes* (1885) and *L'Imitation de Notre-Dame la Lune* (1886), it is clear from his *Moralités légendaires* that his poetics had evolved to embrace the circus performer (clown or acrobat) as a figure whose existential identity is ambiguously double, and to adapt the circus ring as a semantic space in which such impossible incompatibilities can emerge and be sustained. Most of the collection's *nouvelles* possess a few carefully chosen and carefully placed circus-related words that signal moments of existential limbo in which the tales' characters become both themselves and their opposite. As with his *mots-valise*, whose individual components retain their distinctiveness, Laforgue creates characters whose dual natures establish textual space as that other arena in which the impossible paradoxically occurs.

In the final chapter, I look at the work of Octave Mirbeau, who, unlike Laforgue, is not generally associated with either the acrobat or clown. Like Laforgue, however, he employed the devices of semantic destabilization that he found in the related arts of pantomime clowning and circus acrobatics in order to mobilize an assault on the powerful quintet of social-cultural systems that would constitute his lifelong targets: the state, the military, the church, education, and the social elite. If he never wrote another *chronique* or novel devoted to a circus acrobat (*L'Écuyère* from 1882), there is not a novel in his oeuvre that does not include references to *funambules* or the effects of an acrobatic performance. These references do not function to endow the cultural environment in which he places his protagonists with the form, texture, and solidity of the real. On the contrary, the writer increasingly incorporated the *funambule* and the *funambulesque* into the tools of his *romanesque* repertoire. Over the course of his career, he moved from a faith and reliance on the power of reason and language to shine a reproving light on social inequities and crimes to the transgressive position of agency that desemantization afforded him. Beginning with *Le Jardin des supplices* (1899), his later novels often call upon the metacultural manipulations of buffoonery and acrobatics to neutralize and dismantle systems of power, including formidable literary traditions and conventions.

If the writers and artists that follow him in the twentieth century lack Mirbeau's social outrage, they inherited his joyous liberation from the prison-house of aesthetic convention, a liberation that had been prepared, perhaps even without them ever knowing the source, by the example of the *funambule*.

Note

1 While the term *funambule* technically designates the tightrope walker, since the beginning of the nineteenth century it came to refer to the full range of acrobatic skills, including pantomime, since pantomimists were also

gymnasts, as evident in the name of the famous Théâtre des Funambules which gave us the most celebrated Pierrot interpreter of all times: Jean-Gaspard Deburau. John Stokes remarks that we can explain the all-purpose use of the word "because most performers did more than one thing, but also because the term was always both literal and figurative" (278).

Works Cited

Baudelaire, Charles. *Œuvres complètes*. Ed. Marcel A. Ruff. Paris: Éditions du Seuil, 1968. 370–78.

Bouissac, Paul. *Circus and Culture: A Semiotic Approach*. Bloomington and London: Indiana UP, 1976.

Starobinski, Jean. *Portrait de l'artiste en saltimbanque*. Geneva: Editions d'Art Albert Skira, 1970.

Stokes, John. "*Aux Funambules*: Acrobatics and Aesthetics." *French Cultural Studies* 3.9 (1992): 277–98.

1 1857, Part I

Plays with Sad Clowns

The year 1857 saw the publication of Théodore de Banville's *Odes funambulesques*. That same year, Thomas Couture painted *Le Duel après le bal masqué* and Jean-Léon Gérôme *La Sortie du bal masqué*, both based ostensibly on the same event, a duel in the Bois de Boulogne after a masked ball.[1] And while art historians have been at pains to identify the origin date for a great many of Honoré Daumier's drawings and paintings, one can safely assume that he drew or painted at the very least one of his circus arts-related subjects in that year.[2] What is certain is that while "clowns crowded the walls of the Salon," the works of these five artists and writers contributed each in his own way to preparing a paradigm shift toward a modern aesthetic in which the *funambule* held a privileged position (119) (Figures 1.1 and 1.2).[3]

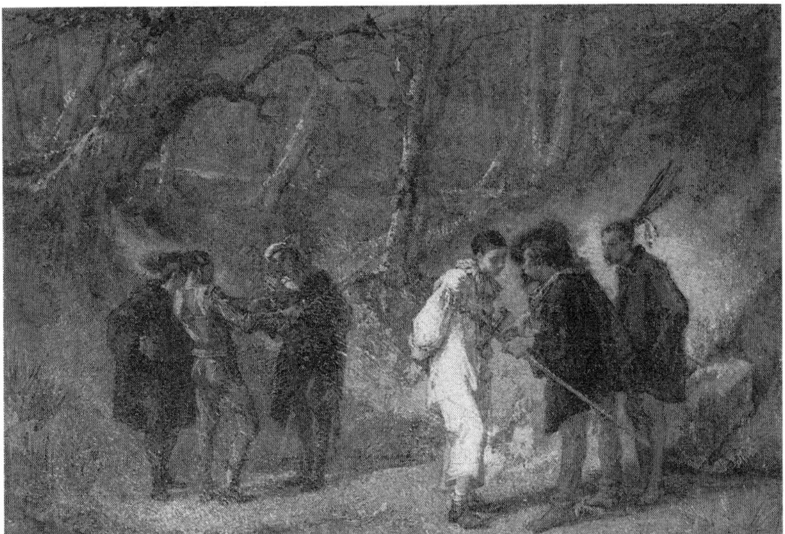

Figure 1.1 Thomas Couture, *Le Duel après le bal masqué*, 1857. The Wallace Collection, London.

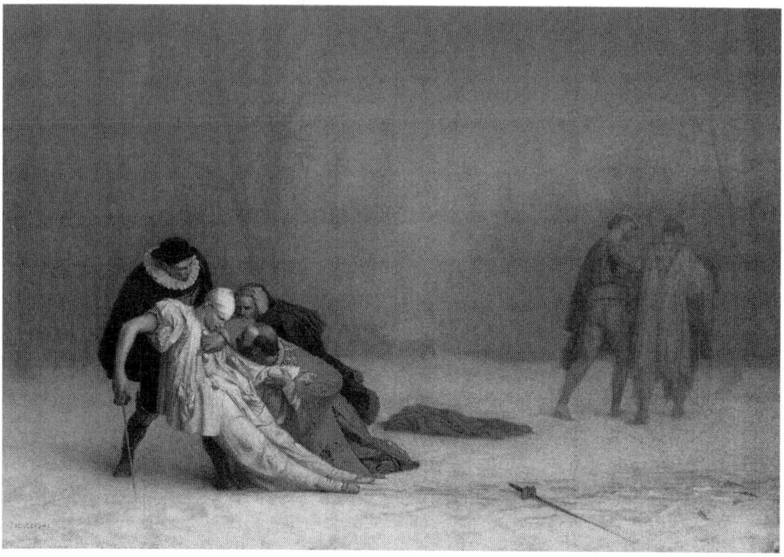

Figure 1.2 Jean-Léon Gérôme, *La Sortie du bal masqué*, 1857. The Walters Art Museum, Baltimore.

In the introduction to the special issue of *Études françaises* "1857. Un état de l'imaginaire littéraire," Geneviève Sicotte identifies 1857 as an extraordinary year for literature. There appeared not only Banville's *Odes funambulesques*, but also Jules Champfleury's treatise on *Le Réalisme*, Gustave Flaubert's *Madame Bovary*, and Baudelaire's *Les Fleurs du mal*. The trials for the latter two authors' affront to public decency took place during that year as well. The historical moment was pivotal on multiple levels:

> Tout se passe comme si les événements et les œuvres contribuaient à la donner pour une année-charnière au cours de laquelle s'exposent les grandes tensions qui structurent le champ littéraire au long du XIXe siècle – tensions entre le romantisme et le réalisme, entre la poésie, le théâtre et le roman, entre les discours littéraires et journalistiques ou essayistiques, entre l'art et l'argent, entre l'art et la morale. (Sicotte 9)

The figure of the clown offered a model for the expression of many of these tensions. "Clowns are," as Louisa E. Jones notes, "[...] figures of boundaries and crossroads" (25). Clowns from the circus or pantomime erase barriers, obscuring the lines separating persona and person, performer and spectator, and dream and reality (Jones 17, 20). Clowns are equally figures representative of crossroads. They establish sites at which shifting – aesthetic, semantic – may occur.

In the first half of the nineteenth century, clowns, depicted graphically or in literature, mirrored the social and cultural climate; in the second half, clowns and their acrobatic colleagues – *funambules* – became in many instances agents of social and cultural change.[4] In the first half of the century, clowns functioned thematically: writers, in particular, imagined their problematic heroes as fools or jesters whose grotesque masks hid their princely qualities. A notable example is Victor Hugo's Triboulet in *Le Roi s'amuse* (1832).[5] In the second half of the century, *funambules* were figures of an existential doubling that placed them both within a specific historical moment as well as outside of time. They were increasingly transformation tools, too: artists and writers transposed the experience of the *funambulesque* into the very form of their works.[6]

It is not just a coincidence that *funambule*-centered works by Banville, Baudelaire, Couture, Gérôme, and Daumier appeared in the same year – 1857 – since mid-1850s French culture was saturated with *funambules*: Paul Legrand entertained audiences as Pierrot at the Folies-Nouvelles; Charles Deburau continued his father's legacy as Pierrot at the Théâtre des Funambules until the late 1850s[7]; the Cirque de l'Impératrice (the future Cirque d'Été) and the Cirque Napoléon (the future Cirque d'Hiver) were at their height; and readers of illustrated journals were sure to enjoy caricatures featuring politicians as circus performers (Daumier) and *commedia*-inspired carnival revelers (Paul Gavarni). Starting in the 1850s, Pierrot imagery figured strongly in the "premières tentatives de *marketing* généralisé," from "encre Deburau" (a reference probably to Charles Deburau) to Desfossé wallpaper reproducing Couture's *commedia*-themed *Souper à la Maison d'Or* (1855) (Boime, *Couture* 302; Rykner 25). The ubiquity of the figure signaled its passage into the cultural imagination. This period also marked the beginning of a deeper, more complex association between artist/writer and the *funambule*, one that will extend into the late 1920s with the waning of Surrealism.

Formal innovations initiated by these artists and writers in 1857 anticipate Decadence. To Théodore de Banville, the Decadents will owe, among other things, the notion of imagining and even realizing formally the impossible as epitomized by a feat executed by an acrobatic clown. Banville proposed as well a unique conception of the real that has nothing to do with realism and everything to do with the manipulation of time and space that occurs uncannily during acrobatic performance. Decadents will trace the image of the "gouffre d'en haut" and "d'en bas" to Banville and Baudelaire, images that provoke a certain existential vertigo that will thread, for example, through the novels of Octave Mirbeau.[8] Baudelaire cites his own experience of vertigo, one which occurs during a *funambulesque* performance or from crossing "la frontière du merveilleux" (377). With Daumier and Couture, one encounters troubling paradoxes that function like photons[9]: when the viewer approaches one of their *funambule* paintings or drawings as allegory, they behave like social commentary, and when one interprets them as anchored in a specific historical moment, they offer themselves instead as timeless symbols.

How and why, one could wonder justifiably, does Gérôme's painting fit into this group? While art historians often include his painting in a discussion of the artist as sad clown, *La Sortie du bal masqué* was Gérôme's sole contribution to the theme, and its dying clown hardly expresses the degraded condition of the artist vis-à-vis his public. One would be hard pressed to find in Gérôme's work – a representative of the *art pompier* – the type and degree of innovation associated with the others. Nevertheless, he is discussed here because his one clown-themed painting, far from getting lost in the sea of clown paintings that one could find at the Salon, was so enormously popular an image throughout the rest of the nineteenth century that its conceptual weight would have been difficult for any artist revisiting the figure to shake.[10]

In his seminal "The Sad Clown: Some Notes on a 19th Century Myth," Francis Haskell wonders parenthetically if Gérôme was the first artist to paint a sad clown with his *La Sortie du bal masqué.* "Sad Clowns," as he notes, played a "significant role" in French painting beginning in the 1850s with Gérôme's tableau and continuing into the twentieth century with works by Georges Rouault and Pablo Picasso, two painters with whom we customarily associate the figure as an allegory of the artist. Haskell does not place great value on Gérôme's painting's position as initiator of the sad clown myth: the painter did not identify with his dying Pierrot, nor does he invite the viewer to do so. Gérôme would represent, however, an actualization of the nascent trend. Haskell wonders, however, what factors trigger the clown's sadness and why this figure's unusual and unexpected melancholy emerges in art, particularly in the 1850s (3). Gérôme's painting serves in Haskell's essay primarily as a historical marker whose quality pales considerably in comparison to the handling of the very same subject by Couture, a greater painter, just a few months prior to Gérôme's interpretation. If Haskell does not discuss the two very different treatments, it is because Couture's painting depicts an earlier stage in the story of two dueling masqueraders and therefore does not offer an example of the sad clown.

In addition to identifying the significance of this particular historical moment, Haskell distinguishes two "distinct, but closely associated, contributions" to the myth of the sad clown, the second of which he finds in the series of works depicting fairground acrobats by Daumier from the late 1850s to the mid-1860s (13). For him, the perceived sadness of Daumier's *saltimbanques* stems from the very real precariousness of their profession and itinerant existence.[11] The metaphysically sad clown and the economically vulnerable one, Haskell proposes, merge later in the century with Félix Larcher and Paul Margueritte's efforts to revive classical pantomime, particularly with the creation of the Cercle Funambulesque in 1888 (13). I propose that there are less two distinct contributions that eventually come together than two temporally parallel variants with fundamentally unrelated ideological trajectories. Their paths cross in only a few clashing encounters during the last half of the century, encounters that, in keeping with the subject of both Gérôme's and Couture's paintings, I view as aesthetic duels. One thread follows a theatrical use of the sad clown theme, beginning with Jules Champfleury and his application of bourgeois realism to pantomime – a radical revision that is given visual authentication in Gérôme's painting – and continuing through to the pantomimes of the Cercle Funambulesque. The other thread takes inspiration in the formal innovations of non-theatrical *funambulesque* performance, beginning with Banville, Baudelaire, Couture, and Daumier, and continuing through to early modernism.

If Gérôme had no investment in the figure of the sad clown, one wonders how fiercely independent artists of the likes of Banville, Baudelaire, Couture, Daumier, and the many artists and writers that followed them in the next forty years – in this instance, men in pursuit of creating nothing short of wholly original and modern works – were willing and able to work with the figure of the *funambule.* One need only think of the disdain many writers held for those objects that they deemed debased precisely for their easy accessibility and pervasiveness. For example, in Banville's short story "Les Féeries du zinc" from 1853, the narrator categorically refuses to read Harriet Beecher Stowe's *Uncle Tom's Cabin* (1852) precisely because of its ubiquity in Paris:

> où il n'y a plus d'autre livre que l'*Oncle Tom*, plus d'autres gravures que les illustrations de l'*Oncle Tom*, où tous les théâtres ont joué de l'*Oncle Tom*, où les carafes, les verres, les foulards et les bas-reliefs d'armoires à glace représentent exclusivement l'*Oncle Tom*. (*Pauvres saltimbanques* 59)[12]

We find another notable example later in the century among the Decadents in Joris-Karl Huysmans's *À rebours* (1884). In des Esseintes's efforts to select jewels with which to incrust the shell of his tortoise, he dismisses many gems precisely because of their popularity among members of the lower middle classes. Diamonds had become "singulièrement commun[s] depuis que tous les commerçants en portent au petit doigt," and topazes and amethysts, the latter especially, were anathema because one could find them "aux oreilles sanguines et aux mains tubuleuses des bouchères" (133–34). So, how is it possible that, given the saturating presence of *funambules* in the French, primarily Parisian middle-class culture of the 1850s, these artists and writers adopted what should likely have been a highly unattractive subject by virtue of its very ubiquity and commerciality?

One consideration is the extent to which relations with the marketplace and an awareness of having to please an audience provoked engagement with the figure of the *funambule*. The works from 1857 by Banville, Baudelaire, Daumier, Couture, and Gérôme address this encounter in some fashion. As regards the first three of these artists/writers, the tension between the quest for artistic authenticity and the demands of the market will be discussed more extensively in Chapter 2. For Couture, his series of Pierrot and Harlequin paintings, which signaled his renunciation of *grande peinture*, were a source both of personal and aesthetic fulfillment as well as ambivalence toward the fact that they were commissioned by private buyers and were completed with a view to financial gain. As for Gérôme, in his review of *La Sortie du bal masqué*, the art critic Edmond About claims that the artist seemed less interested in "dessiner que de réussir" (69). Celebrity and financial success so appealed to the painter that, About concluded, he sought only to "renouveler ses succès sans renouveler son talent" (77). We find the difference between these two artists in that the former faced the market with hesitation and trepidation but accepted it as a reality of modern artistic production, while the latter embraced and exploited it.

We can trace to the 1850s the sources of the Decadents' own conflicted relation to the market. The image of the Decadent author who makes ends meet by writing for revues and periodicals (reviews, short stories, serialization of novels) is one that he worked to his advantage. He promoted himself as a martyr to his art (Macleod 47). Representative of the 1850s, the image of Daumier's *saltimbanques* and Baudelaire's *vieux saltimbanque* come readily to mind: Daumier's performers struggle to attract a paying audience and Baudelaire's simply gives up. From the 1890s, one thinks curiously of Marcel Schwob, but not because he experienced ambivalence toward his career as a journalist. Expecting nothing less than this fin-de-siècle mindset, it is rather his scholars who have done much of the work of promoting the myth of him as a poet-martyr by insisting that Schwob conceived of his short story collections according to a uniting theme prior to their publication in the press. The feeling has been disbelief that Schwob could have possibly found his journalistic work rewarding or incredulity that he could have entertained a more semantically rich relationship with the medium.[13]

It would have been hard to escape an awareness of Gérôme's *La Sortie du bal masqué* in the last half of the nineteenth century. It would have been difficult as well to avoid being moved by its depiction of the death of Pierrot, if only because the result is so unexpected. The work was immensely popular, a popularity fed, first, by the innumerable print reproductions in the variety of formats and mediums that circulated over a forty-year period and, second, by the numerous theatrical stagings that spanned just as much time and banked on familiarity with the painting by invoking the emotional power of its *mise-en-scène*, thereby considerably extending its shelf life.[14] The doomed protagonist of the painting is a masquerader, not a melancholic clown in the same way one generally assumes Picasso's itinerant circus performers are, nor even a tragic clown, as in Hugo's Triboulet. He is a masquerader as well in almost all the plays that subsequently reproduce the canvas in a *tableau vivant*. And yet the emotional force of the death scene's *mise-en-scène* comes clearly from the viewer/spectator's knowledge that Pierrot is a clown whose traditional medium is comedy. As is evident from the painting's original frame, which depicted the masks of comedy and tragedy, Gérôme tapped the Hugolian and ultimately Romantic opposition between comedy and tragedy to provoke a *coup de théâtre*. The contrast lacks, however, the depth that emerges in the isolation of the Romantic hero whose mask, metaphorical or real, hides a noble soul.

One explanation for the inability of Gérôme's painting's overwhelmingly popular reception to discourage the four other artists and writers may lie in the important distinction between the low-brow and the commercial, between a popular character drawn from stock pantomime or circus, associated with low humor and appealing to disenfranchised social groups (and writers living in self-imposed class alienation), and a character exploited for popular consumption, enjoyed by a mass public. The Théâtre des Funambules was the birthplace of modern pierrotic pantomime, and owed the origins of its mythical status to the many Romantic era men and women of letters who slummed there in admiration of the venue's star performer Jean-Gaspard Deburau and the pantomimes in which he appeared. Of course, part of the attraction was the knowledge that the reviled bourgeoisie (ironically, the class from which most of these writers came) would never deign to set foot in such a place, and if it did, would not survive an entire evening within its walls before being repulsed by the smells and the coarse tomfoolery. As for Gérôme, he, on the other hand, was representative of the modern popular artist. His Pierrot belonged to the 1850s when Pierrot became "middle class and respectable" (Jones 63). From the 1860s through to the end of the century, one could find inexpensive photographic copies of the painting decorating the living and dining room walls of middle-class homes. Christopher Knight notes that "Gérôme stands at a kind of crossroads. He was there at the dawn of popular culture," highlighting the way in which the painter "engage[d] with commerce" ("Art Review"). While he does not fault Gérôme for engaging with commerce, the painter's error, Knight comments, was in having "disengage[d] with art's possibilities" ("Art Review").

The artists and writers who turned to the *funambule* in 1857 saw in the figure precisely its means for exploring and extending "art's possibilities." This alternate use signals that originality emerged in spite of the overwhelming presence of Gérôme's painting, and in some instances (e.g., Auguste Villiers de l'Isle-Adam's short story, "Le Convive des dernières fêtes" and the Hanlon-Lees' *Le Duel*), this came about in its interstices, through the metaphoric cracks of its paint. These artists and writers steered their *funambules* away from the very crowd that Gérôme sought to please, an image that Daumier depicted in some of his *saltimbanque* drawings and paintings and Baudelaire in his *vieux saltimbanque*. A crossroads representative of this artistic bifurcation offered itself in 1857 in the form of a *fait divers*, a duel that took place with adversaries and seconds still dressed in their masked ball costumes. Gérôme took the path of popular acclaim with his *Sortie du bal masqué* and Couture followed the path of personal and aesthetic fulfillment for his *Duel après le bal masqué*.

Gérôme's *Coup de théâtre*

Couture's *Le Duel après le bal masqué* and Gérôme's *La Sortie du bal masqué* depict the same event at different moments: the duel at dawn after a masked ball between Deluns-Montaud, Empire *député*, and Symphorien Boittelle, the future prefect of police (1858–66) and afterwards senator (1866–70).[15] Couture's painting, conceived and completed months before Gérôme's, portrays the moments preceding the duel and accordingly cannot be the source of the many subsequent representations of the death of Pierrot throughout the rest of the century, although it, too, like his *Souper à la Maison d'Or*, was probably "reproduced [...] in various sizes and media to supply an enthusiastic audience" (Ives, *Romanticism* 168). Gérôme's more famous *Sortie du bal masqué* portrays with considerable dramatic license the duel's conclusion: while Boitelle's wound was not mortal, that of Gérôme's Pierrot is.[16] While the composition of the two camps differs somewhat in the two versions of the encounter, without a newspaper account it is impossible to ascertain to what extent either painter reproduces the factual details of the episode.[17] One constant in the two tableaux is that the participants – duelists and seconds – wear their ball costumes: in one group Harlequin and in the other Pierrot, echoes of the stock characters' often adversarial relations on the pantomime stage. True to the mask's notorious cunning in nineteenth-century pantomime, Harlequin's side emerges the victor in Gérôme's staging.[18] That victor, however, is not Harlequin but a Native American, as evidenced by the feathers scattered across the space of the duel. Although featuring these farce figures, his painting does not make light of the moment, however potentially humorous the details of a political and/or personal quarrel coming to a head at a masquerade, a quarrel so heated that the two opponents dispense with going home to change their clothes before defending their honor. Indeed, the intense pathos of the scene is heightened by a familiarity with these pantomime characters and by the very knowledge that they generally come miraculously back to life contrary to their flesh-and-blood counterparts.[19]

An important difference between Couture's and Gérôme's paintings emerges in the artists' personal and professional relations to the theme. For Couture, the clown – Harlequin or Pierrot – belongs among his works that cast a critical eye on contemporary French society and art, whether through classical moralizing, as in his *Romains de la décadence* (1847), or through caricature and satire, as in his *Lawyer Going to Court* (1860) and *Le Réaliste* (1865). Excluding his *Sortie du bal masqué*, in which Nadar was perhaps the only one to find "comme une légère tendance caricaturale" – Gérôme had rejected Academic moralizing early in his career – one will not find clowns or caricature elsewhere in Gérôme's *œuvre* (10). Indeed, the narrator's distance prevents the viewer from taking Gérôme's Pierrot as a mask for the painter himself ("Salon" 246).

It is ironic that of the two paintings, the one whose creator in no way cultivated the allegory of the artist as *funambule* is the one that left a greater cultural impression on his century through his sole *funambule*-themed painting and that may have single-handedly sealed the fate of the figure of Pierrot in pantomime in the Paris of the latter half of the nineteenth century: neither the victims of a murderous Pierrot nor Pierrot as victim of murder can be revived. Gérôme's striking opposition of "le comique des costumes au tragique de la situation," comments Gustave Haller, "produit une émotion qui se répandit dans tout le public avec une rapidité vertigineuse" (19). Powerful theatrical oppositions determined his choice of theme and not identification with the *funambule*.[20]

Indeed, incompatible performance traditions inform the two paintings' *mise-en-scène*. Couture's painting embraces the illogical performative dynamics of pantomime, which, as Jacques Rancière states, is an anti-theater, from which are absent "tightly knit plots that make unexpected effects emerge from a very simple cause, well-analyzed characters with their complex motives that push them to act, and well-drawn characters like those found in living rooms or in the streets" (80). Couture does endow his Harlequin and Pierrot paintings with a duration possessing a beginning and an ending, but its seeming progression forward always returns to its beginnings: this notion of time is cyclical, not linear. Couture's series comes to a chronological close with the marriage of Harlequin and Columbine, as in the anticipated conclusion of many harlequinades. While in performance there could occur variations in the distribution of roles, according to the harlequinade formula from the first half of the nineteenth century, the last tableau will generally involve a wedding, and it will always occur as if for the first time. The masks' time is in suspension; their situation is in arrested development; they will never age. If Harlequin or Pierrot have children, as in Paul Viard's *Pierrot marié et Polichinelle célibataire* (1847), they will appear in the next entry unmarried and without offspring: the cycle always resets to its core elements. Their personalities may undergo modifications in the hands of different interpreters (Pierrot as played by Jean-Gaspard Deburau, Paul Legrand, Alexandre Guyon, etc.), but once conventionalized for audiences, their basic traits remain relatively unchanged. Pantomime space and time of the first half of the nineteenth century permeate Couture's Harlequin and Pierrot paintings, whose characters find themselves in a duration for which there is a central *before* possessing a constellation of possible *afters* and an inevitable return.

Gérôme's painting also possesses a before and an after, but unlike Couture's, whose existential universe operates according to cycles, his underscores an aftermath and its finality, results of a linear progression from which there is no innocent recovery. The work's central gap separating Pierrot and his opponent visibly replicates the arrangement of the figures in Paul Delaroche's *L'Assassinat du duc de Guise au château de Blois en 1588* (1834) and appropriates its theatricality. The seemingly empty middle areas of both paintings carry visible traces of the moments preceding the assassination (Delaroche) and the duel (Gérôme), communicating a temporal progression, the passage of time. Both works feature an article of clothing cast off in the heat of the action (a cape in *L'Assassinat*, a domino in *La Sortie du bal masqué*), and in place of the blood of Delaroche's painting, Gérôme's offers footprints in the partially melted snow, evidence of recent thrusting lunges and physical parrying. In the lower far right corner of the tableau, one sees four scattered feathers, another remnant of the overpowering forward motions of the Native American.

Gérôme may have been too young to know that the exhibition of Delaroche's *L'Assassinat du duc de Guise* corresponded with the 1834 revival of Louis Vitet's play, *Les États de Blois, ou la mort de MM. de Guise* (1827): the director milked the emotional potential of the dramatic moment immediately following the assassination by reproducing Delaroche's painting in a striking *tableau vivant*, an effect that permitted theatergoers to "compare the scene presented by Delaroche with the one they witnessed in the theater" (Boime, *Art* 341). Nevertheless, Gérôme, whose own *Sortie du bal masqué* would be reproduced in *tableaux vivants* as the dramatic highlight of many plays throughout the last half of the nineteenth century, would have been familiar with his teacher's transmedial relationship to the theater.[21]

The popular reception of Gérôme's painting, however, eclipsed that of Delaroche through its more generally familiar theme featuring *commedia* figures who were ubiquitous on the social landscape of Paris, whether in the pantomimes of the Théâtre des Funambules, the Folies-Nouvelles and the circus, in the legacy of Parisian *bals masqués* (1830–48), captured in the caricatures and illustrations of Gavarni, Daumier, Gustave Doré, Cham, and Auguste Bouquet, or in the myriad collectibles (plaster or porcelain figurines, dinnerware, snuff boxes, etc.) that capitalized on the popularity of the characters, appealing to a wide range of clients of varying purchasing power.

While it is probable that an important frame of reference for both Couture's and Gérôme's interpretation of Pierrot's costume was the *bal masqué* via caricature, it is certain that the source for the myriad visual replicas (costumes, caricatures, and collectibles) was the Théâtre des Funambules's pantomimist Jean-Gaspard Deburau. Around 1830, Pierrot started making his appearance in the *bals de Paris*, an entrance due in no small part to the rising popularity of Deburau. Prior to 1830, as Alexandre Dumas notes in *Mes Mémoires* (1852–56) regarding the *bals de Paris*, "on ne connaissait, comme costume fashionable, ni les pierrots ni les débardeurs; Chicard et Gavarni étaient encore cachés dans les profondeurs de l'avenir et le bal de l'Opéra ne sortait pas du domino traditionnel" (33). The striking sight and focalization in both Couture's and Gérôme's paintings of the Pierrot dressed in a loose and flowing white satin costume and signature skullcap (white in Gérôme, black in Couture) recall without any doubt Deburau's interpretation of the character, a portrayal that made him a sensation in Paris.

One of Deburau's most celebrated pantomimes, the one in which he had his first success in the role of Pierrot, was *Le Boeuf enragé* (1827). Anne Dowling Levillain notes that this particular pantomime "played two hundred successive performances and its popularity was sufficiently solid to warrant its being revived again and again during the next twenty years, nearly always playing to packed houses" (101). If Couture and Gérôme never saw this pantomime, they certainly would have known about it since the last revival was in 1850. It featured notably a duel between Harlequin and Pierrot, with Pierrot being forced by his employer Boissec to fight in his stead, and featuring the typical awkward thrusts (when the arms are rapiers), misfires (when they are pistols), unintended victims, ruses, and evasions of the many duels in Deburau's pantomime repertoire. In *Le Boeuf enragé*, as an inebriated Pierrot and Harlequin fight with swords, the latter fakes being stabbed and collapses, at which point Pierrot and Boissec flee in fear. *Les Vingt-six infortunes de Pierrot* (1832), later known as *Le Duel de Pierrot, ou les 26 infortunes* (another great success that designated Deburau as the uncontested king of pantomime), presents the same scene with a craven Cassandra replacing *Le Boeuf enragé*'s Boissec, with pistols replacing the swords and the bait being money instead of wine (Péricaud 100). Other pantomimes prior to Deburau's death in 1846 repeat with some modification the same duel formula. In all but one, however, neither Pierrot nor Harlequin are mortally wounded.

By the 1840s, however, this popular entertainment was becoming increasingly appropriated and reinvented by men and women of letters, the most notable ones being Théophile Gautier, whose 1842 article in the *Revue de Paris* "Shakespeare aux Funambules" was the inspiration for Cot d'Ordan's *Marrrchand d'habits!* (1842), and Champfleury, who began writing pantomimes for the Théâtre des Funambules in the mid-1840s, his first being *Pierrot, valet de la Mort* (1846). In both pantomimes, there is no fairy to wave her wand and resuscitate Pierrot after he dies: in the first, stabbed to death by the ghost of the clothes hawker whom he had earlier murdered, and in the second, victim of Harlequin's blade in a duel. Neither pantomime was successful with audiences, enjoying only a handful of stagings between them: audiences may not have been ready to follow a more realist construction of scenarios. And depending on one's source, Deburau was either unwell during the period of this production or he categorically refused to interpret this dark revision of his mask. Paul Legrand played Pierrot in his place. The original *Marrrchand d'habits!* was reworked, however, with greater success by Charles Bridault and Legrand in 1853 as *Mort et remords, ou les inconvénients d'assassiner un marchand d'habits grêlé* at the Folies-Nouvelles (Levillain 94). Like the Pierrot of this pantomime, Gérôme's Pierrot dies, mortally pierced by a sword. If Couture and Gérôme had not seen the short-lived 1842 production, it is quite possible that they were spectators at its 1853 incarnation.

Rancière cites Champfleury's contribution to *pantomime pierrotique* as bringing about a monumental shift in the genre toward narrative coherence. In the hands of Deburau and his colleagues in the first half of the nineteenth century, pantomime, highly regulated so as not to compete with the official theaters (no speaking roles, no logical progressions), was a "dramatic art substituting psychological and social plots, which claimed to imitate the reasons of life through chains of causes and effects, with the extravaganza of exact performance that follows the twists and turns of its lack of reason" (83). It is perhaps unfair to lay blame entirely on Champfleury for the introduction of a cause for every effect, since this was perhaps an inevitable evolution of the genre due to a confluence of forces: Champleury's wish to provide (1) rational justification for pantomime characters' actions and scenic transitions, evidence of the gradual eclipsing of Romanticism by Realism; (2) the increasing reorientation and "modernization" of pantomime's scenarios as a result of the patronage and participation of not only other influential men and women of letters besides Champfleury, but of middle-class audiences as well; and (3) the increasing relaxation of the restrictions governing staging and speech, and censorship on small theaters. Pantomime after Deburau became more theatrical, and this is the pantomime from which Gérôme drew to infuse his painting with melodramatic pathos.

Even thirty-five years after the first exhibition of Gérôme's painting, the death of Pierrot still possessed the capacity to shock and awe. In his memoir *L'Homme blanc: souvenirs d'un Pierrot*, the mime Séverin recounts the 1891 performance of his *Pauvre Pierrot, ou après le bal* in Marseille. Pierrot, victim of Columbine's unfaithfulness and object of ridicule, fights a duel to avenge his honor. After 1857, no scene featuring dueling masks could fail to recall Gérôme's painting, and in this instance, the pantomime does so three times: first, in the title; second, in its piteous depiction of the dying clown; and third, in situating the contest after a masked ball, however incongruous the idea of a mask going to a masked ball. Curiously, the provincial audience for this production clearly still anticipated the more traditional pantomime conventions and expected their hero to triumph, but

> Pas du tout, j'étais frappé à mort. Un tel silence régnait dans la salle que j'entendais les respirations oppressées des spectateurs accompagner les râles de Pierrot. Ce fut bien pire quand on me vit, dans les derniers spasmes, presser sur ma poitrine la coupable Colombine et l'embrasser dans l'ultime soupir ... Oh! alors! un chevalier du poulailler fit connaître tout net son opinion en me criant: 'Imbécile! flanque-lui un tas à cette garce!' (178)

After the fall of the curtain, Séverin describes a "moment de silence et de stupeur" at the sight of the lifeless body of Pierrot, after which the audience burst into vigorous applause. While the mime was famous as a champion of classical pantomime, he proved to be poorly versed in the repertoire of the post-Deburau Théâtre des Funambules, for he comments that "Désormais, Pierrot pouvait souffrir et même mourir, comme tout être humain" (179). He saw himself as the innovator of the subsequent fashion among his rivals of killing off Pierrot. So rampant was this narrative twist that he admits having entertained the idea of composing a "satire rocambolesque où j'aurais fait mourir Pierrot quatre ou cinq fois, en le faisant ressusciter pour mourir encore," a scenario that would have brought him, ironically, much closer to the classical routines of Deburau (179).

Shock of this kind was the reaction that Gérôme sought and effectively produced in *La Sortie du bal masqué*. While there is a condensation of several influences – Delaroche's incorporation of *mise-en-scène* in his paintings, caricature, the *bal masqué*, and pantomime – it was familiarity with the conventions of pantomime that delivered the desired effect. This is not the white pantomime of Deburau, but the dark pantomime of Champfleury. While the impulse is to look at Champfleury's writing and production of pantomimes as an integral part of the evolution of the medium during the nineteenth century, an evolution leading up to the works and productions of the Cercle funambulesque, we must remember that the legacy of his pantomime was limited to Paris. Touring and provincial pantomime troupes during the last half of the century continued to stage performances according to a tradition in which illogic, mayhem, and ambiguity, not cause and effect, were the order of the day. Regarding the contributions of some men and women of letters to pantomime before 1850, Jones notes that "they took pantomime so seriously that they very nearly killed it, along with its hero and heroine, themselves ever more pathetic victims" (118). The long-lasting vogue and omnipresence of Gérôme's painting nationally and internationally, however, most certainly surpassed Champfleury and friends' ability to "nearly" kill Pierrot. Indeed, it could function as a visual epitaph for the medium.

Many discussions of Gérôme's *La Sortie du bal masqué* invariably elicit references to Émile Zola's comment about the commonplace of replicas of the work decorating the walls of bourgeois interiors: "Il n'y a pas de salon de province où ne soit pendue une gravure représentant *Le Duel au sortir d'un bal masqué* ou *Louis XIV et Molière*" ("Nos peintres"). Gérôme's painting enjoyed enormous success at the Salon of 1857 and throughout the rest of the century, starting in 1858 when Ernest Gambart exhibited it in London and published the first lithograph reproduction (Lafont 26).[22] The painting was exhibited again at the 1867 *Exposition universelle*, and "again it drew crowds" (Bigorne 83). It was the source of one of only three color photogravures of his paintings and a copperplate etching by Paul-Adolphe Rajon (Lafont 24). Additionally, this was the only one of his works to be lithographed (Lafont 26). In short, it was published "in every conceivable size, format and technique," including *cartes de visite* and cabinet cards, and it was "more widely circulated in photographic than in print form," making it accessible to all pocketbooks, from the more comfortable members of the working class to the upper middle class (Lafont 28; Renié 6). Jules-Émile Saintin's painting *Indécision* (1870) even features a print of it.[23]

The theatrical nature of its *mise-en-scène* lent itself to reproduction in Victorian and French theater, primarily in the practice of the *tableau vivant*, with directors rightly counting on audiences' familiarity with Gérôme's work. Short of recognition, they could still expect to produce the kind of shock that drew audiences to the painting. Nineteenth-century dramatic uses of *tableaux vivants* usually sought to ensure the success of their productions through a positive association with famous paintings.[24] The theatrical re-creations of Gérôme's canvas clearly took advantage of this painting's prestige, popularity, and emotional effect, easily modifying preexisting contexts featuring a *bal masqué*, as in Thomas Hailes Lacy's adaptation of Alexandre Dumas's *Les Frères corses*, or creating narratives expressly for the purpose of reproducing Gérôme's masked duelists in a *tableau vivant*, as in Edward Fitzball's *Christmas Eve; or, The Duel in the Snow* (1860). Gustave Haller admitted that she drew from Gérôme's work in the composition of *Le Duel de Pierrot* (1881), in which ball costumes serve to keep unknown family ties hidden until the emotional moment of unmasking. These reenactments of *La Sortie du bal masqué* tapped the painting's *mise-en-scène* to endow their productions with surplus drama – *tableaux vivants* generally appeared at important moments in a play's narrative – and startling realism.[25] Audiences would not just nod their heads in pleased recognition, they would also relive the melodramatic jolt caused by the striking contrasts that they experienced at the first viewing of the painting, an emotion that could only work to the advantage of the play.

The recognition effect was great, given the number of appropriations of the painting that surfaced in a variety of works and mediums over more than forty years. As mentioned earlier, Edward Fitzball's *Christmas Eve; or, The Duel in the Snow* came on the heels of Gambart's and then Goupil's saturation of London with print reproductions of Gérôme's painting, and clearly aimed to capitalize on the work's popularity. The published play's stage directions in the final moments refer to a "Picture" that the characters reproduce, supported by an accompanying "plate," undoubtedly an illustration of Gérôme's painting (28).[26] Coleman Parsons notes that the artist who made the illustration to accompany the review of Fitzball's play in the *Illustrated London News* respected not the details of the play's dénouement, but the staging of Gérôme's painting, in which there was only one victim, Pierrot, with the Native American "walking away with his second, Harlequin" (320). On the one hand, we can surmise that the illustrator committed a gaffe that betrays perhaps too great a familiarity with Gérôme's painting (it must have been unavoidable at the time), and on the other hand, it was not an error at all. The play was clearly designed around the painting's narrative. Additionally, if the journalist in the *Illustrated London News* referred to the painting and not to the play, this worked to tap into viewer familiarity, giving the production the type of publicity that it sought and on which it depended.

Parsons states that between 1860 and 1864, there was a British production based on a translation of Eugène Grangé and Xavier Aymon de Montépin's *Les Frères corses: drame fantastique en trois actes et cinq tableaux, tiré du roman de M. A. Dumas* (1850), whose stage directions are intended to "realiz[e] the group from the picture of 'The Duel'" (20).[27] Lacy is credited with the unauthorized translation of Grangé and Montépin's play – he was in the habit of doing this to avoid the payment of copyright fees – but given the timing of his actions, he clearly intended to "pirate Fitzball's effects" and to piggyback both on the popularity of Gérôme's painting and the very successful run of Dion Boucicault's adaptation for the stage of Dumas's story starring the celebrated Charles Kean (Parsons 20).[28]

Twenty years later, it was the turn of the French to ride on the coattails of the continuing currency of Gérôme's painting. *Le Duel de Pierrot* (1881) by Gustave Haller explicitly referenced Gérôme's painting both in title and in the reproduction of it in a *tableau vivant*. Appearing at the Gymnase in Paris for 100 performances, the play enjoyed moderate success, of which, Haller admitted rightly, "Tout l'honneur en revenait à Gérôme" (19n1).

Although Charles Marin drew only on the most current title of Gérôme's painting, he felt either genuinely indebted or opportunistic enough to dedicate his 1897 *commedia*-themed play to the "auteur du tableau *Le Duel de Pierrot*" (n.p.). His *Le Duel de Pierrot* reverses conventional character traits with Harlequin as lovesick and ineffectual, and Pierrot as clever and full of initiative. The play features no duel, however; Pierrot does wave his guitar like a swashbuckler his sword. Most significantly, it is the title's explicit evocation of the painting – it was known at that point as *Le Duel de Pierrot* – and the author's inclusion of the painter's permission to draw from it in the 1924 published version that acknowledge the general public's continued familiarity with the painting. This was perhaps the most brazen of the efforts seeking to profit from Gérôme's success.

Marin's and Haller's plays were testimony to the continued relevance of Gérôme's *mise-en-scène* in the last two decades of the nineteenth century and undeniably exploit with confidence the desired recognition effect. As Henry Becque remarked, recognition may have been the only response produced by spectators at Haller's comedy: "La pièce tout entière, on le devine, est dans le duel du père et du fils et dans la reproduction du tableau qui l'a inspiré. Elle se traîne jusque-là et tombe tout d'un coup après" (98). All of the theatrical pieces mentioned earlier, with the exception of Marin's, sought to co-opt the painting's pathos in order to add surplus emotion to their narratives and ensure the productions' success. As in About's critique of Gérôme, these writers seemed less interested in creating original scenarios than in succeeding whatever the cost (69).

Decadent Revenge

Seventeen years after *La Sortie du bal masqué*'s first exhibition and seven years after its triumph at the 1867 *Exposition universelle*, Villiers de l'Isle-Adam could equally count on the continued familiarity of readers with it to deftly trick them by outmaneuvering the painting's manipulation of viewers' emotions in his darkly amusing tale "Le Convive des dernières fêtes."[29] Costumed characters decompressing at the Maison dorée after an earlier evening spent at the Bal de l'Opéra attempt to tease out the mystery of Baron Saturne's pressing engagement at dawn. Villiers directly and indirectly offers the painting's scenario as one of several misleading *effets d'annonce*, with the narrator conjecturing that the baron is expected at a duel in imitation of Gérôme's painting. The narrator refers to it explicitly in his attempt to coax the baron to stay a while longer: "Avant de réaliser le pendant du tableau de Gérôme où vous auriez le rôle du vainqueur, celui d'Arlequin, envoyez le chasseur à votre place, au rendez-vous, savoir si l'on vous attend" (149).[30] The tale's establishing shot seems to anticipate the narrator's later reference to the painting: "Au dehors, il faisait une pluie terne et fine, semée de neige; une nuit glaciale; —des bruits de voitures, des cris de masques, la sortie de l'Opéra" (140). Contrary to the narrator's certitude that, should the auroral appointment indeed involve a duel, the baron would be Harlequin – and his costume may, indeed, be that of that mask – his excessive pallor, his lips, as if painted onto his face like his unmoving eyebrows, suggest Pierrot, the only white-faced *commedia* character ("seulement, en vérité, sa pâleur prenait, par intervalles, des tons singulièrement blêmes – et même blâfards; ses lèvres étaient plus étroites qu'un trait de pinceau; les sourcils demeuraient toujours un peu froncés, même dans le sourire") (140). Armed with this presentation and the evocation of the painting, the reader could well think that the narrator is wrong; that the baron is Pierrot; and that he will die melodramatically in a duel just like the white-faced, white-costumed swordsman of Gérôme's painting.

The reader, who expects to relive the experience of his first viewing of the canvas, has been adequately prepared for being moved by the story's pathos, one that Gérôme built on a series of contrasts that begin upon a first glimpse of comic masks at the poignant dénouement of a duel. About had noted the other mood-inducing oppositions – "On est saisi de voir le plaisir si près de la mort, la solitude si près de la foule, le silence des bois si près de l'orchestre de Musard, la fournaise où l'on danse si près du cimetière où l'on repose" – that all contribute to the theatricality of the scene (72). Villiers skillfully exploits these assumptions to prepare the story's perverse ending, in which the revelers and readers learn that the refined baron is expected not at a duel but at a public beheading at which he will assist the state's official executioner. But rather than set the stage through contrasts that build one upon the other in the movement toward a dramatic finale, Villiers's tale derails the linear narrative of Gérôme's Pierrot tale by having the story's series of revelations emerge in random temporal order.[31] Two narratives are in place, each possessing a different relation to time, with one linear and following narrative conventions (the scenario that follows the masked revelers from the Opéra to the Maison dorée and stays with them until morning) and the other a mosaic (the revelations regarding the baron's identity and macabre predilection) that is a temporal materialization of the pattern of Harlequin's costume and an actualization of one meaning of Baron Saturn's name: Saturn is the Roman god of agriculture, and hence of cyclical time.[32] A dislodged relation to time emerges, one without clear beginnings and endings that challenges, and ultimately suspends, the narrative that could have but does not lead to a reenactment of Gérôme's painting.[33] There is no theme featuring sad clowns here, but an intrusion of mischievous, perhaps even malevolent, clowns into the very form of the tale.

The exhibition of Gérôme's painting coincided roughly with the beginning of the official decline of pantomime in Paris with the closing of the Théâtre des Funambules in 1862 and the destruction of its building as part of Baron Haussmann's renovations. In Paris, pantomime did migrate in diminished form to other theaters, but its salad days were well behind it. Only with the arrival of the Hanlon-Lees in Paris in 1878 did Parisian men and women of letters entertain hope for a rebirth of the genre. Among the pantomimes presented by the troupe in their 1878–79 season was *Le Duel* (1878), which they performed at the Folies Bergère. Vaguely recalling the Gérôme painting in its title, this pantomime represents perhaps the first response by the genre to the tableau's influence. Reminiscent of the perverse foiling of reader expectations that one finds in Villiers's short story, *Le Duel* toyed similarly with its audience. It invoked through its title, only to subvert in its *mise-en-scène*, the lingering image and ascendancy of the canvas.

It is not certain that the Hanlon-Lees' characters were actually Pierrots. Huysmans calls the duelists Pierrots in his *Croquis parisiens* (1880), as does Richard Lesclide in his *Mémoires et pantomimes des frères Hanlon-Lees* (1880). Coquelin Cadet, however, identifies each one rather as a "monsieur en habit noir, masque blanc" (201). That some understood the duelists and many of the characters played by the brothers in their other pantomimes from that season as Pierrot types, especially the one "en habit noir," corresponds first, to the myriad costumes that the character had donned by the time of the waning years of the Funambules and the Folies-Nouvelles, including the signature dark suit of the bourgeoisie of the second half of the century; second, to the stark white make-up associated with the intersection of two clown traditions, one belonging to the French Pierrot, the other to the English Clown conceived by Joseph Grimaldi in the early 1800s; third, to the fact that Pierrot had eclipsed all other *commedia* characters on the pantomime stage in the last half of the nineteenth century in France; and fourth, to the practice of the more successful pantomime companies of adapting their works to local sensibilities and tastes. A troupe member, French juggler Henri Agoust, would certainly have encouraged the English Hanlon brothers to make the most of French audiences' association of the lead pantomime roles with the character of Pierrot.[34] Unlike all the other plays, which welcomed the recognition of and the association with the painting through *tableaux vivants*, the troupe, whose members would certainly have come across at least one of its many reenactments throughout their years of performing, may have encouraged false assumptions about the scenario behind the familiar title. After all, by 1878, the composition of Gérôme's tableau was well known across the spectrum of social classes.[35] There is no doubt that the combination of the performance's medium (pantomime) and the title's reference to a duel would have prepared the spectator to expect the troupe to address the painting in some fashion. The troupe thwarted those assumptions, thoroughly dismantling the iconic painting's conventions, while at the same time reviving and inflecting the conventions of romantic *pantomime pierrotique* with a bit of English. It restores one of Pierrot's defining traits: fear, or fear redoubled, that becomes uncontrolled terror since there are now two Pierrots on stage.[36] In *Le Duel*, the Pierrots are solely agents of self-preservation, whose constant motion makes them impossible targets.

As in Gérôme's painting, the duel is to take place in a forest clearing with the nature of the duel-provoking slight unknown to the viewer. Like the painting, the pantomime dispenses with details regarding what leads up to the duel, focusing solely on the climactic moment. The duelists' seconds give them swords, which the adversaries fail to use properly: first, because they are wholly unskilled in the sport and, second, because they are far too afraid of being hurt. Their seconds replace the swords with revolvers and "ils [the duelists] tirent sur tout ce qui n'est pas eux" (Coquelin Cadet 202). The spraying bullets that hit the seconds restore the stock story lines of pantomime from the first half of the century; if they are mortally wounded, they do not collapse on the ground, but fly away into the heavens.[37] The ascensional motion of the pantomimists' bodies counters the downward movement of the eye toward the fallen figure that viewers could see in the painting. What follows is a comic chasing of a hat, the arrival of harvesters, then of the police, and finally of an ox.[38] The pantomime's illogic short-circuits the emotional shock established by the melodramatic ending of Gérôme's painting and its aspirations toward linear development and realism. Dominique de Font-Réaulx sees Gérôme's creation of a gap between victim and killer as an "artifice théâtral" that permits the spectator to "reconstituer le fil de la narration et donc le temps écoulé" (120). The imprecision in the rendering of the characters' features leaves it to "leurs gestes et attitudes le soin de traduire leurs expressions" (120). This is theatrical gesture performing the work of words in their absence, not the pantomimic gesture associated with the Hanlon-Lees, whose constant and chaotic acrobatic movement resists being captured by language and fixed in a narrative. In their continuous careening, tumbling, and leaping the Hanlon-Lees are "aux quatre coins de la scène," never in any one place long enough for description to take hold (Zola, "Pantomime" 330). "Dans les accidents réels," Zola notes, "on rit d'abord, et puis on s'apitoie," an apt description of the sequence of emotions experienced at a viewing of Gérôme's painting with its pairing of the comic characters in a moment that evokes intense pity ("Pantomime" 330). He continues, and perhaps with a visual of Gérôme's painting in his mind, "Les Hanlon ont compris qu'il ne fallait pas laisser à l'apitoiement le temps de se produire" (330). If the Hanlon-Lees did indeed invoke the authority of the painting, it was only to subsequently destroy it. Narrative description of an acrobatic act, as Paul Bouissac notes, is possible only when there is an accident, "i.e., when the characteristic structure of an acrobatic act breaks down and becomes a 'story'" (43). No such reportable accident materializes, and therefore, no story emerges in the Hanlon-Lees' *Duel*.

Paul Martinetti's *The Duel in the Snow; or, After the Masquerade Ball* from 1889 presents a perplexing acknowledgment of both the enduring relevance of Gérôme's painting on the public imaginary *and* the pre-eminence of the Hanlon-Lees as practitioners of a purer spirit of pantomime. On the one hand, Martinetti's *Duel in the Snow*, which toured at least until 1903, featured a "tableau approximation of the painting as the climax" (Parsons 322n16)[39], and on the other hand, the fear experienced by the pantomime's duelists is reminiscent of that in the Hanlon-Lees' *Duel* and is the source of considerable hanlonesque mayhem on stage. The work equally features a hat chase, which, while a stock routine, may also have come from the Hanlon-Lees' pantomime.

Martinetti, an acrobat and pantomimist of French birth, spent most of his life performing in the US and identified as an American.[40] He and his brothers had joined the troupe of Gabriel Ravel sometime in the late 1850s, early 1860s. The Ravels were from Toulouse, but toured and enjoyed their greatest success in the US, as did the Martinettis. In the 1860s, most likely with the retirement of Gabriel Ravel, the Martinettis inherited his vast repertoire of pantomimes, among which was *The Duel, or, Still Water Runs Deep*. In 1880, the Martinetti troupe offered *The Duel* at the Aquarium Theatre in London, which is perhaps the earlier Ravel pantomime or an imitation of the Hanlon-Lees' Paris production.[41] Many scholars of the medium downplay the acrobatic talents of French pantomimists, preferring to focus on the aesthetic subtleties of silent theater and gesture, and attaching little importance to their moments of fast and furious physicality, but both the Ravels and the Martinettis, like the Hanlon-Lees, were accomplished gymnasts, incorporating trapeze, tightrope walking, and dizzying acrobatics into their scenarios. The Ravels (featuring the Martinettis) and the Hanlons appeared in the same month at Niblo's Garden in New York on at least one occasion. It is certain that they knew their respective repertoires and reputations, and it is also certain that their routines sometimes shared great formal similarities, the result of creative borrowing.[42] The similarities may have continued after the Hanlons-Lees' Paris season, since Agoust left the troupe and worked with the Martinettis for the next few years, and may have shared old routines with them.

Paul Martinetti's re-creation of Gérôme's *La Sortie du bal masqué* in his 1889 pantomime stands as proof of the continued recognition effect of the work more than thirty years after its Salon exhibition. The pantomime is fairly traditional in the comic misunderstandings and misplaced exchange of punches (at the Bal de l'Opéra and in the street before the "Café de Lapai" [sic]), pistol shots, and sword thrusts (in the Bois de Boulogne) (6).[43] Like the plays discussed earlier, *The Duel in the Snow* was designed expressly to end in a reproduction of Gérôme's painting's staging. Until the final moments of the pantomime, it adheres to the traditions of the genre as they had existed since earlier in the century.

The title, however, prepares the viewer for the closing *tableau vivant*, in which Pierrot is dying, run through by the deadly stroke of a blade, a puzzling twist considering that the seconds and the doctor are all pierced and shot repeatedly without a one succumbing to his wounds.[44]

While Martinetti's pantomime obviously enjoyed popular success in Europe, the US, and Australia for roughly fifteen years, it mixes two fundamentally incompatible approaches, which can be summed up in terms of the notion of time that informs them. One belongs clearly to the pantomime format, operating according to cyclical time: main characters never really suffer irreparable harm, nor do they die. The other belongs to the theatricality and realism of Gérôme's painting, which unfolds according to linear time. Unlike Villiers's tale, which skillfully short-circuits the painting's ability to provoke a clichéd emotional response, *The Duel in the Snow*'s final *tableau vivant* does not so much undermine the preceding part of the pantomime's aesthetic grounding but rather feels awkwardly tacked on, as if Martinetti opted for piggybacking on the continued success and relevance of Gérôme's painting to ensure the fortune of his own work.

Pantomime as a primarily silent medium had run its course and would die out within ten years of the last performances of *The Duel in the Snow*, giving way to *féeries* that appealed more to the changing tastes of audiences.[45] Most scholars attribute to Champfleury the introduction of real life into pantomime, in particular the furnishing of logical explanations that eliminated the supernatural twists and turns of the Théâtre des Funambules' scenarios. In an often-cited example, the face and clothing of Champfleury's Pierrot are now white for a logical reason: he is a miller's apprentice (*Pierrot marquis* 1847). It is with Champfleury as well that Pierrot dies so as to restore moral order (Pierrot can come back to life as in *Pierrot pendu* [1846], but only if he has mended his ways).[46] Should Gérôme, however, take some if not most of the responsibility considering the greater reach of *La Sortie du bal masqué* across social classes and national borders and its popular appeal over a forty-year span?

The one pantomime in which acrobatics figured predominantly (the Hanlon-Lees' *Le Duel*) skirted in its own ways the powerful appeal of the painting's dying clown and the temptation to impose logic on the scenario. The same, however, was not true for those pantomimes created by some men of letters in the last two decades of the nineteenth century. While Gérôme's art was often mocked in cultivated circles in Paris, it was in these very groups that the painting had its greatest, however much unacknowledged or unconscious, impact. The Cercle funambulesque's productions (1888–98), many of which featured Pierrot in a duel, perpetuated the trend in linear narratives in which Pierrot dies by the sword or, in a reversal, mortally wounds his opponent.[47] In Camille de Saint-Croix's *Blanc et Noir* from 1888, white Pierrot and black Pierrot fight a duel for the exclusive enjoyment of Columbine's favors. True to Gérôme's painting, Pierrot dies, but this time in duplicate. In Félix Galipaux's *Pour une bouffée de tabac* from 1890, Pierrot is not killed, but rather, in a twist, kills a man in a duel over one too many *bouffées de tabac* in the face. And, of course, in Séverin and Théodore Thalès's aforementioned *Pauvre Pierrot, ou après le bal*, Pierrot dies in a duel after being deceived by Columbine. This last pantomime's subtitle leaves no doubt about the lasting influence of Gérôme's work on pantomime scenarios. And, while Séverin mistakenly concluded that he was the original source for subsequent story lines in which Pierrot dies, it is clear that the real source was Gérôme's *La Sortie du bal masqué.*

*

World War I certainly played an important role in driving in the last nail of the coffin of pantomime, but it is noteworthy that among the last successful pantomimes was one which closed with a *tableau vivant* of Gérôme's canvas. In some respects, one can quip that the last pierrotic pantomime was Gérôme's *Sortie du bal masqué.*

It is ironic as well to consider that Gérôme's painting, whose theme brazenly copied that of Couture's *Le Duel après le bal masqué*, should be either the source or the victim of its own cycle of appropriations by playwrights and hucksters for the next forty years. It is unlikely, however, that Gérôme would have perceived himself as a victim since, as is made clear in the example of Marin's play which cites the painter as inspiration without even reproducing anything from the painting, through all the *tableaux vivants*, Gérôme's name had accumulated enough symbolic capital to effectively consecrate his name.

Gérôme's actions anticipate the opportunism of the fin-de-siècle writer Félicien Champsaur, who recognized the possibilities to be exploited in the figure of the *funambule*, both for making a name for himself and, more importantly, for making him a well-off and powerful man. In *Braves gens* (1886), Jean Richepin's du Glaizat is clearly based on Champsaur. Du Glaizat is

> not an artist; he is a merchant. He does not create, he negotiates, and, when negotiations fail, he pilfers. His literary ambition has for its goal not unfailing devotion to his craft in the creation of an exemplary work, but rather material recognition of him as the creator of an "œuvre d'artiste oseur, original," even if that work of art belongs to someone else, as in the pantomime that 'il filoutait adroitement à Tombre.' (Forrest 105)

The description of Champsaur's objective to succeed whatever the cost by Michel Golfier and Jean-Didier Wagneur echoes strangely that of

Gérôme by About: "Nombre de ces jeunes écrivains [aspiring writers of "la Jeune Littérature" 1875–85] auront les dents suffisamment acérées, et parfois assez peu de scrupules dans l'art de parvenir, en témoigne la carrière de Félicien Champsaur" (38).

If Champsaur represents the most egregious of the literary Rastignacs, he was by no means an isolated case. In the June 13, 1874, *Journal* entry by Edmond de Goncourt, he bemoans how a deplorable number of young writers focus less on developing their own style than on gaming the system to their advantage by learning all the ins and outs of Parisian publishing (particularly the press) from its people to its practices: "ils possèdent, en vrais courtiers de lettres, tous les secrets financiers de l'industrie des lettres. C'est une connaissance commerciale de la place de Paris, qui manquait absolument à notre génération" (580). He makes a monster hybrid of writer with commerce and finance ("courtiers de lettres," "l'industrie des lettres") to signal "la fin de la pure littérature," the end of a presumed utopian age of literature untouched by the market (580). Of course, Goncourt is either mistaken or disingenuous when he states that his generation knew nothing of this type of professional scheming and manipulation since the conditions allowing for such *arrivisme* were in place since the industrialization and capitalization of the press in the mid-1830s with Émile de Girardin's *La Presse* and serialized literature. Similarly, in the art world, it was in mid-century that the gradual shift from the Academic Salon system to the gallery system began. In the worlds of art and literature, regardless of whether one chose the path of fame and fortune or that of devotion to one's art, a practicing artist or writer was aware of and unavoidably *in* the market economy. The path chosen by Gérôme and Champsaur is clear: they seized on a trending subject – the *funambule* – on which they banked to bring them success. As for Couture, Daumier, Banville, and Baudelaire, they chose the same figure precisely because it visually embodied the tension of the artist and/in the market. The *funambule* would also turn out to be an aesthetic device for defusing the power of that tension.[48]

Notes

1 This painting is known under various titles: *La Sortie du bal masqué, Le Duel à la sortie du bal masqué, Le Duel au sortir d'un bal masqué, Suites d'un bal masqué*, and *Un duel après le bal*. Gustave Haller notes that among the public, the painting was known as *Le Duel de Pierrot* (19), a title that probably gained currency among viewers beginning with its exhibition at the 1867 *Exposition universelle. Un duel après le bal* figured as the title on post-1867 photographic reproductions of the painting, "sans doute jugé plus expressif et donc plus efficace" (Font-Réaulx 120). In order to distinguish it clearly from Thomas Couture's *Le Duel après le bal masqué*, however, I use *La Sortie du bal masqué*.

2 As T. J. Clark notes, "No one is sure when the great oil paintings and watercolours of the [*saltimbanque*] series were done: perhaps from the mid-1850s

onwards, perhaps in the 1860s" (119). While Ives, Stuffmann, and Sonnabend of *Daumier Drawings* (1992) offer approximate periods for many of his works, they are nevertheless unable to assign specific dates to them.

3 Paula Hays Harper finds fault with Clark's assertion, having found very few clown-themed paintings in the Salon lists for the 1840s. From my own reading of the paragraph in which Clark makes this statement, I understood him to be referring to the 1850s, when Daumier began his *saltimbanque* series.

4 I draw here from the first three chapters of Louisa E. Jones's *Sad Clowns and Pale Pierrots: Literature and the Popular Comic Arts in 19th-Century France.*

5 Hugo's play was banned because authorities perceived correctly that the protagonist, the court jester Triboulet, was the vehicle for a vehement social critique, particularly against the monarchy of Louis-Philippe. *Le Roi s'amuse* had to wait fifty years before its second performance (having only been performed once in 1832), this time at the Comédie-Française. One would surely have had difficulty staging the play during the Second Empire, given that Hugo lived in exile for writing his scathing political pamphlet "Napoléon le Petit." However, Giuseppe Verdi's opera *Rigoletto*, which premiered in Venice in 1851 and was based closely on Hugo's play, was performed in Paris for the first time in 1857. The opera changed only the jester's name and the narrative's locale to avoid censorship.

6 For example, while the opening and closing poems of Théodore de Banville's *Odes funambulesques* feature an acrobatic clown, the reader will not find any others in the playfully amusing and refreshingly original poems in between. Banville's "acrobatics" were primarily stylistic, not thematic, a fact that his critics made synonymous with empty manipulation of poetic form.

7 The Théâtre des Funambules was torn down to make way for Baron Haussmann's renovations in 1862.

8 In his comments to "Le Saut du tremplin," Banville explains that, "[d]ans ce poème finale, j'ai essayé d'exprimer ce que je sens le mieux: l'attrait du gouffre d'en haut" (*Odes* 385). There are two kinds of poets, he claims, in "À Madame Caroline A.," one "qu'attire le gouffre/Cherche l'abîme," and the other, like he, who "interroge le ciel" (*Poésies* 189). And from Baudelaire's "Le Gouffre" from *Les Fleurs du mal* (1857), the poet, "toujours du vertige hanté," refers to the two abysses, "En haut, en bas, partout la profondeur" (88).

9 In physics, photons behave like waves when one tries to identify them as particles and like particles when one tries to identify them as waves.

10 "In a poll taken in the winter of 1909–1910, Baltimoreans were asked to identify their fifty-five favorite works of art, and *The Duel After the Masquerade* topped the list" ("The Duel After the Masquerade," July 2018, *Wikipedia*, 10 August 2018 <https://en.wikipedia.org/wiki/The_Duel_After_the_Masquerade>). The recognition factor was still great in 1960 when it featured in the introduction of George Cukor's film *Let's Make Love* starring Yves Montand and Marilyn Monroe. One of Yves Montand/Jean-Marc Clément's ancestors is shown as the victor in a duel, with the painting ostensibly depicting that event.

11 I use the term *saltimbanque* here rather than *funambule* for expedience. This is the term employed by scholars when discussing these Daumier works, and his circus-related figures are almost exclusively street and fairground performers.

12 The marketing of all things *Uncle Tom's Cabin* would push back to the 1850s Rykner's assertion that modern marketing techniques in France began in the 1860s.

13 See Cédric de Guido's *Marcel Schwob, du journal au recueil* (Paris: Classiques Garnier, 2015), in which the author situates Schwob's short pieces in a very positive and energetic relationship with journalism.

14 The saturating distribution of reproductions of Gérôme's painting, begun in earnest in 1867, was primarily the work of his father-in-law, the collector, publisher, and critic Adolphe Goupil. One cannot underestimate Goupil's deft marketing of the image, which was probably the key factor in its translation into other genres and mediums in its targeting of an audience covering all social classes over the last half of the nineteenth century.

15 Like Haskell, I have been unable to find a newspaper report of this duel. Haskell drew his information from Coleman O. Parson's "The Wintry Duel: A Victorian Import," whose own source was Victor Guillemin. A half century after this affair of honor, Guillemin provided the names and professions of the combatants in his "Étude sur le peintre et sculpteur Jean-Léon Gérôme (1824–1904)" in a footnote, without, however, citing his source (145). Régine Bigorne wonders if the encounter ever occurred, especially since Boittelle appears several times in the Goncourt brothers' *Journal* without reference to a duel (83). Théophile Gautier, who reviewed the painting in 1857, seems to corroborate Bigorne, attributing the event depicted to impetuous youth: "Des jeunes gens, chauds de vin sans doute, se sont pris de querelle sur l'escalier de l'Opéra ou dans quelque cabinet de la Maison-d'Or, pour un coup de coude, un sarcasme trop vif, une préférence de fille ou tout autre motif frivole" (Gautier, "Salon de 1857" 245). As for Edmond About, he ridiculed Couture's claim to priority with respect to the subject, stating that the situation depicted was a common enough event: "Le bois de Boulogne a vu deux ou trois de ces duels enfarinés, et l'idée est tombée dans le domaine public, surtout si les inventeurs sont morts" (73). As Albert Boime notes, Gérôme was undoubtedly aware of Couture's painting and probably borrowed the topic from him (313). If Bigorne is correct in thinking that the duel never took place, then the shared costumes of the paintings' major players would mean that Gérôme had indeed adopted Couture's theme.

16 In the original painting, the victor is either Harlequin or the Native American. In the two subsequent versions of the painting, Gérôme cleared any confusion by identifying the Native American as Pierrot's opponent: his head turns toward his second, Harlequin, who appears to comfort him. This may not have been, however, his intention, given that he often made slight changes to replicas of his paintings either to establish the first as the original (originals generally sold for more money than replicas), or in response to a request from Goupil, or from the buyer. It is even possible that changes reflected either Gérôme's own "second thoughts" about a particular work or, in this particular instance, an effort to exaggerate the differences between his painting and Couture's to put to rest comparisons between the two (Lafont-Couturier 21). It is worth noting, however, that in his review of the painting, Théophile Gautier, champion of the Théâtre des Funambules, describes confidently the opponents as Pierrot and Harlequin ("Salon" 246).

17 In Couture's painting, Pierrot's seconds are Crispin and a Native American.

18 As with Jean-Gaspard Deburau and his interpretaion of Pierrot, nineteenth-century pantomime interpretations of Harlequin transformed his basic character traits. As Adriane Despot notes, "He is not the perplexing and explosive complex of stupidity and craftiness [of the *Commedia dell'arte*], but he is the daring, determined, clever and energetic hero" (371).

19 Unlike Gautier, Nadar was initially perplexed at how to read the painting: "est-ce une scène sérieuse et ces gens enfarinés et bariolés ont-ils la

colère et la haine qui tuent, ou ne dois-je voir là qu'une farce du Pierrot des Folies-Nouvelles?" (9). Nadar refers to the mime Paul Legrand, who featured at the Folies-Nouvelles, and who was known for his sentimental interpretation of Pierrot, one who could and did shed tears. As noted, the confusion was aggravated by the fact that Gérôme intentionally emphasized the striking opposition of the comic and the tragic, symbolically echoed in the original frame of the painting which featured the masks of comedy and tragedy, separated by a court jester's mock scepter or bauble. The frame motif's echo of the painting's comic masks contrasted with a tragic situation suggests Pierrot and Harlequin as the duel's opponents, prompting Gautier to reproach Harlequin, "Qu'as-tu fait de ton frère Pierrot" ("Salon" 246).

20 Mme Wilhelmine Joséphine Fould was the wife of politician and *homme de lettres*, Gustave-Eugène Fould.

21 Another example is Delaroche's *Les Enfants d'Édouard* (1830), which was the source of a similarly titled play by Casimir Delavigne. As Boime notes, "Delavigne dedicated the drama to Delaroche, and the finale replicates the painting as a *tableau vivant*" (*Art* 341).

22 There were commercial ties between Gambart and Goupil Maison dating back to 1840 when "Belgian-born Gambart arrived in London as an agent of the French print publisher Goupil" (Fletcher 1).

23 *Indécision*, which also depicts one of Saintin's own paintings in print reproduction (*Deuil de coeur*, 1872–73), was distributed by Goupil & Cie, the same company responsible for the publicity blitz surrounding *La Sortie du bal masqué. Indécision* worked double duty for the Maison Goupil in promoting the works of these two painters.

24 The *tableau vivant* appeared on several different "stages" from the sacred to the profane during the nineteenth century: some church masses incorporated them, for example, in nativity plays and in scenes depicting the Last Supper; some society events featured prominent socialites as the heroines of famous paintings; and music-halls had recourse to them as one of several ways to titillate the male spectator without incurring censorship.

25 Ironically, Paul Hugounet notes in *Mimes et Pierrots* that on the walls of the apartment of the mime Paul Legrand, "c'est le *Duel après le bal* de Gérôme offert à l'interprète du *Duel de Pierrot*, par l'éditeur Goupil" (122). The pantomime was not a reprise of Deburau *père*'s *Le Duel de Pierrot, ou les 26 infortunes* from 1832. I have been unable to determine when precisely Legrand performed this pantomime (sometime between 1854 and 1887 according to Robert Storey), but it has no relation whatsoever with the scenario of Gérôme's painting, hence there is no surplus drama in a *tableau vivant* re-creation (330). That said, Goupil's gesture, nevertheless, reflects the art dealer's continued aggressive promotion of the painting, regardless of the relevance, with the suggestion in this instance that all references to a duel featuring Pierrot have their origin, not in classical pantomime but in the canvas.

26 There is no plate, however, in the digital copies that I found of Fitzball's play.

27 I have been unable to find any reviews of this production.

28 Parsons quotes Kean's biographer, who stated that so great was the success of Boucicault's production that it inspired not only Lacy, but other producers to come up with their own version of the story. Although most citations of Lacy's translation estimate its publication date as 1852, all the copies that I have found indicate the placement of the characters in the vision at the end of first act as "realizing the group from the picture of 'The Duel'" (28). This would place the date of the publications that refer to Gérôme's painting after

its London exhibition in 1858, the year in which Gambart exhibited and reproduced it. Lacy's *tableau vivant* most likely served another more economical purpose, as well. It replaced the complicated and costly machinery used in creating the illusion of Louis dei Franchi's ghost at the end of the first act in Boucicault's production. The recognition effect produced by the *tableau vivant* in Lacy's version would have compensated the audience that expected the spectacular illusion of a ghostly apparition with a visual thrill of another order.

29 The tale was first published as "Le Convive inconnu" in the *Revue du monde nouveau* (February 15, 1874). It was included later in Villiers's *Contes cruels* (1883).

30 Certainly, Villiers's memory of the painting was overpowered by his familiarity with traditional pantomime in which the opponents are usually Harlequin and Pierrot, hence his reference to Harlequin's victory and not the Native American's. The poet Charles Burdin, as well, preferred the traditional *commedia* opponents in his "Le Duel de Pierrot, d'après Gérôme" from *Tableaux et paysages* in *Poésies* (1876).

31 The reader could wonder if Villiers will provide the reader, as the plays do, with the details that lead up to the duel, details that we can only infer from the painting.

32 His Greek counterpart is Kronos or Time.

33 See P. W. M. Cogman's excellent article exploring the tale's *récit* as operating according to a mosaic structure: "Masks and Madness: Villiers's 'Le Convive des dernières fêtes,'" *Nineteenth-Century French Studies* 21.1–2 (1992–93): 102–13.

34 Agoust, credited with steering the troupe toward pantomime, did have a background in the art. According to Tristan Rémy, he studied and performed pantomime under "maître Blanc, directeur d'une salle de spectacle au Havre" (55). Rémy got this information from Richard Lesclides's *Mémoires et pantomimes des frères Hanlon Lees*, where he quotes George Hanlon on Agoust's background. Without citing the source of her information, Levillain states, however, that he had been a "juggler and minor mime at the Funambules" (249). She may have been citing M. Willson Disher, who wrote that "Agoust, a juggler who became manager of the Nouveau Cirque, passed on the lessons he had learned at the Funambules to the Hanlon-Lees whom he met in America" (194). Disher also fails to offer the source of his information.

35 As an indication of the continued relevance of Gérôme's painting in the popular cultural imagination, the penny dreadful (juvenile literature) illustrator associated with the British Aldine Publishing Company, Robert Prowse, Jr., did a March 3, 1904, cover for the Spring-Heeled Jack series (*The Terror of the Land; or Spring-heeled Jack at Home and School*) that reproduces much of the painting's *mise-en-scène* with some minor changes. Representing one camp, Harlequin supports a wounded Pierrot in his arms, with Le Rouge (devil costume) and a cowl-clad figure in the other. There is no Native American. The bottom caption reads: "Swift as lightning the bully delivered his thrust, and La Croix dropped into Marchon's arms. 'So much for that insult,' Le Rouge sneered. He had scarcely spoken when from the wood there came a fiendish cry. 'Spring-Heeled Jack!' Le Rouge exclaimed." One can conclude that either Prowse or his father, also an illustrator, possessed a print copy of *La Sortie du bal masqué*. Also, three years earlier, Pathé produced a silent short film, *Un duel après le bal*. In 1908, the Società italiana cines produced *Un duello in maschera/Duel After the Ball*. The Pathé film

was based on the Gérôme painting. I have no information on the Italian film, but given the degree of borrowing and outright duplication that took place in early cinema, it could be a longer "remake" of the Pathé version.

36 This was not the first time that spectators would have encountered multiple Pierrots. Many of Gavarni's caricatures of the *bal masqué* offer many instances drawn from experience. Gautier wrote in 1845 that "Comme nous rentrions chez nous, nous vîmes descendre d'un estaminet une bande de quarante pierrots tous costumés de même, qui se rendaient au bal de l'Opéra, précédés d'une bannière où étaient écrits ces mots: *Que la vie est amère!*" (*Histoire* 188). Nor was this the first time that more than one Pierrot figured on a pantomime stage. In 1849, the Funambules offered *Les Deux Pierrots* (with Paul Legrand and Charles Deburau), a success that led to *Les Trois Pierrots, ou Pierrot le rusé, Pierrot le naïf, Pierrot le dévoué* (with Alexandre Guyon taking the role of the third Pierrot) (Levillain 215).

37 While it is doubtful that the acrobats sought recognition in the audience of Couture's *Le Duel après le bal masqué*, the Hanlons do act on the painter's implicit commentary on seconds as pernicious inciters to action by doing away with them.

38 One could argue that the presence of harvesters and an ox represents a contrary worldview to the realism of the painting, and on a larger scale, of an urban, industrial culture. The pantomime offers a viewpoint associated with seasons, cycles, the carnivalesque, and perhaps even with the return of Mardi Gras.

39 The Library of Congress copy of the pantomime clearly reproduces the staging of the figures in Gérôme's painting, an association made explicit by the pantomime's title.

40 A review in the *Revue encyclopédique* from August 1, 1894, states that Paul Martinetti was born "vers 1855" and that he debuted in the US at the age of seven (Boghaert-Vaché 326). The five Hanlon brothers' birth dates range from 1833 to 1848, situating them generationally in between the Ravels and the Martinettis.

41 I have been unable to find any details regarding the story lines of either the Ravel or the Martinetti pantomimes. The pantomimes that Martinetti had advertised as new and of his own creation were often old productions. For example, his *Robert Macaire* was based on Gabriel Ravel's adaptation from the play *L'Auberge des Adrets* (1832), and his *Jocko* was part of the pantomime repertory that went to Ravel at the death of the pantomimist Charles-François Mazurier, who had adapted the work from either the novella by Charles de Pougens (1824) or the popular ballet-pantomime by Edmond Rochefort.

42 The Ravels enjoyed regular billings at Niblo's Garden. They closed their 1861 billing there on January 7, and the Hanlons started theirs as members of Cooke's Circus on January 16. As for creative borrowing, in 1867, Martinetti performed the "'Zampillaerostation' exercise," a number and an apparatus that the Hanlon-Lees created and debuted in 1861 and later patented ("Amusements, etc." 1; Cosdon 18).

43 Martinetti deposited a handwritten copy in English at the Library of Congress in 1890, perhaps in imitation of the Hanlon brothers' practice. Ironically, Martinetti's submission survives in the Rare Books and Collections Division of the Library of Congress, while those of the Hanlons were destroyed sometime last century.

44 Martinetti's pantomime scenarios in which death and macabre behavior emerge reflect the evolution of the medium in the last half of the nineteenth

century. For example, in a review of an unidentified pantomime featuring the Martinettis, the reviewer describes one in which Paul and his brother Alfred as Pantaloon "kill a policeman (Mr. J Head), and presently, when the murder is out, turn up to assist at the discovery, disguised severally as a doctor and his boy" ("Two Pantomimes" 20).

45 In 1916, the Pierrot mime Georges Wague retired from performance to teach at the Conservatoire national supérieur d'art dramatique. As for the mime Séverin Cafferra, he was able to revive pierrotic pantomime only briefly and sporadically after his stint in the army during World War I; his last role as Pierrot was in his own *Mains et masque* (1920).

46 Leisha Ashdown-Lecointre does not give *Marrrchand d'habits!* the honor of having first killed Pierrot because the pantomime lacks a moral conclusion: "despite the fight to the death between the ghost and Pierrot, Pierrot is not indicted for his crime, nor does he show remorse for the clothes-seller's murder" (191). Death is final, however, remorse or no remorse, and is alien to the marvelous world of *commedia* pantomime.

47 The Cercle Funambulesque, whose membership at its height was roughly 150, was founded by Paul Margueritte, Eugène and Félix Larcher, Paul Hugounet, the mime Najac, and Fernand Beissier. It would soon boast members like J. K. Huysmans, Jules Chéret, Jean Richepin, and more.

48 We see the continued relevance of the *funambule* as an agent of disruption later in the century in the 1886, and especially the 1889, posters that Jules Chéret did for the *Expositions des Arts Incohérents.* In these exhibitions and in the materials advertising them, the Incohérents parodied the official Salon. The clown that figures in the posters is not an allegory of the artist but a graphic representation of an aesthetic tool of disorder.

Works Cited

About, Edmond. *Nos Artistes au Salon de 1857.* Paris: Hachette, 1858.

"Amusements, etc." *Daily Alta California* 19.7068 (1 February 1867): 1.

Ashdown-Lecointre, Leisha. "Pierrot and the Pantomime: Théophile Gautier's Ideal Theater." *Novel Stages: Drama and the Novel in Nineteenth-Century France.* Ed. Pratima Prasad and Susan McCready. Newark: U of Delaware P, 2007. 183–98.

Banville, Théodore de. *Les Pauvres saltimbanques.* Paris: Michel Lévy Frères, 1853.

———. *Les Poésies de Théodore de Banville, 1841–1854.* Paris: Poulet-Malassis et de Broise, 1857.

———. *Odes funambulesques, suivies d'un commentaire. Œuvres de Théodore de Banville.* Paris: Alphonse Lemerre, 1892.

Baudelaire, Charles. *Œuvres complètes.* Ed. Marcel A. Ruff. Paris: Éditions du Seuil, 1968. 370–78.

Becque, Henry. *Querelles littéraires.* Paris: Dentu, 1890.

Bigorne, Régine. "A Publishing Policy." Lafont-Couturier. 77–92.

Boghaert-Vaché, Arthur. "Théâtre: Le Mort." *Revue encyclopédique: recueil documentaire universel et illustré. Année 1894.* Ed. Georges Moreau. Paris: Librairie Larousse. 325–28.

Boime, Albert. *Art in an Age of Counterrevolution, 1815–1848.* Vol. 3 of *A Social History of Modern Art.* Chicago, IL: U of Chicago P, 2004.

———. *Thomas Couture and the Eclectic Vision*. New Haven, CT and London: Yale UP, 1980.

Bouissac, Paul. *Circus and Culture: A Semiotic Approach*. Bloomington and London: Indiana UP, 1976.

Burdin, Charles. *Poésies*. Paris: Librairie des Bibliophiles, 1876.

Coquelin Cadet. *La Vie humoristique*. Paris: Ollendorff, 1883.

Despot, Adriane. "Jean-Gaspard Deburau and the Pantomime at the Théâtre des Funambules." *Educational Theatre Journal* 27.3 (1975): 364–76.

Disher, M. Willson. *Clowns and Pantomimes*. New York and London: Benjamin Blom, 1925.

Dumas, Alexandre. *Mes Mémoires*. 6th edition. Paris: Michel Lévy Frères, 1863.

Fitzball, Edward. *Christmas Eve, or the Duel in the Snow: An Original Domestic Drama in Three Acts*. London and New York: Samuel French, 1868. 6 July 2015 <https://catalog.hathitrust.org/Record/011610739>.

Fletcher, Pamela M. "Creating the French Gallery: Ernest Gambart and the Rise of the Commercial Art Gallery in Mid-Victorian London." *Nineteenth-Century Art Worldwide*. 1 August 2018 <http://www.19thc-artworldwide.org/spring07/46-spring07/spring07article/143-creating-the-french-gallery-ernest-gambart-and-the-rise-of-the-commercial-art-galler>.

Font-Réaulx, Dominique de. "Sortie du bal masqué dit aussi Un Duel après le bal." *Jean-Léon Gérôme (1824–1904): l'histoire en spectacle*. Eds. Laurent des Cars, Dominique de Font-Réaulx, and Édouard Papet. Paris: Skira Flammarion, 2011. 118–21.

Forrest, Jennifer. "Artists Unknown: The Poetics of Anonymity in Jean Richepin's *Brave gens*." *Romance Studies* 31.2 (2013): 101–12.

Gautier, Théophile. *Histoire de l'art dramatique en France depuis vingt-cinq ans*. Vol 4. Paris: Édition Hetzel, 1859.

———, "Salon de 1857, IV: MM. Gérôme, Mottez." *L'Artiste, Tome Premier* (5 July 1857): 245–49.

Golfier, Michel, and Jean-Didier Wagneur. Introduction. *Dix ans de bohème, suivi de Les Hirsutes*. By Émile Goudeau and Léo Trézenik. Eds. Michel Golfier and Jean-Didier Wagneur. Seyssel: Champ Vallon, 2000. 7–79.

Goncourt, Edmond and Jules de. *Journal: Mémoires de la vie littéraire II – 1866–1886*. Paris: Robert Laffont, 1956.

Grangé, Eugène, and Xavier Aymon de Montépin. *Les Frères corses: drame fantastique en trois actes et cinq tableaux, tiré du roman de M. A. Dumas*. Bruxelles: J.A. Lelong, 1850.

———. *Les Frères corses, or, The Corsican Brothers, A Dramatic Romance in Three Acts and Five Tableaux*. Trans. Thomas Hailes Lacy. London: Thomas Hailes Lacy, n.d.

Guillemin, Victor. "Étude sur le peintre et sculpteur Jean-Léon Gérôme (1824–1904)." *Procès verbaux et mémoires, Année 1904*. Eds. Académie des Sciences, Belles Lettres & Arts de Besançon et de Franche-Comté Besançon: Typographie et Lithographie Jacquin, 1905: 134–88.

Haller, Gustave. *Nos grands peintres: catalogue de leurs oeuvres et opinions de la presse*. Paris: Goupil et Cie; Boussod, Manzi, Joyant et Cie, 1899.

Harper, Paula Hays. *Daumier's Clowns: Les Saltimbanques et les Parades. New Biographical and Political Functions for a Nineteenth Century Myth*. New York and London: Garland Publishing, 1981.

Haskell, Francis. "The Sad Clown: Some Notes on a 19th Century Myth." *French 19th Century Painting and Literature with Special Reference to the Relevance of Literary Subject-Matter to French Painting*. Ed. Ulrich Finke. Manchester: U of Manchester P, 1972. 2–16.

Hugounet, Paul. *Mimes et Pierrots, notes et documents inédits pour servir à l'histoire de la pantomime*. Paris: Fischbacher, 1889.

Ives, Colta Feller. *Romanticism and the School of Nature: Nineteenth-Century Drawings and Paintings from the Karen B. Cohen Collection*. New York: The Metropolitan Museum of Art, 2000.

Ives, Colta Feller, Margaret Stuffmann, and Martin Sonnabend, with contributions by Klaus Herding and Judith Wechsler. *Daumier Drawings*. New York, NY: The Metropolitan Museum of Art, 1992.

Jones, Louisa E. *Sad Clowns and Pale Pierrots: Literature and the Popular Comic Arts in 19th-Century France*. Lexington, KY: French Forum, 1984.

Knight, Christopher. "Art Review: 'The Spectacular Art of Jean-Léon Gérôme' @ J. Paul Getty Museum." *The Los Angeles Times*. 21 June 2010. 27 June 2018 <http://latimesblogs.latimes.com/culturemonster/2010/06/art-review-the-spectacular-art-of-j-paul-getty-museum.html>.

Lafont-Couturier, Hélène, ed. *Gérôme & Goupil: Art and Enterprise*. Trans. Isabel Ollivier. Paris: Réunion des musées nationaux; Bordeaux: Musée Goupil; Pittsburgh: Frich Art and Historical Center; New York: Dahesh Museum of Art, 2000.

———. "'Mr. Gérôme Works for Goupil.'" Lafont-Couturier, Hélène: 13–29.

Levillain, Anne Dowling. *The Evolution of Pantomime in France*. Diss. Boston College, 1943.

Macleod, Kirsten. *Fictions of British Decadence: High Art, Popular Writing, and the Fin-de-Siècle*. London and New York: Palgrave MacMillan, 2006.

Marin, Charles. *Le Duel de Pierrot, comédie en un acte et en vers avec chant*. Vannes: Émile Mahéo, 1924.

Martinetti, Paul. *The Duel in the Snow; or, After the Masquerade Ball, a Serio-Comic Ballet Pantomime in 3 Scenes*. Washington, DC: Rare Book and Special Collections Division: The Library of Congress, 1890.

Nadar (Gaspard-Félix Tournachon). *Nadar jury au Salon de 1857: 1000 comptes rendus, 150 dessins*. Paris: Librairie Nouvelle, 1857.

Parsons, Coleman O. "The Wintry Duel: A Victorian Import." *Victorian Studies* 2.4 (1959): 317–24.

Péricaud, Louis. *Le Théâtre des Funambules: ses mimes, ses acteurs et ses pantomimes depuis sa fondation jusqu'à sa démolition*. Paris: Léon Sapin, 1897.

Rancière, Jacques. *Aisthesis: Scenes from the Aesthetic Regime of Art*. Trans. Zakir Paul. London and Brooklyn: Verso, 2011.

Rémy, Tristan. *Les Clowns*. Paris: Bernard Grasset, 2002.

Rykner, Arnaud. *Corps obscènes. Pantomime, tableau vivant et autres images pas sages suivi de Note sur le dispositif*. Paris: Orizons, 2014.

Séverin (Cafferra). *L'Homme blanc: souvenirs d'un Pierrot*. Intro. Gustave Fréjaville. Paris: Plon, 1929. 8th edition.

Sicotte, Geneviève. "Présentation: Que peut l'approche synchronique? Ou quand le littéraire fait date." *Études françaises* 43.2 (2007): 5–12. 14 August 2018 <https://www.erudit.org/en/journals/etudfr/2007-v43-n2-etudfr1779/016469ar/>.

Storey, Robert F. *Pierrots on the Stage of Desire: Nineteenth-Century French Literary Artists and the Comic Pantomime*. Princeton, NJ: Princeton UP, 1985.

"Two Pantomimes." *The Saturday Review of Politics, Literature, Science, and Art*. London LXI (2 January 1886): 19–20.

Villiers de l'Isle-Adam. "Le Convive des dernières fêtes." *Contes cruels*. Ed. Pierre Reboul. Paris: Gallimard, 1983. 134–63.

Zola, Émile. "La Pantomime." *Le Naturalisme au théâtre*. Paris: Bibliothèque-Charpentier, 1912. 327–34.

———. "Nos peintres au Champs-de-Mars." *La Situation* (1 July 1867). 6 July 2015 <http://www.cahiers-naturalistes.com/Salons/01-07-67.html>

2 1857, Part II
Making Clown Faces

Depictions of *funambules* in works by Couture, Banville, Daumier, and Baudelaire exhibit tensions that contribute to making "une année charnière" of the year 1857, as Geneviève Sicotte contends (9). Through them, the *funambule* becomes the contested site of both art and commerce. If these artists and writers chose to embrace and explore an image that one would expect to see dismissed for its very proliferation in mediocre paintings, postcards, photographs, and other objects of industrial production (prints, statuettes, etc.), it was precisely because the figure's relation to the market made it both meaningful and useful. These artists and writers acknowledged through the *funambule* their relation to commerce, a decision that did not serve, however, to mask a critique of the traditions, conventions, and authorities in which their use of the image would have blended almost imperceptibly with all the others saturating the streets and display windows. Their adoption of the figure was a means to drawing back the curtain behind which the grand wizard of society and culture fabricated the artificial laws that we all take to be true and natural. Revealing the arbitrariness of the rules of art and society through the mischievous antics of the acrobatic clown, they situated themselves outside the social-cultural system, whose codes they proceeded to playfully manipulate. Working from both inside (avowal of the commercial conditions of art in 1857) and outside culture (impish derision, including self-mockery), these artists/writers created for themselves a paradoxical duality whose nexus one finds literally and metaphorically in clown faces.

Thomas Couture

The art critic Edmond About expressed regret that Couture's *Le Duel après le bal masqué* was not displayed in the same Salon room as Gérôme's, ostensibly so that the critics and the public could judge for themselves the merits of Couture's assertion to priority in the depiction of dueling pantomime figures.[1] Ironically, he accuses Couture of the kind of commercialism that defined Gérôme's and his future father-in-law Goupil's milking of the *Sortie du bal masqué* cash cow. About implies not only that Couture, by selling his paintings "à la veille de l'exposition" rather than exhibiting them at the Salon like Gérôme, had ambitions more commercial than painterly, but also that Couture feared with good reason that his painting would not have triumphed in a comparison (About 73). About's comment carried some truth since it was at this time that Couture had "no lack of eager American and French purchasers," and the striking *mise-en-scène* of Gérôme's painting made it "[l]e tableau le plus populaire du Salon" (Boime, *Eclectic* 292; Nadar 9).[2]

About's comments reveal the tension at the heart of Couture's aesthetic position as he "veered from the notion of *grande peinture* to a more authentic expression of his talents" (Boime, *Eclectic* 292). The group of works that mark this personal and critical shift – the Pierrot and Harlequin series, which includes *Le Duel après le bal masqué* – is in many ways symbolic of Couture's transition away from the academy-patronage system. For example, a wallpaper manufacturer commissioned the first in the series, and a private clientele commissioned the others. In this undeniable turning away from official painting, Couture, like most artists, may have been conflicted by what he considered debasing financial motivations. We find contemporary echoes of this conflict in Banville's introduction to his *Pauvre saltimbanques* (1853), Daumier's own *saltimbanques* beginning mid-decade, and Baudelaire's "Le Vieux saltimbanque" (1861). These works depict impoverished street or fairground *funambules* forced to perform for money before unappreciative or unworthy spectators. While scholars generally cite the choice of subject as revealing these artists/writers' identification with the lowly street or fairground *funambule* as an embodiment of their experience, and while they were moved by and sympathetic to the real-life conditions endured by these performers, there is an aesthetic consideration that more satisfactorily demonstrates how these particular men were important precursors to many fin-de-siècle and modernist painters, poets, and novelists in their embracing of the figure. It stands to reason that these fiercely independent artists/writers would seek to distinguish themselves and their work rather than be yet one more contributor to what was becoming the "lieu commun" of the artist/writer as sad clown (Starobinski 8). If there is a shared subject by them, it is more likely that they were willing to adopt the figure precisely because it was one that performed the double duty of what I identify as avowal and derision.

On the one hand, becoming the *funambule* allowed them to avow their place in the market in direct violation of their pact with the public, a pact in which artists/writers usually deny the commercial conditions of their work. As About's criticism of Couture makes clear, in foregoing the 1857 Salon and selling *Le Duel après le bal masqué*, the painter contradicted the lie behind the Romantic belief that "real" artists are detached from the commercial side of the art system.[3] Depicting oneself as a *funambule* acknowledges explicitly that while one is an artist, one is also a seller/agent in an exchange of goods. The image of the artist/writer as *funambule* forced to perform represents a sobering assessment of the changing landscape of art and literature in the 1850s: his freedom to create is seemingly hampered by the need to cultivate and please his public. On the other hand, in becoming the *funambule*, the artist/writer also wields the positive and empowering weapon of derision (of others and of oneself), one that sets the stage for the creation of original work. The figure has at its disposal particular tools for challenging the presumed truths of "l'ordre établi" of art and literature (Starobinski 144). Here, the *funambule* opens a breach that frees the artist/writer from the constraints – authorized genre, style, and subject; sanctioned conditions and venues for exhibition and publishing; forms of official recognition, and so on – that academic systems impose on him.

With these innovators, therefore, it is more rewarding to examine what the *funambule* does and less what it means. Indeed, as Jean Starobinski notes, it is an error to "assigner au clown, aux saltimbanques, au monde du cirque une signification définie, une fonction stable" (141). On the contrary, *funambules* represent an absence of meaning – they are fundamentally destabilizers, mischievous thwarters of the power and authority of social-cultural systems – and it is through this absence that these artists/writers created original works of art.

Couture's *Le Duel après le bal masqué* understandably paled next to Gérôme's more dramatic *mise-en-scène*, without a doubt because there is demonstrably less tumult in the preparations for a duel than in its aftermath. From an early drawing depicting a victorious Harlequin standing astride or beside a fallen Pierrot, it is clear that Couture did initially consider depicting the duel's aftermath.[4] His decision to focus rather on the preliminary moments, however, reveals that his composition was of another order. The moment that he targeted, not to mention the subject that he selected, was a far cry from the historical painting with which he had been and stubbornly continues to be associated. Taken straight from the cast of characters of popular Parisian stages and the intimate literary drawing rooms of friends like George Sand and her son Maurice, Couture's Pierrot and Harlequin reflect the mid-century "conversion au réel" described by Starobinski (11).

One influence on the painter was perhaps the hallucinations that he experienced while working on his murals for the Church of Saint-Eustache's Chapel of the Virgin (1851–56). The church is the burial site of the famous seventeenth-century Harlequin Dominique (Domenico Biancolelli).[5] The celebrated pantomimist appeared to him over a period of eight days. Helen Borowitz proposes that Couture may have even come across and taken a cue from Dominique's comic duel scene in *Arlequin roi par hasard* (1672) (29–30). These explanations and the timing of the apparitions – during the execution of an official commission – point to Couture's arrival at a personal and professional crossroads, perhaps even at an epiphany. Whatever the inspiration for his series of seven Pierrot and Harlequin paintings, it is certain that Couture underwent a powerful realization, one that propelled his aesthetic transformation from academic painter to innovative outsider. These seven paintings are the *Souper à la Maison d'Or, Arlequin et Pierrot* (1857), *Le Duel après le bal masqué, La Commandite* (1858–59), *Pierrot malade* (1859–60), *Pierrot à la correctionnelle* (1863), and *Le Mariage d'Arlequin* (1866–67).[6] Unlike Gérôme, in whose works *funambules* were uncharacteristic, Couture's relationship to them was intensely personal (Lafont-Couturier 26).[7]

The two painters' approaches, however, differ noticeably, and not just because they depict different moments of the same event, but precisely because Couture refused the melodrama – or tragedy, as some describe it – of the most climactic moment of the duel: its outcome. While both Gérôme and Couture broke away from academic painting to draw from everyday experience and to try their hands at smaller, more lucrative genre painting, Couture's selection of an incidental rather than dramatic moment in the action is striking.[8] After all, if he had really been on a quest for fame and fortune, then he would have worked from his original sketch depicting a triumphant Harlequin looking down on his pathetic fallen opponent. But he did not. His objective was not to tell a conventional story.

Boime sees the Pierrot of all the Pierrot and Harlequin paintings as a mask for the artist himself, particularly in *Souper à la Maison d'Or* and *Arlequin et Pierrot*, whose clowns resemble remarkably his self-portraits, a gesture that literalizes what Starobinski describes as an "autoportrait travesti" (9). The mask represents more than an association between artist and *commedia* character, however. As examples of a "portrait de l'artiste en saltimbanque," to borrow from the title of Starobinski's book, these are more than just self-portraits; they are "une forme singulière d'*identification*" (9). For these artists/writers to choose to represent themselves as *funambules* is "une façon détournée et parodique de poser la question de l'art" (Starobinski 9). Couture as *funambule* visually reflected on his relation to art, particularly with respect to form and style, and that reorientation included an admission, however conflicted, of his evolving relation to the market. If rethinking one's engagement with art in the 1850s meant coming to terms with being an artist in the market, Couture found a way to put these real conditions to aesthetic use, and in choosing *funambules*, he managed to wrangle some degree of control. The movement away from the grandeur of the historical and religious subject signaled a shift toward another kind of hero, one belonging to the everyday experience found in the streets, fairgrounds, pantomime theaters, and circuses (Starobinski 14). By adopting the *funambule* as that hero like the other artists/writers discussed in this chapter, Couture took a step beyond allegory by challenging "la notion même de héro" (Starobinski 14).

Souper à la Maison d'Or was commissioned by Jules Desfossé, the wallpaper manufacturer who planned a wallpaper series on the theme of virtue and vice (Jacqué 447). Desfossé arranged with the well-known painter Couture to do a series of eight paintings on the theme, of which the first two treatments would be *Les Prodigues* (which became the *Souper à la Maison d'Or*) and *La Prière après le travail*. Apart from *Souper*, neither the series nor the companion piece on virtue ever materialized as wallpaper. The wallpaper based on the *Souper*, presented at the 1855 *Exposition universelle* as an example of industrial wallpaper reproductions of great artists' work, was very well received. Like Gérôme's association with the Maison Goupil that mass-reproduced his *Sortie du bal masqué*, Couture allied himself with a technology that would "mettre les chefs-d'oeuvre de l'art à la portée du plus grand nombre" (Jacqué 448).[9] Couture, however, avowed his connection to the market in each painting in the series; Gérôme did not. As a piece representative of this artist at an aesthetic crossroads, we can understand why Couture never sold this particular painting during his lifetime (Figure 2.1).

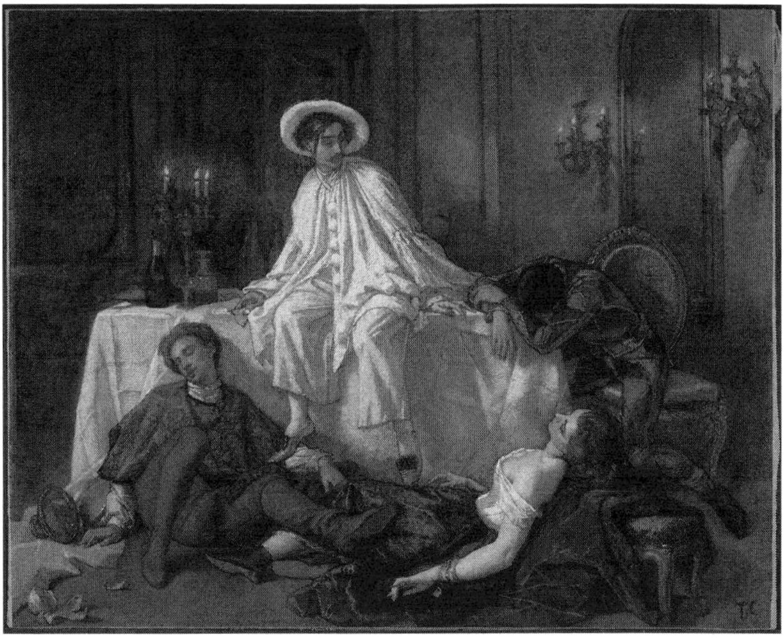

Figure 2.1 Thomas Couture, *Souper à la Maison d'Or (également connu sous le titre Chaque fête a son lendemain*, 1855. Oil on canvas, 120 cm × 228 cm; frame 190 cm × 239 cm × 5 cm. Collection of the Vancouver Art Gallery, presented by Mr. and Mrs. Jonathan Rogers. Photo: National Gallery of Canada (NGC).

For his theme of virtue and vice, Desfossé asked Couture to revisit the orgy theme of two earlier paintings: Couture's début Salon piece from 1840 *Jeune Vénitien après une orgie* and his *Romains de la décadence* (1847). If Desfossé determined the theme, Couture provided the context and details with his *commedia* characters. The vice that Desfossé set for the painting, the commercial nature of the commission, and Couture's own position at a professional crossroads may have functioned as a fortuitous confluence of events: the painter was poised for change, and the conditions surrounding that change may have guided his aesthetic choices – the aftermath of an orgy (a reference to the state of Parisian society in the 1850s) and a clown (a reference to a farce transgressor who inappropriately manipulates cultural codes). This latter element can involve a confusion of "two types of patterned interactions that are mutually exclusive in the cultural context," which are here the codes of the real and the symbolic (Bouissac 168).

As regards the depiction of French society in the 1850s, the contemporaneity of the painting/wallpaper would be lost on today's viewers, but as Bernard Jacqué notes, "la scène est contemporaine et les viveurs qui visitent l'exposition peuvent [...] reconnaître les charmes vénaux de la comédienne Alice Ozy et le décor d'un des cabinets particuliers de la Maison dorée, sur le boulevard des Italiens" (Jacqué 451). Not only can one recognize Alice Ozy as Columbine and Couture as Pierrot, but the figure to the left of Columbine has been identified as the German painter Anselm Feuerbach, Couture's student until 1854. And, as noted, the *funambule*, too, was a figure relevant to the cultural experience of the 1850s. As for the symbolic element, while Gérôme's clown is a masquerader whose facial sweat pierces through his carnival makeup, Couture's is clown eternal. The selection of Pierrot as the central figure in a *commedia* staging taps into the stock character's timeless quality (as serial persona, as myth), which creates confusion with the painting's contemporaneity as established by both the real-life personages, the real venue, and the real-time nature of caricature. Pierrot, Gilles Bonnet explains, "n'appartient pas au temps de l'histoire" (73). He lives in "une utopie-uchronie où le temps des horloges a été destitué de son pouvoir dictatorial" (Bonnet 72). Pierrot as *funambule* and myth is the figure through whom it is possible to perceive the oxymoronic co-presence of the contemporary *and* the timeless in the same space of the composition.

The interaction of the codes of the real (real place and people) and the symbolic (stock characters disconnected in time) that emerge in all the paintings in the series also finds an echo in the mixing of low and high tones. To establish his painting's social and aesthetic commentary, Couture incorporated "low" caricature into "high" art. In this action, he was in line with Gavarni and Daumier, whose caricatures often featured clowns and acrobats (*commedia* costumes from carnival and the *bals de Paris*, satirical send-ups of public figures depicted as circus performers).

On a basic level, we know that caricature is at play in Couture's Pierrot and Harlequin series precisely because moralizing legends accompany many of the paintings, beginning notably with the *Souper*, which cries out "Morts illustres! J'ai vus vos descendants succombant dans l'orgie" (Hôtel Drouot et al. 11). *Souper*'s caricatural element does not end with the legend, however, since it includes a visual quote as well. Boime notes that this painting refers to and condenses the participants from another supper after a masked ball, Paul Gavarni's *Chanson de table* (1853), replicating the principle body positions and arrangement of its exhausted revelers. *Souper* is, as the wallpaper manufacturer Desfossé intended, a modernized pendant to Couture's moralizing *Romains de la décadence*, with Pierrot casting a disapproving eye on the dissoluteness of his companions, and by extension contemporary French society.[10] Unlike the lofty message of his historical *Romains*, *Souper*'s legend insists on the immediacy of its social critique. What Desfossé did not intend, however, is that *Souper* also parodies the earlier painting, that spectacular Salon success, pairing Couture's disapproval of his time with an aesthetic self-deprecation that suspends the painting's message in an interpretive no-man's-land. He mocks his earlier high-minded academic stance of disparagement, while at the same time "rephrasing" and historically situating that same social critique. This ambiguity creates a semantic breach, one that would signal to viewers to pay more attention to the way in which Couture's parody plays out formally and stylistically. The *commedia* figures, in particular, announce the artist's first steps toward liberating himself from academic painting in a movement toward new artistic expression.[11]

In the seven Pierrot and Harlequin paintings, there exists a semblance of narrative continuity, forming what could be described as a sequence of scenes in a pantomime. I use the word "semblance" because, while the order of the tableaux chosen here replicates the sequence of their creation, this is not the only possible arrangement. Indeed, the image of the mosaic might suit best the imprecision of the series' virtual narrative potential. True to the spirit of *la pantomime sautante*, there need not be any logic to the transitions from one tableau to the next. Couture may or may not have planned *Souper* as the first in a series, indeed commissions from his private, primarily American, clientele may even have been the important deciding factor subsequent to its success, but since it is the first, it assumes a performative role as the opening scene of a pantomime that charts Couture's aesthetic transformation over roughly a twelve-year period.

In *Souper*, Pierrot is still conscious, while Harlequin, Columbine, and Lélio/Léandre (an *inamorato* of traditional *commedia* casts) are passed out after a night of overindulgence. With the knowledge that the stock character Pierrot has traditionally an excessive fondness for wine and food, we stop to consider Couture's reformulation of the conventions of pantomime farce. It is in Pierrot's nature to jump off the table and go through his companions' pockets in search of money or to finish off the contents of the wine bottles on the table and collapse into a drunken slumber like his fellow masks.[12] In *Souper*, the depleted state describes his companions, however, not Pierrot, which is the first of several signals to the viewer that Pierrot is not just a stock character involved in the debauchery. He is also detached from it. This duality facilitates an aesthetic transformation that comes about through semantic interference of meanings, meanings normally set by context. Only here, context is ambiguous. A breach opens creating dualities in the viewer's perception of identity, time, and genre: the viewer is aware of "real" masqueraders *and* mythic farce characters; of the present *and* the timeless; and of "low" caricature *and* "high" art in the same piece.

The pantomime ostensibly begins at the celebrated Maison d'Or on the night of a *bal masqué* and, in keeping with the genre's classical tradition, ends with *Le Mariage d'Arlequin.* The second tableau in the series, *Arlequin et Pierrot*, could be, as suggests Boime, the prequel to *Le Duel après le bal masqué.* Made in the same year as that work, *Arlequin et Pierrot* features Pierrot and Harlequin reading an issue of the conservative *Le Moniteur universel.* In the background, one sees a poster advertising a *bal masqué*: "Bal Molière à Grrrrrrrand Orchestre/Galop Final/ Avec Accompagnement de Coups de Canons." Directing the viewer's reading of the painting, the repeated "r"s of "Grrrrrrrand" recall the clothes hawker's cry (heard both before and after Pierrot murders him) from Cot d'Ordan's *Marrrchand d'habits!*, the Théâtre des Funambules pantomime.[13] While the contemporary newspaper and poster as well as the top hat and cape piled on a table at Harlequin's side situate the scene neatly in the period of the painting's execution, the masqueraders are also pantomime characters who muddy the contextual waters established by all the *effets de réel*, here with the introduction of ahistorical time. In addition, as caricature, Boime interprets this painting as a critique of the bourgeoisie, whose sole preoccupation is business when they should be reveling. The derision, however, may be directed not only at the bourgeoisie, but at the painter himself, too. With Couture offering his self-portrait for Pierrot, he depicts himself as an artist *and* businessman. After all, the painter did sell his own paintings. In this way, he succeeds in blurring the separation between the social-cultural registers of art and commerce.[14] This ambiguous position anticipates that of Jules Laforgue's Pierrot from *Pierrot fumiste*: in the list of characters of this unpublished pantomime, Pierrot is described in similarly oxymoronic terms: he is a "poète très lyrique et boursier" (Laforgue) (Figure 2.2).

Although not chronologically next in the series, *La Commandite* also plays visibly with the codes of art and commerce in presenting an officer, a judge, and a nobleman as victims of an investment scam (a nineteenth-century Ponzi scheme) perpetrated by Harlequin and Pierrot, with

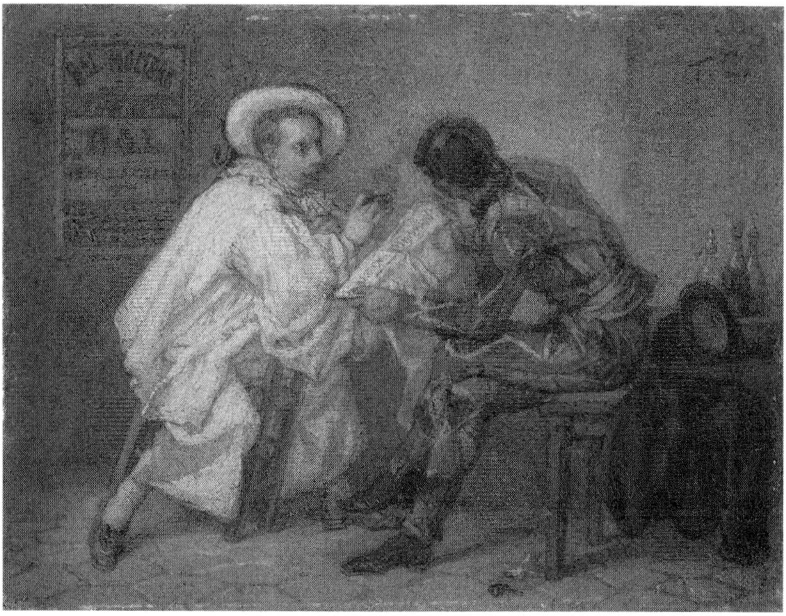

Figure 2.2 Thomas Couture, *Arlequin et Pierrot*, 1857. The Wallace Collection, London.

plentiful comestibles on display as proof of the misdirection of funds. While such "respectable" social figures were targets of Couture's attacks here as elsewhere, it is fruitful to consider this painting as a companion to *Arlequin et Pierrot*, since it revisits the duality artist *and* businessman (self-derision on the part of Couture). All the while avowing Pierrot and Harlequin as perpetrators of a con game, Couture also allows them to comically recuperate their subversive farce roles of duping powerful authority figures.

According to Boime, Couture mocks dueling, and in particular targets the pernicious role of seconds in *Le Duel après le bal masqué*[15]: seconds were more often than not instrumental in the direction negotiations took, pushing their friends or colleagues into tragic encounters rather than advising reconciliation (*Eclectic* 316).[16] While Harlequin's second does appear to counsel against an armed engagement, Pierrot's second has given him a hefty sword that is obviously (and comically) too unwieldy for him to brandish and certainly not a regulation arm for dueling. If duels between masqueraders in the Bois de Boulogne were so common as to fall into "le domaine public," as About claimed in his review of the Salon of 1857, then it would have been indeed quite interesting to "voir le tableau de M. Couture exposé en concurrence dans la salle de M. Gérôme" (73). The subtle power of the painting is perhaps lost on us today, as we assimilate it with other pieces treating the theme of the clown, but had it been exhibited at the Salon in 1857, the daring mix of low and high, of the transitory and the eternal (the depiction of an event taken out of the newspapers *and* the treatment of that event as high art), it could have caused a minor scandal. Had Couture chosen to depict the pathetic moment of the engagement, the effect would have been tragic instead of *funambulesque*.

With the oxymoronic pairings that Couture had established in the two earlier paintings, we anticipate as well a repetition of the uncomfortable cohabitation of art and finances. This duel creates semantic confusion by depicting both the figurative and literal meanings of a *règlement de comptes* – a settling of scores *and* a settling up (of financial accounts). In this way, Couture both acknowledges and disparages his position as artist in the market (his Pierrot is a social and financial *naïf*, much like the inept Auguste of late nineteenth-century clown pairs) in the same breath in which he disparages dueling as a code as pernicious and arbitrary as any other social system.[17]

Couture's pantomime in seven tableaux comes to a close with *Le Mariage d'Arlequin,* which carries no moral as do the earlier paintings, but rather ends in the marriage of Harlequin and Columbine like many *commedia* farce scenarios from the first half of the nineteenth century, a match made possible by the substantial dowry that Harlequin is miraculously able to provide the bride's greedy father, Cassandra. The painting, however, does not present the figures in a joyous gathering of all the pantomime's characters in celebration of the event with the happy couple joined before a priest at a church altar. This marriage is as dry and businesslike as can be.[18] It depicts the official signing of the marriage contract in an office featuring a notary and his secretary in eighteenth-century dress with Harlequin and Columbine solemnly standing at opposite ends of the notary's table as Cassandra kneels over the bags of money. On the wall behind Columbine, we make out a few public notices, with the sole legible one announcing in big letters the sale of some property ("*Vente*"), a notice that situates this scene in its historical moment like the poster in *Arlequin et Pierrot*, while also emphasizing that it involves more a financial transaction in a "marriage" of art and commerce than an exchange of vows. The absence of a legend may be just because the painting appears incomplete with only the face of Harlequin and the head of Cassandra in a "finished" state, with Harlequin's hat and neck and the back of the Cassandra's head bathed in light coming from an unseen and impossibly placed high window. Boime makes a good argument for Couture's transposition of *commedia funambulistes*' ability to invent on the fly within the basic framework of their stock material, "introducing topical jokes, capitalizing on slips of the tongue," and commenting on current events to the degree censorship would allow (*Eclectic* 297).

In Boime's reading of all the paintings in the series, but in particular the *Mariage*, Couture would have transposed the medium's openness to spontaneous ad-libbing in order to give his "'finished' conceptions the look of an improvised performance" and that touch of contemporary relevance (297) (Figure 2.3).

Couture saved the best for last in targeting for his ridicule the academic art system that was to no small degree the inspiration for the series, the system that purported to hold the right to determine the cultural value and place of a work of art. It is probably no coincidence that the completion of this last "scene" in his pantomime in seven tableaux comes during the same year in which Couture published his *Méthode et entretiens d'atelier* (1867), a work that officially severed his ties to academism. One function of the *funambules* in *Le Mariage* is to reveal the arbitrariness of that "right": is it possible that Cassandra (Couture?) bypasses the Salon, goes into the market, and sets his own price for his beautiful daughter (work of art)?

The painting may perhaps have had another contemporary target. In the incomplete *Le Baptême du Prince impérial*, which was commissioned by Napoléon III to commemorate the baptism of his son in 1856, and abandoned by Couture in 1862, there is a striking resemblance between the preparatory sketches and treatments of the emperor and

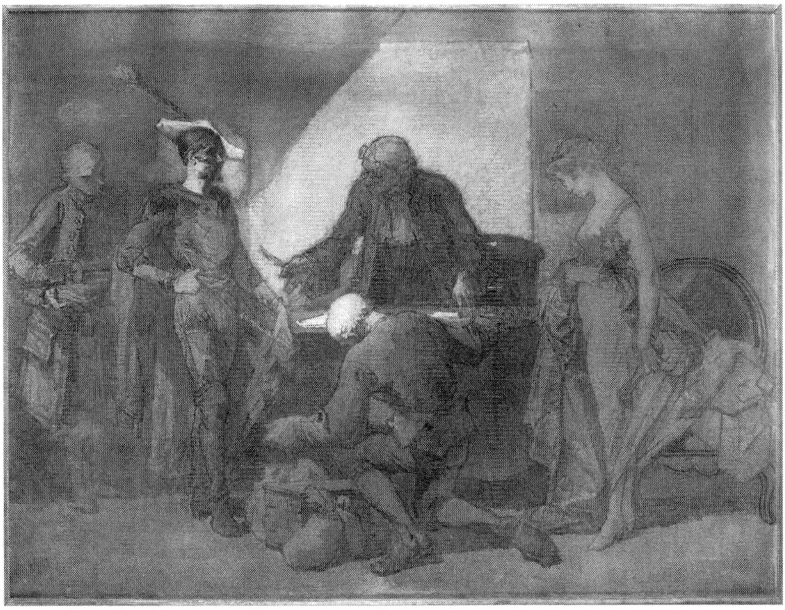

Figure 2.3 Thomas Couture, *Le Mariage d'Arlequin*, 1866–67. Musée d'Orsay, Paris.

those for the Harlequin of *Le Mariage*: the right leg slightly forward, the right hand on the hip, the left hand balanced on the hilt of a sword, the head cocked slightly to the left.[19] As was true with Daumier, it was not uncommon for artists to reuse figures from previous works. From his *Méthode et entretiens d'atelier*, we learn that even in 1867, Couture still talked about completing the commission. It is what happens afterwards to the depiction of the emperor, however, that is remarkable: Couture was not content to just leave the painting undone. He deliberately removed the identifying traits of the emperor, erasing his head and his right hand.[20] It is possible that, as Boime claims, Couture was just dissatisfied with his execution of the study depicting the emperor and its integration with the flags "behind and to the left" of him (*Eclectic Vision* 275). The educational dossier for the Palais de Compiègne conjectures that the problem may have been of another order: in the original study "le peintre contourna de cette manière une difficulté à représenter le regard du souverain, souvent décrit comme vague par les contemporains" ("Dossier" 23). It is also plausible that the notoriously curmudgeonly painter simply took his revenge by effectively stripping the emperor of his individuality (Figures 2.4 and 2.5).

In addition to the close resemblance between the body positions of Napoleon III and Harlequin, there are compositional similarities between the two paintings as well. The imperial family, with the emperor at the left, is replaced by the *commedia* family; the officiating religious dignitary (the Papal nuncio) is substituted by the notary, who both lean forward with an outstretched right arm; and the infant is supplanted by

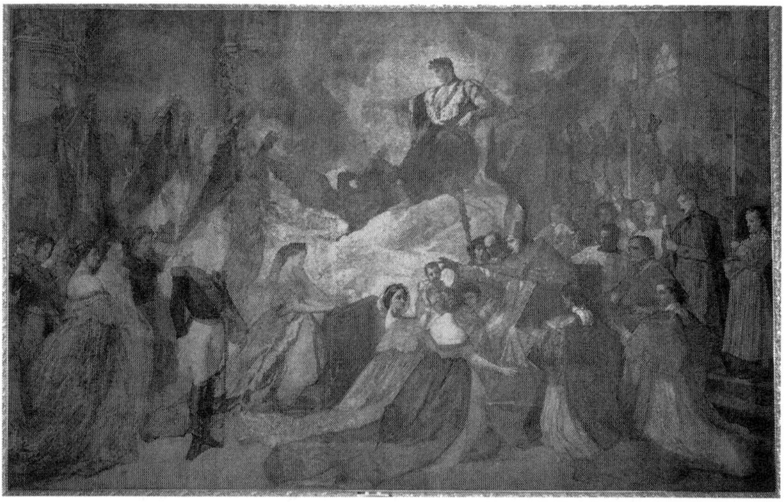

Figure 2.4 Thomas Couture, *Le Baptême du Prince impérial*, 1856–62. Palais de Compiègne, Compiègne.

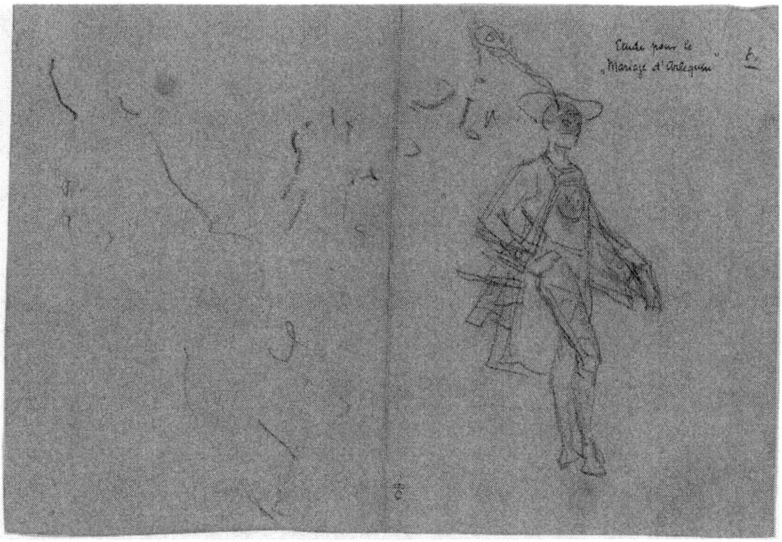

Figure 2.5 Thomas Couture, Étude pour *Le Mariage d'Arlequin*, 1866–67. Palais de Compiègne, Compiègne.

sacks and a chest of money. The upper, unfinished, central area of the *Baptême* depicts Napoleon I in a halo of light blessing the event and consecrating the imperial lineage of the infant prince; the light falling from above and illuminating the back wall in *Mariage* is its parodic and uncompromising echo, thereby resolving the "confused combination of unsparing realism and idealized sentiment" of the baptism painting (Boime, "Evolution" 49).

Couture's revenge was therefore *funambulesque*, with the artist transferring the portrait of the emperor from the *Baptême* to the *Mariage*. If the painter concealed the emperor's distinctive features, however vague they were, in his favorite *commedia* character Harlequin, it was also to open a temporal breach permitting the movement back in time to the Napoleon plays of the presidential campaign and the first year of the empire. Through the figure of Harlequin, Couture reverses Napoleon III's "canny politics of image and what we might today call 'marketing,'" divesting him of that fabricated public image and returning him unceremoniously to the site of those plays which he exploited to develop a cult of personality: the Cirque National (Truesdell vii).[21] While the authors and producers of these military spectacles glorifying Napoleon I did not intend their work to be comical, the circus space as inherently productive of feelings of wonderment and amusement could not help but give a comic turn to the plays' reception, imbuing them with all the sights, colors, sounds, and odors associated with a popular entertainment. In an August 30, 1859, entry in their *Journal*, the Goncourt brothers exploit the connection with great humor and cynicism,

> Lorsque Louis-Napoléon était à l'Hôtel du Rhin, au commencement de ses grandeurs, il fit venir un acteur, Pastelot, pour s'entendre avec lui pour promener dans la province, avec une troupe, tout le répertoire du Cirque, des guerres de l'Empire. Et ils étaient là, le cabot et le futur César, cherchant l'homme pour porter la redingote, le petit chapeau et le nez en cire de feu Gobert, l'homme rare, l'homme unique pour monter le coup aux futurs médaillés de Sainte-Hélène. Enfin, Pastelot se souvint de Rhozevil. Napoléon fournit l'argent de la troupe. La grosse caisse de sa candidature était trouvée.[22] (471)

In inverting Louis-Napoleon's real-life trajectory from circus ring publicity (milieu of the clown) to imperial court by depicting him as Harlequin, Couture reduced him to a caricature featuring the "coat, the little hat, and the wax nose" of the actor Gobert (who did not die until 1873). In a displacement which substitutes Gobert for Napoleon I, there is not so much a *mise en abyme* than a mirrored kaleidoscope of overlapping reflections in which the actor Rhozevil becomes the imitator of an imitator (Rhozevil modeled his performance on that of Gobert, who himself impersonated the gestures and tics of Napoleon I) and Napoleon III the imitator of his uncle. To add insult to injury, in *Le Mariage*, Harlequin, perhaps sporting the beard of Louis-Napoleon, wears the bicorne hat associated with Napoleon Bonaparte and his generals. In this scenario, the continuity and legitimacy that Napoleon III sought to establish between himself and his uncle volatilizes, leaving him unanchored in a play of reflections that has no source to which to return him.[23]

Théodore de Banville

Banville resorted to similar methods to defang the literary critic Paulin Limayrac in "L'Ombre d'Éric" in the *Odes funambulesques*.[24] Deciding against a duel of words fought in the press in which he would challenge the forceful critic's dismissal of great Romantic writers, Banville opted to "détourner les chiens" by making him the subject "de la *romance en général*, de ce genre faux et absurd," absurd because the mode's characters behave as if they were "birds or flowers" (266–67). In placing an unworthy contemporary personage in a classical poetic form, Banville achieved a discomforting mix of the comical and the lyrical not unlike the encounter of caricature and academism in Couture's Pierrot and Harlequin paintings, and in this way orchestrated the critic's character assassination. All of Paris learned the poem by heart, Banville claims.[25] So entirely was it on everyone's lips that when Limayrac appeared in the great hall of the Opéra on the evening of a masked ball, the conductor Philippe Musard momentarily stopped the music as all eyes turned to look at the critic, and the voices of these "chicards, pierrots, caciques, masques aux guenilles furieuses, débardeurs aux culottes de soie, taillés à la Rubens" chanted in unison "Si Limayrac devenait fleur" (267).[26] Banville made the supercilious Limayrac the object of ridicule, and doing so transmogrified his identifying traits, those very traits for which he was known and of which he was most confident: his wit and his eloquence. Barbara Bohac notes that "Les *Odes funambulesques* dessinent en effet une vaste scène de féerie où les êtres et les choses sont en métamorphose constante" (42). "Beings and things" may be less in "constant metamorphosis," however, as caught in a semantic breach opened up by form and rhyme themselves, a result of being in a state of the *funambulesque*, not to be confused with a state of metaphor. The semantic register of "Limayrac" allows for a continual contamination of categories, a constant slippage in which the critic's detachable collar is the flower's corolla (shared shape), a boutonnière a medal of honor (shared site), and fluttering birds a garland (shared movement). Limayrac is turned not only into a flower in "L'Ombre d'Éric," but in "Âge de M. Paul Limayrac," he is cut down to a little boy, and in "Villanelle de Buloz," an undefined thing identified as "mon Limayrac."[27] In the latter poem, the critic's name is reduced to an incantatory word that is the source of a dizzying concatenation of amusing rhymes ("sac," "cornac," "almanach," "micmac," "havresac," "cognac," even "Balzac"). Limayrac's name accrues importance only in its ability to produce rhymes, ones that the reader anticipates with the passage of each stanza. With each successive rhyme, the reader forgets the person and focuses on the verbal acrobatics and experiences an exuberance, both of which progressively rob the critic of his personhood (Banville 201–02).[28]

Banville had been in search of a new poetic form (3). What he devised was one that mixed the painting of contemporary times and classical genres, the comical (rhyme) and the lyrical (form) (Banville 4). He insists on the oxymoronic nature of the poems' composition: they are "un essai de pamphlet en rythmes," an ambiguous blend of the prosaic and the poetic (16). Like Couture, he espoused the *funambulesque* model of avowal and derision. Avowal of his situation emerges specifically in the opening and closing poems that frame the collection and initiate the state of the *funambulesque*. In both "La Corde roide" and "Le Saut du tremplin," the poet offers himself as a performing acrobatic clown, a "baladin" who "deigns" to dance on the "corde funambulesque" and who creates ever increasing distance between himself and "ces épiciers et ces notaires" below him in the stands, but who nevertheless acknowledges the conditions of his work in a gesture of self-derision (19, 243). This is, after all, how he earns his living, and his audience, hardly a gathering of fellow writers, artists, and intellectuals, is composed of "boursiers à lunettes d'or," critics, young ladies, and "réalistes en feu" (244). The targets of his derision – not so great "hommes d'État" and not so illustrious "écrivains éminents" – all belong to the transitory details of his era, hardly the worthy subjects of the classical poetic forms in which they find themselves (15).[29]

Honoré Daumier

The inclusion of low in high art is mirrored inversely in the *saltimbanque* paintings of Daumier, which Paula Hays Harper characterizes as "high caricature," the incorporation of high art into low caricature (200). As in Couture's Pierrot and Harlequin series and Banville's *Odes funambulesques*, Daumier's series offers the confusing notion of time that accompanies the ambiguous co-presence of the ephemeral details of daily existence and an enduring theme. The artist suspends his figures ambiguously in both the specific moment of the real *saltimbanque* and a general one associated with the literary and artistic tradition of the *funambule*. For Clark, the specific moment relates to the real condition of street performers who were the targets of a series of laws and regulations beginning in 1849, controls designed to curb, if not eliminate, their presence in urban spaces.[30] Here, the *saltimbanque* is a social outcast. According to Harper, however, "[b]y the late 1850's and 1860's, when Daumier did the majority of his saltimbanque and parade pictures, the parade in Paris was, in fact, an outmoded remnant of a golden past" (41).[31] To complicate matters, she notes, while he did base depictions of *saltimbanques* on the observed "appearance and activities of actual nineteenth-century performers," physical observation may not have been contemporaneous with the execution of particular caricatures or paintings (39–40). Indeed, Daumier often worked from muscle memory, with the artist repeating gestures, physical positions, and figures from earlier caricatures and paintings over decades (Harper 58).[32] Finally, Harper points out that the perceived degree of realism based on first-hand knowledge that one finds in his drawings and paintings lessens when one realizes how much they owe as well to "illustrative prints and contemporary descriptions of nineteenth century clowns" (39).

Daumier's engagement with the figure of the *funambule* spans his entire career, ending in his self-portrait as clown in 1870, but particularly after the 1848 Revolution and throughout the Second Empire. In his caricatures, there can be no question of identification on the part of Daumier, since his objective was to lampoon a political or social figure or political events.[33] For Clark, in the *saltimbanque* series, "[t]he clown is his hero, and his central image of the artist, just because he is an outcast" (122). But if, as in the work of Couture and Banville, the *funambule* is more an aesthetic device, a way of posing the question of art in the 1850s, and less a pointed reference to the social-cultural conditions that the artist shares with the figure, he is also less an outcast, the passive victim of social repression and ostracism, and more an outsider, who like the *funambule* actively "manipulates a cultural system" (Bouissac 8). However, as Bouissac contends, the circus, a group which includes circus-related performers like the fairground *saltimbanque*, is "both 'within' and 'outside' culture," which would make Daumier both an insider *and* an outsider, conditions that reflect the oxymoronic duality that scholars have remarked in the artist and his work (7).

Clark describes Daumier's duality as "living in the interstices of the new social order" – the Second Empire but also the state of art in the 1850s (103, 118). Daumier chronicled through his caricatures, drawings, and paintings the historical moment that he witnessed in the streets, some events of which he was a supporter if not participant, but he and his *saltimbanques* were also strangely detached, much like the *funambule* that plays with social-cultural codes (Clark 102). For Clark, Daumier was "neither worker nor bourgeois," but it might be more apt to describe him as being paradoxically both (102). In his *Ratapoil* statuette and caricatures (1850–51), he was "directly political in subject and intention, but in its style stepping out of the nineteenth century" (116). He parodied tradition while also working within it (116). He mixed the genres of caricature and high art. Daumier was a bundle of contradictions.

For Clark, the strange mixture of the specific and the general – the "real" clown observed in the streets and persecuted by authorities and the myth of the clown in literature and art – within the same work of art raises "the question of meaning and intention" (118). Harper's study of Daumier's clowns, too, is peppered with questions about the nature of the artist's relationship to his clowns and *saltimbanques*. Like Clark and Harper, other scholars have assumed that there is a meaning behind them, but are nevertheless "not certain what this significance was" (Harper 5–6). The series elicits many questions, for which the fallback response has been to refer to the real clown as a symbol of the artist's personal or lived experience or to the cult of the mythical "sad" clown in artistic and literary circles. Daumier himself did not offer an explanation for his recourse to these figures.

Starobinski describes the *funambule* as a "vide" and a "vacance," as an absence or in some instances a suspension of meaning (141–42). Suspension of meaning comes through in many of the faces of Daumier's *saltimbanques*, suggesting that the very semantically disruptive properties of the *funambule* determined his choice of subject. The *saltimbanque* painting series began probably in the mid-1850s and continued into the 1860s. Perhaps one of his earliest is *Un Hercule et un Pierrot dans les coulisses*, which Harper dates to the "late 1850's or around 1860" (142). It presents an inconsistency – Pierrot's indistinct head – for what is otherwise considered a completed painting (Figure 2.6).[34]

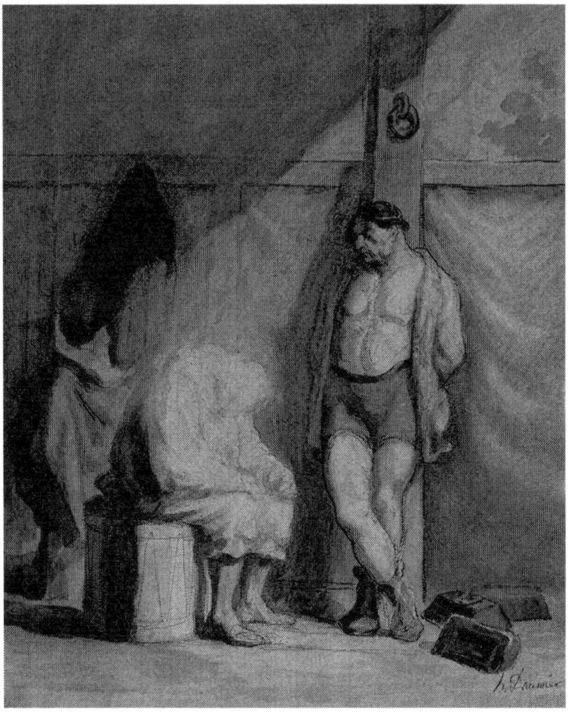

Figure 2.6 Honoré Daumier, *Hercule et un Pierrot dans les coulisses*, (n.d.). The Private Collection of Michael and Judy Steinhardt.

In this watercolor, one finds a strongman looking down from a standing position upon the collapsed figure of a Pierrot, whose head is so bathed in white light that his distinguishing features almost disappear. The clown's absence of meaning, graphically depicted as blinding light, is a symbol of Daumier's own troubling, and I would say willfully cultivated, indeterminate identity in a truly singular relationship with the clown. Indeed, the identification is at first glance one of anonymity. For Clark, Daumier embraced anonymity "part by choice, part by necessity" (122). He offers as evidence Daumier's actions of withdrawal – his secretive painting, the refusal to put dates on his pieces, and his reluctance to exhibit (122). These strategies as listed by Clark describe a man who did short stints in prison and was repeatedly harassed for his political caricatures. As Robert J. Griffin notes, "by enabling the hiding of one's identity, one of the dominant functions of anonymity over the centuries has been protection" (891). The beauty of anonymity is also that it "guaranteed integrity because it freed writers from social and political pressures" (884). But while Daumier was certainly at pains to protect himself from prosecution in general, the *funambule* of his paintings more specifically reflects identificatory instability. Indeed, the uncertainty of generic, temporal, and existential identity translates not into garden variety anonymity, but into suspended identity, which is not necessarily a state of crisis. A suspended identity exists in a state of complete freedom, a freedom not related to the integrity to which Griffin refers (being true to one's moral principles), nor to the integrity of being whole and undivided, since the *funambule* is fundamentally double.

Banville's refusal to affix his name to the first edition of the *Odes funambulesques* offers an example of the dynamics at work. To Peter Edwards, Banville's letters to his publisher show that the poet's insistence on the collection appearing without his name was for "des raisons stratégiques et esthétiques" (376). Banville acknowledged that many of the poems that had already been published in the press had carried his name: he could not have been seeking the protection of anonymity since he "ne voulait ni se dissocier du livre ni feindre de modestie" (Edwards 377). All of literary and artistic Paris knew the identity of the author. For Edwards, this was a striking tactical move that surrounded the collection with the mystique of a "livre malicieux," assuring it a "succès de scandale" (377). Banville already recognized himself as a commodity in the frame poems, but here he exhibited keen marketing skills. He did not, however, prevent his publisher Auguste Poulet-Malassis from listing his name as the author of the *Odes* in an advertisement on the last page of *Poésies de Théodore de Banville, (1841–1854)*, which was published in 1857 as well. The *Odes*, therefore, expressed suspended identity through their very *funambulesque*-ness, a qualification that did not apply to his *Poésies*. Banville, like his unnamed acrobatic clown (and the public figures that receive the clown treatment of being de-named by effacing rhyme), is as ambiguous as Daumier's, poised precariously in an identificatory no-man's-land. He is both real poet and acrobatic clown.

In all of Daumier's *saltimbanque* paintings and drawings, the artist has become two entities in much the same way as the composite persona/person commonly referred to as Pierrot-Deburau by scholars. Deburau, the pantomimist, was for Paris the incarnation of Pierrot, and Pierrot, the serial character, was inconceivable without Deburau. Indeed, the mimes that followed in his footsteps had difficulty establishing an interpretation that could stand on its own without invoking the specter of the powerful precursor. This duality emerges in the three artists/writers studied in this chapter: Pierrot/Harlequin-Couture, *funambule*-Banville, and *saltimbanque*-Daumier.

Circus acrobats and clowns inhabit this identificatory no-man's-land in the bewildering co-presence of their real persons and personas in the same moment. For small traveling circus performers, as Yoram Carmeli has written, their real names are the same as their performer names, with real names as part of a performance (198). Inversely, stationary or big circus performers often have an assumed name, but the real person, one that engages directly with spectators, is also incongruously part of performance.[35] Carmeli makes the distinction that the danger of which the spectator becomes aware during a performance is not the one described by the anthropologist Mary Douglas in *Purity and Danger* (1966), in which impurity threatens the social order: it is taboo to name that which is impure (212). With circus danger – and there are many forms it can assume – the spectator is simply *unable* to identify, to name, and to classify.

Fluid identity is just one way of imagining the danger associated with the *funambule*, and in Daumier this manifests itself through his figures' faces: sometimes they turn their heads away, sometimes their faces are not visible due to the slumped position of their bodies, and sometimes they are blurred, twisted, or deformed. And when the faces are clearly visible, the expression is often one of defiance, a defiance not unlike the one associated with Édouard Manet's *Olympia* (1863).[36] In *Un Hercule et un Pierrot dans les coulisses*, the head of his clown is obscured almost entirely in a pool of light. In the painting and related drawings of *Les Saltimbanques*, believed to have been executed sometime during the first half of the 1860s, Harper suggests that the slightly turned-away face of the clown playing a drum may in fact be a self-portrait of Daumier, a gesture that recalls Couture's own self-portraits as Pierrot in *Souper à la Maison d'Or* and *Arlequin et Pierrot*. And in the fairground barker paintings, the faces are disturbingly distorted, shapeless, almost viscous (Figure 2.7).[37]

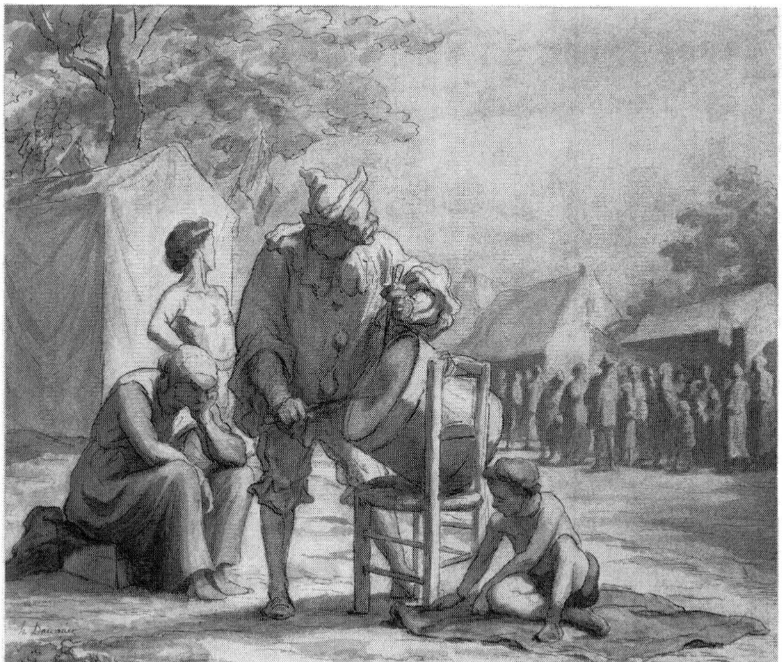

Figure 2.7 Honoré Daumier, *Les Saltimbanques*, (n.d.). The Victoria and Albert Museum, London.

The tendency is to view these faces and their ambiguousness in terms of disintegration, even decomposition, but as Starobinski notes, the acrobat/clown *emerges* into our reality "d'un autre espace, d'un autre univers," and this passage takes place "sous nos yeux, au moment du bond, du saut périlleux, de l'obstacle surmonté" (139). Juxtaposed with the image of Daumier as an artist who withdraws from the world is one in which he crosses the threshold separating the *funambulesque* beyond our here and now. His clowns may be interpreted as retreating materially, but they may just as easily be caught at the moment of entering our world, a form of crowning like that fetal head that appears during the second stage of childbirth. Starobinski likens the white paper hoops through which acrobats and trained animals leap to a symbolic incarnation of the passage between these worlds – the elsewhere of the acrobat and our world (139–40).

Daumier's blurry Pierrot visually activates the dynamics of the relationship between *funambule* and spectator. For Gilles Bonnet, Pierrot-Deburau was a blank screen onto which spectators projected their primal desires and dreams (63). I propose that the very whiteness raining upon Pierrot's head is an apt imagining of the nothingness described by Starobinski, and it replicates the spectator's experience during a viewing of an acrobatic or pantomime performance. Likewise for Carmeli, the "[b]right, shining material" of acrobats' costumes "reflect back on the public and discommunicate the performer," disrupting one's certainty about one's perceptions and suspending one in existential limbo (199). Whether through the clown's white face or the stock character's impassive mask, the *funambule* becomes separated from himself, introducing a suspension of identity (hence, meaning) that short-circuits the spectator's certainty about his own identity (Starobinski 144). The result is an experience of vertigo.

Charles Baudelaire

For Baudelaire, in his 1855 essay "De l'essence du rire," the spectator experiences vertigo – that phenomenon involving a spinning sensation and a loss of balance – when the pantomime fairy waves her wand (377). For Baudelaire, and by extension for acrobats, clowns, and artists, this feeling is exhilarating because it is the moment when marvelous, indeed impossible, things happen: clowns waving their arms become windmills; they tumble turbulently over each other without breaking a bone; and they miraculously survive volleys of punches and kicks that themselves are surprisingly given and taken "sans rancune" (377). The essay also describes a performance of astounding pantomimic violence when a clown is gruesomely guillotined. It offers the portrait of a deliciously terrifying English clown as a most uncommon Pierrot, no longer uniformly pale and silent, but sinister and unsettling: his make-up features blotchy red cheeks and an equally red mouth that looks like an enormous gaping wound on his face. These fleshly gashes are physical manifestations of the semantic breach described by Starobinski. Baudelaire's discussion of this pantomime in the context of the *comique absolu* identifies the pantomime stage as a space marked by "le vertige," a term that can be explained as a place of absolute confusion regarding cultural codes, a space where, for example, a headless clown's torso defies all the laws of natural science by retrieving his bloody and butchered head and pops it into his vast pocket (375).

Baudelaire was the first to attempt to critically analyze what happens during a clown's performance. His study appears within the framework of the creation of a theory of the comic in the arts, with caricature as its primary focus (Champfleury 296). While much has been written on Baudelaire's notions of the *comique significatif* (humor produced through caricature) and the *comique absolu*, and while scholars use them as valuable models for textual and cultural analysis (this is, after all, one of the most important, perceptive, and influential of poets and aesthetic critics), the features of the *comique absolu* – in particular, the vertigo effect experienced when one perceives the seemingly impossible, man's feeling of superiority over nature, and the highly creative conditions that they bring into play – do not reside solely in the production of humor. Laughter, as the expression of a "sentiment double, ou contradictoire," can have as a source the clown, but ambiguous duality, along with vertigo and the sensation of being "freed from the constraints" of social and cultural codes (the equivalent of man feeling superior to nature), occur as well during acrobatic performances (Bouissac 9). The resulting sensation is existential limbo.

Michele Hannoosh sees the *comique absolu* at play in Baudelaire's "Une mort héroïque," but identifies the theory's requisite *dédoublement* in the Prince, not in Fancioulle the clown (53). I propose, however, that it is Fancioulle's marvelous performance, marvelous in the sense of the otherworldliness that Baudelaire gives the word in his essay, that ultimately dooms the clown, not his involvement in an assassination attempt on the life of the Prince. Indeed, Baudelaire deliberately contrasts two dangers with the express purpose of demonstrating that the act that we would ironically assess as the least threatening is in fact the most sinister: the danger of a political act of assassination pales in comparison to the danger of a pantomime performance. Baudelaire plays on what constitutes real power in his juxtaposition of an assassination plot, in which one attempts to wrest power from a ruler (there is no threat to the underlying system structuring and bolstering power in its shift from one group to another), and an act that thoroughly invalidates the perceived naturalness of all power. During that unforgettable pantomime, the narrator speculates that the Prince experiences both "de la jalousie et de la rancune" at the sight of the clown's play of freedom – freedom from natural and man-made rules – that poises him and his spectators in limbo between law and disorder, between the real and the supernatural, between low pantomime and high art, between the *gouffre d'en bas* (the tomb) and the *gouffre d'en haut* (paradise) (Baudelaire 167–68). Fancioulle's body makes the impossible materialize as real before everyone's eyes, culminating in what can only be interpreted as a visible and palpable challenge to the naturalness of the power of the Prince. The Prince does not begrudge Fancioulle his greater artistic talent. Rather, he must destroy the clown who demonstrates an absolute freedom – however momentary – that volatilizes the "truth" of the social and natural laws that validate his rule.

*

The artists and writers of the mid-1850s who adopted the figure of the *funambule* in their work did so in spite of the prevalence of commercial versions of the image from Deburau statuettes to Deburau ink. They pinpointed the source of the disorientation experienced during the performances of real *funambules* and adapted it to (their) art in the creation of a new aesthetic: they acknowledge their position in the market (avowal); they mock themselves as well as the power systems – artistic and political – that they are undoing (derision); they assume a double nature, being both within and outside their society and culture (duality); they play with accepted beliefs regarding society and culture, making the impossible appear as real (manipulation of cultural codes); and, as a result, they exist in and instill in the reader/spectator a sense of existential ambiguity (vertigo). Banville took familiar names from the 1840s and 1850s, most of them well known but minor actors from the Parisian literary, artistic, and theatrical landscape, made them the subjects of old fixed poetic forms, subjected them to antic rhymes, and in doing so created a new genre, the oxymoronic "ode funambulesque" (Edwards 367). Banville, like Baudelaire, Couture, and Daumier, deliberately chose to be "toujours entre deux esthétiques" (Sicotte 11). If, as Sicotte notes, Banville "inaugure l'exploration de nouvelles voies" in literature, we can say that Baudelaire, Couture, and Daumier, too, found themselves at the crossroads at which aesthetic approaches "se chevauchent et s'affrontent" (11–12). Because of their unique recourse to the device of the *funambule*, "l'année 1857" is not only "poétiquement 'funambulesque,'" it is aesthetically *funambulesque* (Bertrand 83).

Notes

1 Unlike About, who figuratively placed the two paintings in competition, an echo perhaps of the rivalry between Couture and Gérôme, Victor Luciennes described them as two faces of the same event, with one drawing

from comedy, the other from drama. In pairing them as the *Deux Duels de Pierrot*, Couture's painting serves as *Le Premier Duel de Pierrot* and Gérôme's as "son dernier duel" or as "Pierrot qui commence et Pierrot qui finit" (50–51).

2 The Belgian-born Englishman, Ernest Gambart, courted both artists during that period. Gambart exploited with considerable success Gérôme's duel painting in London, sponsoring its exhibition there in 1858 and in the distribution of a "widely popular print" (Boime, *Eclectic Vision* 313). In 1860, he requested Couture's *La Commandite* for another exhibition. As regards comparing the two duel paintings, it is interesting to note that Nadar suggests a comparison between Gérôme's work and another that figured in the Salon of 1857: Louis-Alexandre Eustache-Lorsay's *Pierrot malade* (1855) (24). Interestingly, Boime refers to this latter painting in his discussion of Couture's *Pierrot malade*, noting that whereas Eustache-Lorsay's painting presents a "pictorial joke of which Pierrot is the butt," Couture's transformed the lowly clown into the stuff of high art by the expression of a moral that transcends the comic component of the scene (*Eclectic Vision* 325).

3 In a criticism of Couture, Eugen Weber adds the quest for fame as the companion vice to seeking money. Weber refers to him as a Second Empire toady "attracted to the rewards and glories" of Napoleon III's court until he fell out of favor (703–04). Like About, Weber writes off Couture as a disgruntled artist.

4 This drawing figures in the collection of the Cleveland Museum of Art.

5 Domenico Biancolelli (1636–88) performed with the Comédie-Italienne at the Palais Royal. This *commedia* troupe alternated performances with Molière's troupe.

6 As with Gérôme's painting, critics used other titles to refer to Couture's. Like other critics commenting on the retrospective exhibition of Couture's paintings after his death in 1876, the unnamed reviewer of the "Chronique des Beaux-Arts" referred to it as *Le Duel de Pierrot et d'Arlequin* (180). Other paintings in this series carry several titles as well.

7 That Couture had painted two earlier Pierrot and Harlequin paintings gives credence to the claim of precedence in his dueling masks canvas. What also favors the idea that Gérôme borrowed his painting's theme from Couture is the fact that this was not the first time that one of the latter's paintings served as inspiration. Boime cites Gérôme's *Combat de coqs* (1846) as a translation of Couture's *Le Fauconnier* (1844–45). *Combat de coqs*'s "success at the Salon of 1847 was second only to that of Couture's *Romans [of the Decadence]*" (Boime, *Eclectic* 114). Ironically, in a parallel to the "competition" between Gérôme and Couture and their duel paintings, with the former's version making him a wealthy and famous artist, it was Gérôme's *Combat de coqs*, influenced strongly by Couture's *Le Fauconnier*, that "first made Gérôme's reputation" (Johnson). The tale of two paintings with borrowed themes that were instrumental in establishing Gérôme as a painter to the point of him eclipsing Couture recalls Fyodor Dostoevsky's novella *The Double* (1846), in which a meek civil servant's doppelgänger takes over every facet of his social and professional life. Gérôme was certainly the more confident and socially adept of the two artists. Boime points out another possible influence on the appeal of the duel theme in the April 1857 exhibition of the work of Couture's and Gérôme's mutual teacher, Paul Delaroche. Delaroche's *Suite(s) d'un duel* from 1827 figured in the show. In his review of the exhibition, Gautier makes no reference to this painting. I am unable

to comment on its relevance beyond the titular elements shared with the paintings under study, having been unable to locate an image of it.

8 Nadar describes the paintings that Gérôme submitted to the 1857 Salon as reflecting his desire to "définitivement rompre avec la fâcheuse école qu'il a créée, après le premier et le grand coupable feu Ingrès" (10). In a glance at Gérôme's work after 1857, this painting was not a clean and enduring break with academic painting. One can wonder if this surprisingly small work represents Gérôme's cooptation of Couture's own rupture beginning with the two earlier Pierrot and Harlequin paintings, yet one more instance of a deliberate effort to overshadow his rival. Critics ridiculed Couture for claiming precedence in his dueling masks painting (Gérôme probably copied the idea), and if Nadar's comments reflect the general response to Gérôme's painting, Couture was not recognized for breaking with academism before him. On the contrary, Gérôme's "break" was much louder: his presumed "schisme fait, dit-on, grand scandale dans la petite paroisse" (Nadar 10). Finally, Gérôme's commitment to painting a contemporary subject in his *Sortie du bal masqué* was perhaps not so strong after all. About commented that, "Il est peut-être à regretter qu'un chapeau de l'année, un habit noir, une pièce du costume de nos jours ne marque pas la date de son tableau" (73).

9 Desfossé, however, played the high art game of the dealer professing disinterest in the market: "Un travail ainsi conçu n'est pas, on le comprend bien, une pièce faite en vue de plaire au grand public; elle ne s'adresse pas au vulgaire" (Bourdieu 75; qtd. in Jacqué 447).

10 Recall that *Romains de la décadence* triumphed over Gérôme's *Combat de coqs*'s, itself a borrowed subject, at the Salon of 1847. Boime contends that Couture's masterpiece, "[t]hanks to a carefully orchestrated publicity campaign, [...] received more public attention than any other painting in the nineteenth century" (*Eclectic* 131). The painting's success parallels Gérôme's *Sortie du bal masqué* in that its "intrinsic appeal" guaranteed its popularity throughout the rest of the century (Boime, *Eclectic* 131). The historical distinction between the two paintings plays out, however, much along the lines established in this and the preceding chapter: while reproductions of Gérôme's work (photographs, prints, and *tableaux vivants* in various plays and pantomimes, etc.) concealed what was essentially the Gérôme franchise, keeping to the semblance of commercial disinterest indicative of the art system, those of Couture invoked the dynamics of avowal and derision associated with the Pierrot and Harlequin paintings: in addition to the Desfossé wallpaper, there were fin-de-siècle circus reenactments, "featuring *tableaux vivants* of the *Romans* with acrobats and even baboons and chimpanzees" (Boime, *Eclectic* 131). It is to be hoped that Couture would have appreciated this unique form of recognition.

11 There is perhaps a more literal representation of a breach in another painting from the period: *La Lecture* from about 1860. An example of Couture's continuing experimentation with genre painting, it features his wife reading a book as she walks through a gate in her garden. According to information for the 2016 exhibition of Couture paintings in the collection of the museum of the Palais de Compiègne, this painting not only signals the new directions that the artist was exploring, but it may contain a deeper symbolic meaning as well: "Si la figure est dans l'ombre, une vive lumière éclaire la porte treillagée vers laquelle elle se dirige et plusieurs colombes sont perchées sur des branches en fleurs de l'autre côté de la clôture" ("Dossier" 6). For the writer(s) of this brochure, the symbolism is linked to Couture's wife's pregnancy

with their first child, indicative of a "temps de calme et de repos préludant au printemps d'une nouvelle vie" (6).

12 One senses behind the calmness the potential for pantomimic pandemonium in almost all of the paintings in the series. The farce potential of *Le Duel après le bal masqué* offers a Pierrot who could take the heavy blade, wave it maladroitly to the point of losing control of his motions and, in doing so, accidentally injure or even kill the seconds, as often happened in pantomime duels from the nineteenth century. Given that Harlequin is wilier and stronger than Pierrot, however, the latter will probably lose the contest. He will not die, however, for the Pierrot of a classic *scénario féerique* always recovers miraculously from dismemberment and horrific physical trauma. With *La Commandite*, we must remember that Pierrot's "great passion," as comments Irene Mawer, "is kitchens and their scents" (qtd. in Levillain 77). This kitchen's array of pots, pans, vegetables, and meats promises a scenic development in which their potential as projectiles and clubs are fully utilized, if and when Harlequin's crafty explanation goes south. With *Pierrot malade*, we find echoes of Champfleury's pantomime *Pierrot, valet de la Mort* (1846). The canvas's doctor could decide to take some of the valuables in the bedroom as payment for treating a penurious Pierrot, upon which the latter would leap out of bed and beat the doctor soundly with those same objects, including the bottles from the prior evening's debauch. In *Pierrot à la correctionnelle*, Harlequin could put an end to the civil nature of his defense and pull out his not so carefully concealed bat and start thrashing the (sleeping) judges and the plaintiffs, a restaurant chef and his assistant.

13 The original *Marrrchand d'habits!* was a considerable flop, enjoying only two (or seven, depending on the source) performances before closing. It was reworked, however, with greater success by Charles Bridault and the mime Paul Legrand in 1853 as *Mort et remords, ou les inconvénients d'assassiner un marchand d'habits grêlé* at the Folies-Nouvelles, and the poster refers to that production (Levillain 94).

14 In a May 20, 1857, *Journal* entry, the Goncourt brothers expressed frustration at the blurring of distinction between, indeed the monstrous hybridity of, the seemingly incompatible occupations of businessman and artist. Nadar introduces a man to them whom he dismisses as "un homme de Bourse," but whom they learn is Pierre-Charles-Auguste Lefranc, one of the authors of the "immortel" *Un chapeau de paille d'Italie*: "Ce temps est étrange: on vous présente un homme d'affaires, c'est un vaudevilliste. Il y a un mélange d'états incroyable, c'est la confusion de métiers" (262).

15 Boime sees these first three paintings as linked thematically as well (*Eclectic* 641n90).

16 Ironically, John Leigh cites the perception of a similar reproving tone in Gérôme's painting:

> Critics and commentators thought it a moral piece, apparently reflecting scandalous French mores, a response to recent duels conducted in the Bois de Boulogne. The popularity of this moving, intriguing picture was soon attributed to its timeliness in exposing the horror and frivolity of contemporary duelists. (256)

Unfortunately, Leigh does not cite any of those critics and commentators. I have not come across such references in reviews from the period. Nadar, however, does perceive "une légère tendance caricaturale" (10). If there is the merest hint of caricature, the source can only have been Couture.

17 In Baudelaire's *Le Peintre de la vie moderne* (1860), the poet states that "[l]e dandysme est une institution vague, aussi bizarre que le duel" (559). Like dandyism, the duel is "une institution en dehors des lois," but which "a des lois rigoureuses auxquelles sont strictement soumis tous ses sujets" (559).

18 Boime notes that *Le Mariage* shares many elements with Jean-Baptiste Greuze's *L'Accordée de village* (1761), in particular the focus on the signing of the marriage contract (*Eclectic Vision* 296).

19 In the execution of the body's position in the painting, Couture deviated from the sketches that he had taken at the ceremony and decided not to place Napoléon III's right hand on his hip. He left what there is of it hanging at the emperor's side.

20 The date of the defacing is unknown, if it is even a question of defacing. According to Boime, Couture continued to work on the painting even into the Third Republic ("Evolution" 52). The Palais de Compiègne pedagogical pamphlet for the *Thomas Couture, Romantique malgré lui* exhibition (2015–16) states that Napoléon III's face was "effacée" ("Dossier" 21). Boime, however, categorizes it as simply incomplete or unfinished, since "it was not unusual for painters of Imperial portraiture – or any portrait for that matter – to leave the head for last since the costume details and badges of rank had to be carefully rendered and required complex study" ("Evolution" 51; *Eclectic* 276). In the baptism painting, Couture would have encountered technical and compositional difficulties that he found himself unable to resolve. Given the charged significance of Couture and Daumier's deformation of the heads and faces of *funambules* – and I would add Banville in this list, considering his treatment of names as form of defacement – I am inclined to think that Couture deliberately removed these facial details from the sketch preparation of the large canvas.

21 We can never, however, pin Couture's political position down since, as Boime points out, the painter attempted to "portray himself as a rugged republican individualist" but was an "avowed Bonapartist during the Second Empire" ("Evolution" 53).

22 The actor Gobert played the role of Napoleon I in military dramas from 1830 to 1852.

23 In his section "L'Expiation" of *Les Châtiments* (1852), Victor Hugo does not so much ridicule Napoleon III by comparing him to a circus equestrian as return him, like Couture, to the source of his political campaign:

> Tu mourus, comme un astre se couche,
> Napoléon le Grand, empereur; tu renais,
> Bonaparte, écuyer du cirque Beauharnais. (286)

24 "L'Ombre d'Éric" was first published on November 23, 1845, in *La Silhouette*. The title in the first edition of the *Odes* was the first line of the poem "Si Limayrac devenait fleur" and was placed in the collection according to its poetic form, the "balancelle." For all subsequent editions, Banville used the title of Limayrac's failed novel "L'Ombre d'Éric" (1845). The Goncourt brothers offer a wry example in their *Journal* of Limayrac as toady for Napoleon III: "Flaubert nous cite cette critique sublime de Limayrac sur *Madame Bovary*, dont le dernier mot: 'Comment se permettre un style aussi ignoble, quand il y a, sur le trône, le premier écrivain de la langue française, l'empereur?'" (518).

25 "L'Ombre d'Éric" was not the only poem that Parisians committed to memory. From an anonymous introduction to the publication of "La Corde

roide" in the *Gazette de Paris* (September 28, 1856), the author claims that "chacun les [the collection's poems] sait par coeur" (Banville 444).

26 How ironic that the *funambulesque* participants of the Paris Opéra's *bal masqué* perpetuated the *funambulesque* defacement executed by the poem, slipping from the pages of the volume into the streets of Paris.

27 Among other transformations in the volume, the publisher and former manager of the Opéra de Paris Louis Véron is transformed into a coquettish girl and a caterpillar in "V … le baigneur," which appropriates fondly the form and rhythms of Victor Hugo's "Sara la baigneuse."

28 Curiously, Banville also makes the very mercurial Couture's name and person disappear all the while explicitly naming him and enjoining others to do the same in "Nommons Couture!" The inspiration for the poem was three letters supposedly written by the painter to the editor in chief of *Le Figaro*, Hippolyte de Villemessant. Miffed by the reference to a portraitist "C" in a newspaper article, and even angrier when his first letter was not published, Couture wrote Villemessant claiming to be the "seul artiste véritablement sérieux de notre époque" (Banville 155). Taking this arrogant claim as his creative springboard, Banville depicts Couture trying as he might to throw his shadow over the work of other painters and doom them to oblivion (compared to him, they are "des farceurs"), but the artist's name and person nevertheless fall victim to a "fatalité" and are effectively removed – "Couture ôté" – by the rhyme (Banville 155, 159). In this letter business, Couture claimed to be the victim of a hoax. In his 1857 preface, Banville expresses regret for having believed that Couture was the author of the first two letters. Edwards concludes, however, that Banville's remorse was insincere and that his apology for the poetic "javelot" that he threw at the great painter and his considerable pride was mere expedience, since Banville never removed "Nommons Couture !" from subsequent editions of the *Odes*, and since in his 1873 commentary he promises to withdraw the poem if ever Couture should withdraw his letter (15, 637, 279). Despite the innumerable contradictory stances and comments made by Couture during his lifetime, there might be some validity to his claim. The satirized component of the letter was his boast of being the most "serious" painter of his time, but it may be this word that vindicates him. As Boime writes, "Couture shared Delacroix's disdain for the academic style, which both mocked as 'peinture sérieuse.' Couture wrote that the 'serious' in painting is an 'assemblage de certains sujets, toujours les mêmes, qui compose ce baggage; il va sans dire que le naturel en est exclu.' He noted that his failure to be 'sufficiently serious' cost him the Prix de Rome when he was a pupil at the École" ("Evolution" 55). I am inclined to interpret Banville's appreciation of Couture's talent as sincere, since the Goncourt brothers, close friends of the poet, admired Couture, and, according to Boime and Helen Borowitz, based the painter Anatole from *Manette Salomon* (1867) on him (*Eclectic Vision* 298; 31). It would not be a stretch to conclude that the brothers expressed their support of the painter to the poet.

29 Banville's parodies of poems by Victor Hugo, particularly from *Les Orientales* (1829), do not fall under the category of derision, since it is clear that he found the lyricism of the Hugolian model sublime.

30 Harper discounts Clark's citing of the enforcement of the 1849 laws and the persecution of street performers as the contemporary circumstances that caught Daumier's attention, stating that, "[a]ll of the historians of the parades and saltimbanques of the nineteenth century mention regular police interference with their activities dating from the late 18th century" (32n39).

31 This claim is inaccurate, as many paintings from the last two decades of the century prove, notably Georges Seurat's *Parade de cirque* (1888).
32 One could say that he had arrived at a mental glossary of gestures, much like the glossary that Raoul de Najac had destined for society people who staged salon pantomimes: *Petit traité de mime à l'usage des gens du monde* (1909).
33 Daumier's circus-related caricatures are numerous. In an early caricature, his "Mr Chose, premier saltimbanque d'Europe" targeted Louis-Philippe as a pear on a tightrope (August 1, 1833, in *La Charivari*). Later in his career, Daumier depicted an aerialist Adolphe Thiers of the Comité de la rue de Poitiers supported on his pole by an old woman in "La Perche: Exercice renouvelé du cirque" (March 9, 1870 in *Le Charivari*). "L'Écuyère" (around 1864 in *Le Journal Amusant*) and "Au Cirque: C'est sa fille ! ou l'art de casser ses enfants et de s'en faire des rentes" (January 16, 1875 in *Le Journal Amusant*) appear to feature the same unidentified politician. "La Pyramide humaine" (May 7, 1868 in *Le Charivari*) featured a Prussian carrying a big sword atop a pyramid of figures representing Hanover, Holstein, and Nassau. One can find these caricatures and more on the comprehensive online Daumier Registry (http://www.daumier-register.org/login.php?startpage).
34 The effect is strangely reminiscent of the effacing of Louis-Napoléon's face and hand in Couture's *Baptême*.
35 As Carmeli notes, "Unlike dancers or actors, who from the very start are disclosed to the public in performance, the circus performer introduces himself to the townsfolk by waving from the ring to the public seated in different sections. His real, human, communicative nature is thus indicated" (198–99).
36 Manet was Couture's student from 1850 to 1856.
37 Gustave Doré's undated *Pierrot grimaçant* reveals similar liquid features.

Works Cited

About, Edmond. *Nos Artistes au Salon de 1857.* Paris: Hachette, 1858.

Banville, Théodore de. *Œuvres poétiques complètes.* Ed. Peter J. Edwards. Vol. 3. Paris: Honoré Champion, 1995.

———. *Les Pauvres saltimbanques.* Paris: Michel Lévy Frères, 1853.

Baudelaire, Charles. *Œuvres complètes.* Ed. Marcel A. Ruff. Paris: Éditions du Seuil, 1968.

Bohac, Barbara. "Poésie lyrique et caricature dans les *Odes funambulesques* de Théodore de Banville." *Études françaises* 51.3 (2015): 27–52. 11 June 2018. doi: 10.7202/1034130ar

Boime, Albert. *Thomas Couture and the Eclectic Vision.* New Haven, CT, and London: Yale UP, 1980).

———. "Thomas Couture and the Evolution of Painting in Nineteenth-Century France." *The Art Bulletin* 51.1 (1969): 48–56.

Bonnet, Gilles. *La Pantomime noire, 1836–1896.* Paris: Hermann, 2014.

Borowitz, Helen O. "Painted Smiles: Sad Clowns in French Art and Literature." *The Bulletin of the Cleveland Museum of Art* 71.1 (1984): 23–35.

Bouissac, Paul. *Circus and Culture: A Semiotic Approach.* Bloomington and London: Indiana UP, 1976.

Bourdieu, Pierre. *The Field of Cultural Production: Essays on Art and Literature.* Ed. Randal Johnson. New York, NY: Columbia UP, 1993.

Carmeli, Yoram. "Performing the 'Real' and 'Impossible' in the British Traveling Circus." *Semiotica* 80.3–4 (1990): 193–220.

Champfleury. *Contes d'automne.* Paris: Victor Lecou, 1854.

"Chronique des Beaux-Arts." *L'Illustration: journal universel.* 11 September 1880. 180.

Clark, T. J. *The Absolute Bourgeois: Artists and Politics in France, 1848–1851.* Berkeley, Los Angeles, London: U of California P, 1973, 1982, 1999.

"Dossier Pédagogique: Thomas Couture dans les collections du Palais de Compiègne." 5 August 2018 <https://palaisdecompiegne.fr/sites/palaisdecompiegne.fr/files/dossier_enseignant_couture.pdf>.

Edwards, Peter J., ed. *Œuvres poétiques complètes.* By Théodore de Banville. Vol. 3. Paris: Honoré Champion, 1995.

Gautier, Théophile. "Salon de 1857, IV: MM. Gérôme, Mottez." *L'Artiste, Tome premier* (5 July 1857): 245–49.

Goncourt, Edmond and Jules de. *Journal. Mémoires de la vie littéraire, 1851–1865.* Ed. Robert Ricatte. Vol. I. Paris: Laffont, 1989.

Griffin, Robert J. "Anonymity and Authorship." *New Literary History* 30.4 (1999): 877–95.

Hannoosh, Michele. *Baudelaire and Caricature: From the Comic to an Art of Modernity.* University Park: U of Pennsylvania P, 1992.

Harper, Paula Hays. *Daumier's Clowns: Les Saltimbanques et les Parades. New Biographical and Political Functions for a Nineteenth Century Myth.* New York and London: Garland Publishing, 1981.

Hôtel Drouot, Charles Blanc, and Émile Bergerat. *Catalogue de tableaux modernes et de tableaux anciens composant la collection Laurent-Richard dont la vente aura lieu Hôtel Drouot, Salles nos 8 et 9 les jeudi 23, vendredi 24 et samedi 25 mai 1878.* Paris: Pillet & Dumoulin, 1878. The Open Library. 10 August 2018 <https://archive.org/stream/detablauren00htel?ref=ol#page/n8/mode/2up>.

Hugo, Victor. *Œuvres complètes. Poésie IV. Les Châtiments.* Paris: Hetzel-Quantin, 1882.

Jacqué, Bernard. *De la manufacture au mur.* 2003. Diss. University of Lyons II Lumière. 1 August 2018 <http://theses.univ-lyon2.fr/documents/lyon2/2003/jacque_b#p=0&a=top>.

Johnson, Ken. "Art Review: A Return to the Junction of Art and Commerce." *The New York Times.* 20 April 2001. 8 August 2018 <https://www.nytimes.com/2001/04/20/arts/art-review-a-return-to-the-junction-of-art-and-commerce.html>.

Lafont-Couturier, Hélène, ed. *Gérôme & Goupil: Art and Enterprise.* Trans. Isabel Ollivier. Paris: Réunion des musées nationaux; Bordeaux: Musée Goupil; Pittsburgh, PA: Frich Art and Historical Center; New York: Dahesh Museum of Art, 2000.

Laforgue, Jules. *Pierrot fumiste.* 13 August 2019 <http://www.laforgue.org/Pierrot.htm>

Leigh, John. *Touché: The Duel in Literature.* Cambridge, MA: Harvard UP, 2015.

Levillain, Anne Dowling. *The Evolution of Pantomime in France.* Diss. Boston College, 1943.

Luciennes, Victor. "Le Premier duel de Pierrot." *Musée des familles. Lectures du soir.* Vol. 30, November, 1862. 49–51. 14 July 2018 <https://books.google.com/books?id=QbM_AAAAcAAJ&pg=PA51&lpg=PA51&dq=Victor+luciennes+%22Le+Premier+duel+de+Pierrot%22+Mus%C3%A9e+des+familles&source=bl&ots=lb_R3A3WTU&sig=ACfU3U3UPTH3Du7XSbC5i5sUh4xkDlqOhw&hl=en&sa=X&ved=2ahUKEwi4lue10sPgAhWEITQIHRqID14Q6AEwA3oECAcQAQ#v=onepage&q=Victor%20luciennes%20%22Le%20Premier%20duel%20de%20Pierrot%22%20Mus%C3%A9e%20des%20familles&f=false>.

Nadar (Gaspard-Félix Tournachon). *Nadar jury au Salon de 1857: 1000 comptes rendus, 150 dessins.* Paris: Librairie Nouvelle, 1857.

Sicotte, Geneviève. "Présentation: Que peut l'approche synchronique? Ou quand le littéraire fait date." *Études françaises* 43.2 (2007): 5–12. 14 August 2018 <https://www.erudit.org/en/journals/etudfr/2007-v43-n2-etudfr1779/016469ar/>.

Starobinski, Jean. *Portrait de l'artiste en saltimbanque.* Geneva: Editions d'Art Albert Skira, 1970.

Truesdell, Matthew. *Spectacular Politics: Louis-Napoléon Bonaparte and the Fête Impériale, 1849–1870.* New York and Oxford: Oxford UP, 1997.

Weber, Eugen. "Review of *Thomas Couture and the Eclectic Vision*, by Albert Boime." *The Journal of Interdisciplinary History* 12.4 (1982): 703–05.

3 1879, Part I

Suspending Identity with the Hanlon-Lees

In their 1878–79 season in Paris, the acrobatic troupe the Hanlon-Lees made an immediate and lasting impression on their Parisian audiences. Jacques Noiray surmises that

> Ces cinq frères, mimes, acrobats, créateurs de féeries poétiques et bouffonnes, ont inspiré à de nombreux écrivains de l'époque des pages enthousiastes, à tel point qu'il n'est pas exagéré de parler d'un véritable thème des Hanlon-Lees, autour de 1880, dans la presse et dans la littérature. (96)

The troupe's performance season was the creative spark of considerable influence on the literary and visual arts. Their undisputed sphere of aesthetic influence recalls 1832 when literary and artistic Paris discovered Deburau as Pierrot – soon the only Pierrot for roughly a decade – at the Théâtre des Funambules, thanks to the *succès de scandale* of Jules Janin's biography of the pantomimist in *Histoire du Théâtre à quatre sous*. The biography was such a hit that celebrities from a variety of artistic mediums flocked to the tiny theater on the Boulevard du Crime, among whom the songwriter Pierre-Jean de Béranger, Théophile Gautier, Victor Hugo, Gérard de Nerval, Champfleury, and the actresses "Mlle Mars, Mlle Georges, and Marie Malibran" (Jones 62). Several writers even developed relationships with the theater and its star attraction. Charles Nodier wrote reviews of Deburau's pantomimes as early as 1828, and to him is attributed authorship of the pantomime *Le Songe d'or, ou Arlequin et l'avare* (1828). Gautier's 1842 review "Shakespeare aux Funambules" was the inspiration for Cot d'Ordan's *Marrrchand d'habits!* from the same year. Champfleury, too, wrote the first of many pantomimes for the theater in 1846 (*Pierrot, valet de la mort*) in the hopes of prolonging the life of a genre threatened by the increasing popularity of vaudeville. Janin's book, and perhaps equal measures of serendipity, however, brought creative Paris to the little theater on the Boulevard du Crime. Janin's biography of Deburau had another distinction as well. It was not only a biography; it was also part manifesto against the classical tradition represented by the Théâtre Français, part description of the pantomime genre and the conditions of the theater's productions, all of which in combination worked to account for the Deburau effect, an explanation that, rather than demystify its subject, enshrouded him in a cloud of paradox (Jones 67). As for the role of happenstance, Hugo's *Le Roi s'amuse* came out in the same year as Janin's *Histoire du Théâtre à quatre sous*. Hugo's jester Triboulet, like Deburau's Pierrot, embodied the duality of the Romantic hero: he was grotesque *and* sublime. The elements necessary for making Deburau the poster child of an aesthetic revolution were present.

Roughly fifty years later, the Hanlon-Lees produced another singular entertainment sensation, and like Deburau, the materialization of the right conditions at the right moment drew artist and writer spectators to their pantomimes at the Folies Bergère.[1] They had had successful engagements before in Paris. In 1870, before the Franco-Prussian War, they had a steady billing at the Théâtre du Châtelet and in the pantomime ballet *Fiamma*, and they returned in 1872 at the invitation of Léon Sari, director of the Folies Bergère, where they featured for almost a year (Cosdon 40, 43). There, they began to develop the repertoire of pantomimes that would make them the talk of creative Paris seven years later. The electric atmosphere and the half a million visitors of the *Exposition universelle* of 1878 helped set the stage for the enthusiastic Paris reception of the brothers.[2] One could find in the audience on a given evening Banville, Coquelin Cadet, Huysmans, Léon Hennique, Charles Cros, Villiers de l'Isle-Adam, Edmond de Goncourt, Paul Margueritte, and Zola. Jules Chéret captured the spirit of their brand of antic acrobatic pantomime in his poster *Folies-Bergère/Do Mi Sol Do/Les Hanlon-Lees* (1878).[3] While the Hanlon-Lees effect would be felt throughout the 1880s, their performances inspired a flurry of works either conceived or produced in 1879: Richard Lesclides's biography and transcription of the *Mémoires et pantomimes des frères Hanlon Lees* (with the famous preface by Banville), Goncourt's *Les Frères Zemganno*, Huysmans's "Les Folies-Bergère en 1879" in his *Croquis parisiens* (1880), and Villiers's fantastic tribute "Les Hanlon Lees" in *L'Étoile française* (25 December 1880). If we cannot trace Edgar Degas's *Miss Lala au Cirque Fernando* and Catulle Mendès's two-volume *La Vie et la mort d'un clown* directly back to the Hanlon-Lees, we can still feel their influence in the novel use of space in both works and in the conceptualization of the perversely malevolent but sublimely accomplished acrobatic clown Aladin/Papiol/Marquis Papioli in the latter. We can identify the impetus for the revival of the *pantomime pierrotique* in the creation of the Cercle funambulesque in 1888 to the Hanlon-Lees troupe. A Hanlon-Lees-inspired pantomime was Huysmans and Hennique's *Pierrot sceptique* (1881), itself a significant source for Jules Laforgue's *Pierrot fumiste* (circa 1883).[4] Like Janin's *Histoire du théâtre à quatre sous*, Goncourt's *Les Frères Zemganno* was, in the spirit of realist documentation, partially an attempt to dissect and classify the mystery of the acrobat. For his collection of material, Goncourt went straight to the horse's mouth, interviewing Victor Franconi of the Cirque d'Été and the Cirque d'Hiver; Léon Sari of the Folies Bergère; and, of course, the Hanlon-Lees.[5]

"Deux Ordres d'Idées Diamétralement Opposés"

Four writers recorded their recollections of pantomimes performed by the Hanlon-Lees and described, each in his own way, exhilarating and often disconcerting moments of existential limbo: Banville in his preface to Lesclide's *Mémoires et pantomimes des frères Hanlon-Lees*, Huysmans in "Les Folies-Bergère en 1879," Zola in "Pantomime" in *Le Naturalisme au théâtre* (1881), and Coquelin Cadet in *Une vie humoristique* (1883).[6] Each reports the baffling but also exciting production of contradictory emotions and the lack of cohesion between the actions grounding the pantomimes. Banville marvels at the acrobats' grace and precision while executing turbulent physical actions as well as at "la sereine douceur et la céleste innocence de leurs visages [qui] contrastent avec la violence de leurs sauts, de leurs tordions [sic], de leurs luttes et de leurs gambades" (12). Commenting on *Le Duel*, Huysmans relishes the oxymoronic impression produced by "ces désopilants et funèbres acrobates": their performance is a "farce lugubre" and a "bouffonnerie sinistre" (23). Coquelin Cadet echoes Huysmans's assessment of the same pantomime in applying literally the figurative "On meurt de rire," pairing death with laughter. This exclamation prompts his antithetical conclusion, "C'est de l'Edgar Poë à crever de rire!" (202–03). Recounting the series of actions constituting *Do mi sol do*, Coquelin Cadet also emphasizes the pantomime's droll mixture of impassiveness and extreme agitation. He finds sublime humor in the conductor played by Agoust, who, while attacked in every possible manner by his musicians, maintains a serene calmness throughout the madcap pantomime, oblivious to the mayhem taking place around him.

In his review of the Hanlon-Lees' *Le Voyage en Suisse* at the Théâtre des Variétés in 1879, Zola remarks on the disturbing mixture of laughter and fear that the acrobats' performances produce. The result is "un au-delà troublant" (329). Zola's response is perhaps the most visceral of all the eyewitnesses in his characterization of the Hanlon's antics as "la négation de tout" and "le néant humain" (329). The "fou rire" that erupts from him leads him to have "de sourdes inquiétudes pour sa propre raison" (329, 331). Oxymoronic blends – laughter *and* fear, precision *and* unpredictability, facial stillness *and* violent physical activity, gracefulness *and* frenzied movement, "cruauté" *and* "gaité," "la finesse et la force" – all contribute to the loss of one's bearings as one falls into an indeterminate state that is neither the one nor the other, and yet perplexingly, impossibly, and simultaneously both (Zola 333). Recalling the

Hanlon-Lees pantomimes that he saw earlier in the year at the Folies Bergère, Zola characterizes the experience of this limbo as inducing a "petit frisson froid de la vérité," a truth that can be shown but not spoken, and therefore inaccessible to the Naturalist writer (329, 334). He concludes that this is a truth, one grounded in a nothingness that cannot be adapted to the writing of literature.

In his comparison between the superior troupe-authored silent program at the Folies Bergère from earlier in 1879 and the commercially successful but critically mediocre Ernest Blum and Raoul Toché talking farce *Le Voyage en Suisse*, Zola singles out as the funniest moments common to all these productions those scenes in which the acrobats frolic cheerfully amid "des membres cassés et des poitrines trouées," a frolicking that he describes here as the "apothéose du vice et du crime," and later as "une négation absolue de la justice," and "une absolution du crime par l'adresse" (329, 333). Zola's references to the acrobats' reveling in "vice" and "crime," however, not only represent a targeted "revenge against authority" (which we as spectators enjoy vicariously) but are indicative of a greater manipulation of the codes of human culture and society, an absence of natural and empirical laws that is produced through the visual and conceptual pairing of contradictory qualities (332). For Banville, this "jeu double," this expression of "deux ordres d'idées diamétralement opposés" is the modus operandi of the Hanlon-Lees (12). If Banville claims about the acrobat – all acrobats – that "[c]'est dans l'impossible qu'il habite; ce qu'il fait, c'est l'impossible," he only partially accounts for the Hanlon-Lees effect (9). Acrobats make the impossible paradoxically possible. As Carmeli explains,

> It is not, however, the possibility that something like that is really taking place and time, and really is part of the world, that attracts and provokes the public time and again; rather, it is the witnessing of, really seeing that which does not and cannot take place, bearing witness to that which is otherwise not witnessed, playfully touching the ontological foundations of the public's everyday life. Circus travelers do not, then, do the impossible in their performances of real danger and feats. ("Performing" 215)

Zola identifies such an impossible moment in asserting that, in defiance of empirical laws, the Hanlons "sont à la fois aux quatre coins de la scène," a claim that, while obviously an exaggeration, is also very real. They are both everywhere and nowhere in a flurry of leaps.

In his 1880 *chronique* "Les Hanlon Lees," Villiers echoes Zola's perception of the general lawlessness and the "miracle d'ubiquité" of the troupe members, the latter epitomized by the impossible vision of their heads popping up in "vingt lucarnes à la fois" (739). But whereas Zola expresses hesitation at the audacity of their antics, particularly their ridicule of policemen, Villiers heartily embraces their transgressions, reveling in the execution of even greater acrobatic capers that flout all known human and natural laws. He pictures the ubiquity of the five brothers bleeding beyond the four corners of the stage as they expand the "frontière du merveilleux" to encompass the larger "theater" that is the city of London, breaking the barriers separating outside and inside, the real and the fantastic (Baudelaire 377; Villiers 739). Theirs is a topsy-turvy world in which "[l]a réalité actuelle ne peut que dépasser toute fiction" (Villiers 738). They treat the ordinary objects of the urban landscape as familiar stage props, from those related to interior spaces (the armoires from which they emerge or into which they customarily dive) to the exterior (windows, roofs, fences, underground tunnels, boats, and gutters) (739). They create and are also propelled by their own momentum, a dual state in which they possess human agency (subjectivity) *and* let their body function as objects. Villiers figures that duality as a split of the troupe name into the Hanlon(s) and the Lees, with the former slipping between the legs of the policemen (the Hanlons) and the latter leapfrogging over their heads (the Lees). The context of Villiers's *chronique* is precisely the commission of the type of crime described by Zola and the fruitlessness of all efforts by the police to arrest the Hanlon-Lees. Were they ever to be caught, it would be with their cooperation in anticipation of the joy of escaping. George Hanlon abducts a consenting young hostage ("une vraie jeune fille!") from her respectable family, and he and his brothers, in imitation of their "abracadabrantes performances des Folies-Bergère et des Variétés," figuratively and literally fly off with her – they are bluebirds and sylphs whose taunting laughter, "pareil à un battement d'ailes," comes from the stars above, the realm of Banville's "gouffre d'en haut" (Banville 385; Villiers 738, 740).

Perceiving as real the impossible feat of normally gravity-bound bodies careening and ricocheting off solid objects as if they themselves were rubber balls blurs the neat separation of spectator and performer (333). Indeed, the acrobat's presentation of the impossible as really happening invades the everyday reality of the spectator's space, that space ruled in daily experience by natural and empirical laws. This moment arrives like a "coup de vent," and although Zola does not indicate the precise length of its duration, it is over in a flash, for the perception of the performance of the impossible-witnessed-as-possible takes place outside of "social time" (Carmeli, "Performing" 216; Zola 333). Carmeli points out that in order for the perception of the impossible to occur, circus acts have to be short. "The need 'to cut the acts' (i.e., to make them not only separate but also very short in duration, experienced as witnessed rather than as sharing in real time)," he explains, "was often stressed in circus and imposed on the performers" ("Performing" 216). Zola bemoaned the middle-class mediocrity of Blum and Toché's *Le Voyage en Suisse*, a farce written specifically to showcase the Hanlon-Lees, stating that he would have preferred the pantomime format offered by the Folies Bergère, where the Hanlons were "livrés à eux-mêmes" in the execution of their brand of "fantaisie sombre" (329). Distinguishing between the tastes of English and French audiences, he claims that the former are able to sit through "une grêle de gifles et de coups de pied tombant pendant quatre heures," while the latter demand that the pantomime be secondary to a greater unifying narrative and that there be "points de repos" that give spectators a moment to breathe (Zola 328). However, short flashes of dizzying acrobatics of the Hanlon-Lees variety are the only solution for the periodic, because unsustainable, production of non-time and non-space.

Pierrot Times Two

Huysmans, who demonstrated in many of the *Croquis*' prose poems that he was receptive to and capable of producing through literature the magical but short-lived nature of being out of time and place, describes this ephemeral experience in "Le Geindre" as his narrator watches two men knead dough in a bakery basement before dawn. The scene is prepared in advance with the narrator catching sight of one of the baker's assistants on the street: tall and thin like in the illustrations of Deburau by Auguste Bouquet (although Huysmans's narrator's express reference is to Watteau's Gilles) and dressed all in white, the worker dangles a bottle (of water? of wine?) as he walks to the bakery workroom, visually recalling the cunning figure of Pierrot. Here, the worker just *resembles* Pierrot. As the narrator watches the two kneaders through the basement window, they become increasingly powdered in white flour in the execution of a very physical and silent "pantomime" marked only by grunts and cries, and there is an instant – a fleeting instant – when, drinking from their bottles after their exertions, they *become* Pierrot: "—Ah! Je le reconnaissais, ton type de larron et d'ivrogne, Watteau! je le retrouvais enfin, ce sacripant et ce goinfre, mais ce ne fut vraiment lui que pendant quelques secondes" (69). In that moment, time and space as the narrator knows them cease to exist, allowing for the miraculous apparition of Pierrot times two, an echo of the two Pierrots in the earlier poem on the Hanlon-Lees' *Duel*. The boundaries separating art from reality become momentarily fluid, freeing the viewer such that she witnesses a painting figure come to life.

Zola's conclusion is that Naturalist novelists (a group to which Huysmans still technically belonged) fail to account for the full complexity of human social experience because they do not or are unable to go as far as the Hanlon-Lees and English caricaturists. He cites as an example a scene of drunkenness that demonstrates "toute une psychologie de l'ivresse" superior in all details to the analyses that Naturalist novelists can offer (232). But, however much the word *pantomime* is related to the Greek word *mimesis*, Zola mistakes the Hanlon-Lees' physical movements solely for imitation, for acting, for being modeled on life, a mistake he did not make when he compared the acrobats to English caricaturists, referring to their ability to present well-known persons in a recognizable fashion while also distorting their features such that they risk no longer being themselves. As the Goncourts claimed twenty years earlier, unlike actors and actresses who pretend to have talent, acrobats' talent is undisputable and their performances real (491). They were perhaps referring to Jules Léotard whose feats, upon introducing the flying trapeze in 1859, "font courir Paris [...] au cirque de l'Impératrice" (Ricatte 587n5). Ironically, when they describe acrobatic precision as "absolute like mathematics," they quickly correct themselves: it is absolute "plutôt comme un saut périlleux," inviting no other comparison except to itself (491). Acrobatics have no referent outside of the circus ring or its equivalent. As Carmeli notes, the completed trick is "its own evidence. It points, in fact, to itself" ("Performing" 202).

The Goncourts anticipate as well Carmeli's identification of the ambiguous relation that materializes between acrobat and spectator ("Performing" 210). At the same moment in which the acrobat does incredible physical exploits, the performance of the impossible (something that the spectator cannot do in *real* life) is also an event which paradoxically includes the spectator within a shared space of experience (the spectator *really* sees it happening before her eyes). The Goncourts corroborate this phenomenon through the duality of their own impressions: acrobats really risk their lives (they are exceedingly, almost inhumanly, strange – "férocement étrange"), *and* the public perceives them as being like us (they are also at the same time "sympathiquement apitoyé, comme si ces gens étaient de notre race") (491).[7] Banville understood this in his qualification of the acrobats' helter-skelter gymnastics as intrinsically double. When he interprets their pell-mell physicality as "voilà précisément la vie comme elle est," he imagines the Hanlons rhetorically correcting him with "Oui, voilà comme elle est; mais aussi, tu vois, je m'exerce à m'envoler dans l'éther, plus loin que l'azur et les oiseaux là où sont les astres" (13). Mimesis and the distance produced by the performance of the seemingly impossible must both be present.

The Hanlon-Lees' performance of inebriation in *Le Voyage en Suisse* is inflected so as to create a similar double experience composed of opposites, with, on the one hand, the acrobats displaying their human nature in their ability to mimic and, on the other hand, establishing distance through their seemingly uncanny skill. Zola marvels at the high degree of mimicry on the part of the Hanlons without, however, including distantiation into the equation. As his praise of their depiction of drunkenness demonstrates, communication with the spectator is indeed established. A barrier, however, is also erected between the Hanlons and spectators in the moment of executing what seems impossible. In their attempt to turn on a light, the acrobats "perdent successivement les allumettes, la bougie, le chandelier," demonstrating expert mimicry of a loss of physical control, but there is also distantiation, with the latter emerging in a complex juggling routine that no true drunk could ever perform, precise choreography and acrobatic expertise being the opposite of failed motor skills in drunken fumbling and bumbling. In this way, the Hanlons maintain without resolving the contradictions of their performance.

Rancière finds that Tombre from Richepin's *Braves gens*, while not Naturalist in method, was one effort to transpose into writing the Hanlon-Lees' penetrating analysis of the deleterious effects of alcohol.[8] For him, Tombre in his final incarnation as a Happy Zigzag is a composite of "Zola's alcoholics (Coupeau and Macquart) and his painter who sacrificed everything in search of the absolute work (Claude Lantier)" (Rancière 87).[9] Be that as it may, Richepin most certainly took inspiration from the scene of drunkenness in *Le Voyage en Suisse*, the one that struck Zola with its inimitable realism. If Tombre, unlike the Hanlon-Lees and unlike his contortionist co-performers, employs neither the same skilled gymnastics nor expert juggling, his performance is still disconcertingly double. He experiences real alcoholic delirium tremens during his performance, but not in a demonstration of keen Naturalist observation. On the contrary, "C'était la figure même de l'alcoolisme" (Richepin 461). Tombre, the man, is an alcoholic, but his alcoholism serves on stage to bring about a separation from himself. He is both alcoholic and performer of his alcoholic condition:

> Je siffle une absinthe. Paf! Tableau! Tout devient clair. Illumination! Feu d'artifice! Et je retrouve, et je trouve encore. Le geste se met au bout de mon bras, tout seul, comme si on me le posait dans la main. Il n'y a pas d'erreur. C'est aussi net comme deux et deux font quatre. La physionomie se fixe, se transforme, toujours juste. Je la sens passer sur ma face, en équation avec mes pensées. Il me semble qu'on m'y colle et qu'on m'en arrache cent masques à la minute, comme des changements à vue entre cuir et chair. Et qui, on? Lui, parbleu! Lui, le génie de l'alcool. (Richepin 120)

While Tombre attributes to alcohol the separation of his person from his body-become-object (the gestures and facial expressions materialize by themselves, as if someone else or something is manipulating his body), the description conforms to the "separation of human subjectivity from bodily objectness" that occurs during a circus or acrobatic pantomime performance (Carmeli, "Performing" 210). The willful performance of delirium tremens possesses an involuntary component such that the tremors control Tombre's body as much as he controls them, turning him into an object. This detachment repeats itself in other ways during the pantomime. For example, his spastic movements on stage – real delirium tremens *and* the performance of delirium tremens – are complimented by his overall cadaverous appearance, as Tombre is a living skeleton *and* "[i]l joue les squelettes pour de vrai" (Richepin 443).

Performing real alcoholism and real skeletons does not exhaust, however, the complexity of Tombre's entertainment, since he is accompanied by the Happy Zigzags. His two "gnome" partners may have been inspired by Richepin's attendance at a Hanlon-Lees pantomime in early 1870, when the troupe featured the Hanlon Midgets at the Théâtre du Châtelet (Cosdon 40).[10] He may equally have come into contact with dwarves in his encounters with the traveling circus or gypsy caravans.[11] Or, he simply saw performers "at the circus or the music hall, which he attended regularly, [where the performers] discreetly acknowledged his presence" (Sutton 83).

There are also, however, elements distinctly reminiscent of the Hanlon-Lees' *Duel*, the first being the two Pierrots, with one being tall and thin, and the other being short and stocky, details provided by Huysmans in *Croquis parisiens* (21).[12] While the Pierrot who is "plus ramassé, plus boulot" is not a dwarf (no one in the troupe was), the comedy does turn partially on the disproportion of their sizes (Huysmans 21). As Carmeli points out regarding the modern traveling circus in Britain, when a company does hire a dwarf, it is generally as a clown and for the purpose of having him perform his real smallness (and not his real person) against the "normal" size of the other clowns ("From Curiosity" 73; "Wee Pea" 143).[13]

The other resemblance with *Le Duel* is in the extreme emotions that visibly take over the acrobats' bodies. Huysmans observes a terror so powerful that it produces severe muscular disturbances in the Pierrots: "[l]e tremblement de leurs mains s'accentue, les jambes flageolent, le cou suffoque, la bouche remue, la langue bat sans salive et cherche haleine" (22). It becomes so overwhelming that "les nerfs déjà rebellés se détraquent d'un coup et s'emportent sans qu'on puisse les tenir" (22). Drawing on this disturbing display of fear, Richepin shifted focus from the spectacle of emotional panic on stage to the extreme distress in the audience at the sight of frenetic and spasmodic contractions, contortions, and tremors. Accordingly, his Tombre and the dwarves sow "un long frisson d'épouvante" among their spectators (462).

There is a reason why Richepin selected two dwarves to accompany the skeletal Tombre in the Happy Zigzags. Regardless of Tombre's conception of his persona as a new kind of Pierrot ("Le Pierrot qui fait frissonner, et penser"), the troupe's performance falls in no way within the pierrotic pantomime tradition (Richepin 61). This is not an entertainment that tells a story, it is one that functions as, in J. L. Austin's term, a performative: it effects a transition during the time of a performance from one state to another. Historically, when dwarves were exhibited in fairgrounds, they were lumped together with other curiosities of nature.

Exhibition was entirely passive on their parts, as they were treated as aberrations among other strange oddities (giant, exceedingly obese people, three-legged people, etc.) (Carmeli, "From Curiosity" 70–71). Beginning in the nineteenth century, to the passive exhibition was included an active component with dwarves presenting or displaying themselves, what Carmeli describes as the "playing and miming" of their own selves ("From Curiosity" 75). In the context of a clown and dwarf performance, the dwarf ultimately serves as a foil to the "normal" size, hence humanness of the clowns. As such, he functions solely as the "sign for whatever is little," which reduces him to a tool or prop (Carmeli, "Wee Pea" 141).

In *Braves gens*, the dwarves establish their object condition – the first contorts into a rubber centipede that turns into the shape of a zigzag and the second into a ball that flattens out and becomes a stink bug. Tombre enters after this transformation sequence and, although the narrator comments in horror that "[c]e n'était pas un clown, celui-ci," he is the clown in terms of his position in the dwarf/clown dynamic (Richepin 460). The dwarves' small size sets off his humanness, a reality that contrasts disconcertingly with the narrator's description of each aberrant body part that constitutes the monster that is Tombre. He is both man and monster, living and dead, real person and object, a deliberate paradox in Tombre's own description of himself as a "fantôme réel," and in the narrator's as "l'homme-fantôme," who is "fantastique à force de réalité" (61, 41, 460).

In an echo of Villiers's comments about the pantomimes of the Hanlon-Lees, Tombre creates new art characterized by fluidity between, here, the real and the fantastic, but also between other oppositional qualities. Richepin probably fashioned the Happy Zigzags along similar lines as those associated with the British acrobats: they are capable of producing the conflicting emotions (serenity and horror, "le rire maladif," etc.) and perceptions (the acrobat or clown as both real person and person playing himself) that he himself must have experienced as a spectator of their pantomimes (462). This is, after all, the effect observed by Huysmans, Banville, Zola, and Coquelin Cadet in their recounting of Hanlon-Lees pantomimes.

It is customary to read the final stage of Tombre's life and art as that of a sad clown in its alarming portrait of alcoholism. In this depiction, Richepin's biographer Howard Sutton sees a parallel, as did Rancière, with a Naturalist exploration of the "brutal and ugly aspects of his subjects" (239). He determines, however, that the writer goes too far in his analysis (further, one assumes, than Zola and the Naturalists were willing or able to go). According to Sutton, instead of seeking to achieve a "more truthful representation of life," Richepin was more interested in shocking his readers, in pushing that perception of the real to the absolute limits of perversion and depravity (239). He finds fault with most of Richepin's works, particularly those in which "one finds a deliberate deformation of reality, an accumulation of anomalies, horrors, and monstrosities, characters who are abnormal, eccentric or criminal, and an unpruned chaotic style in keeping with the disordered subject matter" (240). Tombre more than satisfies Sutton's reproaches, imbuing his aberration with an odor redolent of fairground entertainment and Hanlon-Lees pantomime. They also echo the comments of contemporaries like Jules Lemaitre, who referred to Richepin as an "écuyer de cirque, ou plutôt un beau saltimbanque," all flourish and no substance (345). These are critiques reminiscent of those thrown at Banville throughout his entire career after the publication of the *Odes funambulesques*, the acrobatic poet who literally did things with words.[14] The preoccupation with the "violence and vulgarity" found in Richepin's work obscures the fact that there is much more to his innovative formal acrobatics than meets the eye, just as there is more to Tombre's performance than a pathetic alcoholic pantomime (Sutton 239). We must remember that Tombre dies a happy, not a sad, Zigzag, having refined and put into practice a revolutionary aesthetic theory that does things with bodies.

On a simple level, the zigzag of Tombre's aesthetic reproduces the staggering, teetering walk of the drunkard. But distantiation is just as important an ingredient in the production of the full Hanlon-Lees effect. Rancière describes Tombre's signature theory "zig, zag, paf!" as a "pure graphic flash," the visual equivalent of which appears during the Happy Zigzag performance when the centipede dwarf, separated from his real self, assumes the shape of the letter "Z," transforming his own body into an inanimate object (Rancière 88; Richepin 477). Tombre, too, literally and paradoxically, embodies his revolutionary formula for art by performing his own zigzagging walk at the same time that he is *really* inebriated. As a "graphic flash," it recalls the spatial displacement of the Hanlon-Lees through "l'air qu'ils déchirent" while also approximating the short duration of the existential limbo that the acrobats and the Happy Zigzags produced (Banville 18). In an echo of Zola's disoriented reaction to the frenzied movement of the Hanlon-Lees across the stage, the abrupt alternations, in which frozen facial contortions become inexplicably "frénétique" and discomforting immobility leads into a "ronde enragée," all leave Yves seriously worried for his sanity (Richepin 462, 463).

Mirror Doubles

At the moment that Tombre the real alcoholic begins to perform his alcoholic self, there is desemantization, a putting into question of all that one thinks that one knows as real and of all that one takes for granted in society and culture (Carmeli, "Performing" 211). Tombre's performance of his real alcoholic self is a stepping outside of and a looking at himself (distantiation) that puts even his identity into question. Zola's assumption that the Hanlon-Lees' analysis of drunkenness is modeled on actual drunkenness is contradicted by their characters' failure to reference a clear signifier. If Tombre can perform his own real drunkenness, then his distinguishing characteristics are not so distinguishing after all. This is one source of Yves's, and by extension the spectator's, feeling of losing his mind, a condition that is not mental instability, but ontological uncertainty. Nowhere is the insistence on the separation between signified and signifier more evident than in a pantomime from the Hanlon-Lees' 1878–79 season. One of the things mentioned about the Hanlon-Lees was the impassibility of their facial expression, which created a striking contrast with their frenetic acrobatics. Their impassive white faces recall the ambiguous white face and costume of Deburau-Pierrot ("most of the character's power lay in the very emptiness of his oval face, his expressive silence, his agile immobility, a great whiteness which lent itself to many styles, many forms, many interpretations") and Couture's and Daumier's white-faced, sometimes distorted-faced, clowns (Jones 116). Rather than protect the integrity of the clown in a cloud of anonymity, a blanket of facial whiteness makes distinguishing traits disappear altogether. The sameness that the white faces establishes – one brother looks like the other, even when one Pierrot in *Le Duel* is tall and thin and the other shorter and stockier, as Huysmans remarks, because they are both Pierrots – makes indistinction and confusion the reigning principle of the pantomime.

In *Une soirée en habit noir*, two swells, each with an elegant lady holding his arm, arrive at an evening party. Four Hanlon brothers play both the male and female characters, and the fifth plays either the servant or the painter. Coquelin Cadet describes the setting and its guests as part of a fashionable "salon du faubourg Saint-Germain," which falls victim to the acrobat's ability to upset social etiquette (315).[15] Chairs are pulled out from under women as they attempt to sit; the domestic serving dishes of ice cream drops them into guests' laps, a mishap that leads to an ice cream fight; when guests want to hear music and dance, all rush to the piano whose lid becomes the site of trapped garments and bodies as well as crushed hands and fingers. In the midst of these shenanigans arrives a painter with "de longs cheveux blonds, la figure blême et l'air inspiré" (Coquelin Cadet 216). At one point, this painter sits down to continue work on a portrait of one of the ladies. According to Lesclide, the Naturalist who makes connections between actions where there are none, the painter, frustrated by not being able to capture the resemblance, punches his canvas and puts in its place the real head of the portrait sitter (164). In Coquelin Cadet's version, nothing motivates the switch from portrait to portrait sitter's head because this is, as he says elsewhere, "un monde à part" (217): "soudain la tête du portrait disparaît, et la dame, qui était sortie, accourt mettre sa tête à la place de la tête du portrait" (218). In both instances, the painter treats the framed face as part of the canvas, applying shade (Lesclide) or coating with white paint (Coquelin Cadet). The painter does not perceive that the portrait sitter is multiple people (the servant takes the place of the lady), nor does he distinguish between inanimate portrait and human sitters, and this even though both lady and servant stick their tongues out and make faces at the artist with each stroke of the brush.

The scene seems to adapt the classic clown mirror routine, featuring here the very pale painter and the white-faced portrait, lady and later servant, a mirroring effect that the family resemblance of the acrobats only supports. The scene, more importantly, puts in question the nature of identity not only in the portrait but in general. The portrait as a painting genre insists on the uniqueness of the sitter: it does not just reproduce a likeness but reveals the sitter's character. Of course, while some portraits tell us about a sitter's personality, others reflect painters' attempts to flatter their subjects. This is because portrait sitters are generally people possessing some social standing or substantial fortunes, and these paintings serve to commemorate them for state or family records. *Une soirée en habit noir* short-circuits the ability of the portrait to record any identifying markers. The portrait that should distinguish its sitter becomes interchangeable with the other faces, including that of the painter, thereby nullifying personal singularity, stripping the portrait of its ability to differentiate, and erasing social distinction. And this is doubly so in that the other faces are all white. This fluid whiteness is further complicated by what I suspect was the family resemblance between the pale painter and the white-faced sitters, a resemblance that erased for the spectator the separation between the painter/subject and his object relations/portrait and series of portrait sitters. Here, the term "object relations" refers specifically to the subject/object dynamic, but it draws very loosely as well on psychoanalytic psychology's understanding of how a child builds her future interactions with others based on internalized records/images of those she had in infancy with her caretakers, usually the mother and/or father. In this loose application of "object relations," they are just one aspect of one's overall acceptance of what is determined to be real and possible. In addition, the word "relations" complicates matters by retaining the real-life blood connection between the brothers. In the same moment that the painter interacts with the portrait/portrait sitters, he both constitutes himself as a subject painting an object and a subject whose object/painting (through resemblance) is also himself.

One finds one of the best examples of the mirror routine in the twentieth century in the Marx brothers' film *Duck Soup* (Leo McCarey, 1933) where a black-mustachioed Harpo, wearing the same style of glasses as Groucho and dressed in the same white nightcap, nightshirt, and socks as Groucho, reproduces correctly all the signature grimaces, gestures, and jigs that Groucho makes into his "mirror." The real Groucho undergoes desemantization as he performs himself for his mirror image.

At one point, both "Grouchos" emerge from the side of the "mirror" with different hats behind their backs, leading the viewer to assume that the hats will bring identity resolution and an end to the pantomime of doubles. Groucho holds a straw hat in order to trip up his mirror double. He is not usually associated with any particular hat, however. Indeed, in most publicity stills featuring the three brothers in character, Chico wears a Tyrolean hat, Harpo a top hat, while Groucho wears none. The straw hat that Groucho hides behind his back is, therefore, not linked to his character's identity. In the *Duck Soup* mirror scene, Harpo enters the mirror frame with his own signature top hat. However, when he turns to face Groucho and places a hat on his head at the same time as Groucho, that hat is no longer the top hat, but a straw one, just like the one that Groucho places on his. The mirror game that levels identifying traits operates on both sides such that even Harpo is stripped of one of his most identifiable character traits. He, too, gets caught in the play of desemantization. One would be tempted to locate the moment in which the scene's "mirror" image cracks and in which Groucho recovers his identity when Harpo drops his hat and Groucho picks it up and returns it to him, but even this cannot undo the identity confusion. The scene (and the routine) cinematically ends when Chico, in the same moustache, glasses, white nightshirt, cap, and socks enters into Harpo's space, displaying two "Grouchos" in the frame. The sketch ends because the suspension of certainty regarding identity, like the suspension of disbelief imposed on the spectator during the viewing of an acrobatic act, cannot be prolonged indefinitely.

Groucho's suspicion that something is not quite right with his mirror image compels him to try and trip up his double, only the latter faithfully reproduces his signature traits, and in doing so puts into question just how singular these traits are. With the arrival of a third "Groucho" and the possibility that there are even more "Grouchos" on the other side of the mirror, his presumed singularity is further threatened. The success of this particular sketch was enhanced by the resemblance between all the brothers. This disorienting resemblance effect, shared and exploited by the Hanlon brothers, undoubtedly contributed to the spectator's perception of a blurring of the boundaries between subject and object in *Une soirée en habit noir.*

The mirror double scenario appealed to the aesthetic sensibilities of many Decadent patrons of Hanlon-Lees' performances, circus, and pantomime. The routine contradicted accepted belief in a natural link between outward signifiers and identity, separating those signifiers from their signifieds, perhaps initially causing ontological uneasiness, but subsequently revealing liberating qualities that permit for the exploration of expanded limits of the experience of reality. The source of this discovery may have been the Hanlon-Lees' *Une soirée en habit noir*, but it could have just as easily come from other incarnations of the mirror routine at circuses, circus-related fairground entertainments, or pantomime theaters, since each venue offered spectacles grounded in desemantization. Whatever the source, the mirror double became a signature aesthetic image of Decadence.

The attraction did not come, however, from distorting mirrors like the concave and convex ones in carnivals where "on s'y aperçoit cagneux ou obèse, trop long ou trop large" (Rodenbach 23). There is nothing physically wrong with the mirrors of many Decadent tales, seemingly perfect in construction, performing their function as impartial eyes faithfully and accurately reflecting back images of the people and objects in their ambit. They echo our own perceptions, confirming the context of our existences: the mirror reproduces the very same décor and objects that I, too, find in the room in which I am standing. And yet, in Georges Rodenbach's "L'Ami des miroirs" (1899), the protagonist who needs mirrors "capable[s] de lui exprimer son visage intégral, jusqu'à la plus minime nuance," first sees his reflection as "un autre lui-même," and then begins to wave at this other person each time he sees him, having progressively lost "la conscience de son identité" (23–25).[16] If he is unable to cross into the looking glass like Lewis Carroll's Alice, he is nonetheless certain that his double is real, not an image. There is not just one double, however, but hundreds, as he has filled his entire apartment from floor to ceiling with mirrors such that "la seule silhouette du solitaire fut multipliée à l'infini," creating a "foule innombrable," a considerable augmentation of the three white-faced look-alikes in the Hanlons' *Une soirée en habit noir* (25). Where the average spectator feels strangely anxious at how clowns turn identity into an ambiguous state in which singular characteristic traits become typical, Rodenbach's protagonist embraces a world where paradoxically everyone is "pareil à moi" (26). The narrator, a more prosaic person, diagnoses this lover of mirrors as crazy, a conclusion at which society arrives as well, and accordingly he ends locked up in a mental asylum. The protagonist, however, seems happily liberated by the action of viewing his other in a mirror, an action in which he is both observing subject and his own object. In his lone hospital room mirror he sees "des choses merveilleuses" and follows mysterious, certainly beautiful women "qui allaient l'aimer," perhaps the same ones that he would glimpse in his apartment mirrors as they passed quickly from one mirror to the next in an effort to throw him off their scent (26). He lives perhaps in that "grand monde absolument nouveau" described by Coquelin Cadet regarding a Hanlon-Lees pantomime (219). In his desire to enter that world, he hurls himself into the glass, only to crack open his head.

Richepin's Pierre Lurier in "L'Assassin nu" from *Les Morts bizarres* (1876) is not a Decadent aesthete like the lover of mirrors, but he shares the same fate. His life turns on varying degrees of recognition, one of which ends in an encounter with his mirror image. After getting out of prison, Pierre finds himself in his native Champagne where, out of hunger and poverty, he plans a crime. He is first apprehensive about being in a region where he risks being recognized ("On allait le reconnaître!") but realizes that enough time has passed to render him unrecognizable (44). He chooses to rob the Berlots, a miserly elderly couple from the village of Nizy-le-Comte in whose service he had been as a boy. His familiarity with their house and their habits plays a big part in his selection of the Berlots because he can rely heavily on his extensive memory of the yard and interior of the house for the nighttime execution of his crime. He enters their bedroom – contrary to every other room in the house, this is a room that he knows only from the point of view of the doorway – murders them in their beds, and takes the money from the armoire. As he prepares to leave, however, he sees at the door a man, naked like himself, carrying an ax, a lantern, and a feed bag full of money around the neck like he does, and rushes head first to kill the "apparition" (60). Although it is dark in the bedroom, he can make out the details of another carefully planned crime possessing all the signs of his own. He leaps into a full-length mirror whose glass gashes his carotid artery.

Pierre Lurier's perceptual confusion begins much earlier, however. During the stakeout from his tree perch, he sees a boy that the Berlots employ that makes him shudder from shock: "Il lui semblait qu'il sortait lui-même de la cuisine" (Richepin 50). The boy, around ten years old and "rose et blond" like Pierre was at that age, is also called Pierre (50). In addition, while sitting in the tree, his mental review of his life – a review which continues into a projection into the future in which his robbery fails, leading to his arrest, trial, and death sentence – takes him so far outside of himself that he "ne voyait ni le jardin, ni la cour, ni la maison, mais une place pleine de monde, et une guillotine dans le trou de laquelle il grimaçait" (53). In the multiple instances of self-recognition – one from the past (the boy) and the other in the future (the mental projection) – he is both himself and another person, and this well before the murders, such that it follows that his mirror image during the murders is yet another externalized, objectified self. Indeed, young Pierre, Pierre under the guillotine blade, and the nude assassin are all mirror images of a sort. But, in this play of simulacra, the boundaries separating reality and another dimension disappear, allowing Pierre's mirror double to emerge through the looking glass and murder him.

In Rachilde's "L'Araignée de cristal," the split between viewing subject and externalized self is so complete that recognition is a deception and becomes a source of danger not only for one's identity, but for one's life as well. *L'épouvanté* relates to his mother that he experienced as a ten-year-old boy the "sensation bizarre d'entrer dans cette glace comme dans un lac limoneux" (22). Feeling himself both outside looking into the mirror and inside, he watched the approach of a white spider that, as if in a dream, took on the appearance of a silver-carapaced crab that planted itself on top of his scalp, extending its legs over his entire head and robbing him progressively and alarmingly of his identity: "elle envahissait mon front, me fendait les tempes, me dévorait les prunelles, effaçait peu à peu mon image, me décapitait" (23). The nightmare continued as the crystal spider assumed octopus-like features as it took position on his shoulders, stretching tentacles that were so powerful that they broke the mirror. The rational explanation is that the gardener, working with a bit-brace, sent a nail flying through a window pane that then shattered the mirror. But this is not the only explanation, nor is it necessarily the most plausible. This incident was followed by others, a particularly disturbing one occurring when he was helping his mother with her fur cloak and saw a woman in the mirror who resembled his mother and was smiling sensually, and another when, through a slightly open door, he glimpses a cheval glass reflecting his cousin Sylvia nude and posing seductively (27). These unsettling visions serve to incriminate *l'épouvanté* by revealing his true desires, reversing the viewer/reflection relationship, establishing the metaphorical mirror image as the protagonist's authentic identity and invalidating his own, the hypocritical and duplicitous one (Ziegler 125).

But this tale also possesses a fantastic, playful quality in which Rachilde borrows her sinister mirrors not only from the mirror routine, but from the haunted furniture of the circus, pantomime, and *féerie* as well, entertainments that offered the vision of a porous boundary separating the natural from the supernatural worlds. Indeed, without the example provided by the genres' eerie play of desemantization, the author would have had to express the idea behind the metaphor of a mirror image representing *l'épouvanté*'s split identity with more conventional tools. Instead, Rachilde's mirrors are quasi-animate entities capable of producing manipulative shapeshifters that take on and pervert the physiognomy of those who make the mistake of gazing into them. In this tale, one's mirror image is not an objectified version of oneself; it is another being altogether. Rachilde's opening paragraphs make this clear in the description of a living room bathed in the semi-darkness of a summer evening. The vague lighting – half day, half night – allows for the materialization of a portal connecting the real and the supernatural. While the looking glass appears to reflect the moonlight, closer examination reveals that the angle for the glow is physically impossible. The narrator's familiarity with common sense physics is put in the service of proving the unthinkable: the mirror emits its own light. The malevolent psyche orchestrates *l'épouvanté*'s death; he meets his end like Pierre Lurier with his throat cut.

The prose poems in Huysmans's *Croquis parisiens* feature multiple mirrors, a motif that Joël Loehr interprets as indicative of the work's exploration of a general "réversibilité du sens" (238). These mirrors figure in a series of "jeux spéculaires," which serve to frame "toutes les possibilités de retournement et d'inversion du sens" (Loehr 238). In "Damiens," however, where the theme is specular confusion, the mirror motif supports less as an exploitation of reversible meanings than the splitting and rearrangement of signifers and signifieds, prefigured in the first sentences's oxymoronic words "douloureuses délices," one of many Huysmansian "accouplements contre-nature" (Huysmans 109, 23; Loehr 236). In this poem, the reflection of the narrator's own body supine on a bed plays with his perceptions to the point that he mistakenly sees himself as Robert-François Damiens, the would-be assassin of Louis XV. In an eighteenth-century illustration of his judgment, Damiens is depicted in restraints on a mattress. The mirror is the nexus where a memory trace of this print is placed neatly over the eerily matching lines of the real image of the narrator such that they become one, producing a visual presentation of the "douloureuses délices"; the bedroom in which he finds himself is now surprisingly consistent as a site of both the pain (*douleur*) and pleasure (*délices*) to which he refers in the opening sentence. Through the mirror, the narrator creates an ambiguous double state in which he is aware of himself *and* perceives an externalized projection of himself as another, thanks to shared details (mattress, body position, white shirt, stiff arms, drawn features, etc.). If Huysmans's narrator is initially startled by a sense of unease and uncertainty regarding his identity, a quandary that the mirror, usually a reliable gauge of the presence of concrete reality, fails to resolve, he demonstrates a willingness to enter into, indeed, seek out, this porous and undifferentiated space of astonishing analogies. Huysmans's narrator need not attempt a leap into the looking glass because that barrier has already volatilized.

Marcel Schwob's "Ilsée" from *Le Livre de Monelle* (1894) is a hauntingly beautiful tale of the eponymous protagonist's life-long relationship with her mirror double. *L'autre Ilsée* (alternately called *l'Ilsée du miroir* and *la dame du miroir*) fulfills numerous roles: cherished playmate, feared rival in love, estranged friend, and companion at her death. It is a stunning illustration of creativity liberated from the myopic conventions of mere metaphor. Ilsée's world is one in which the frontiers of the animate and the inanimate, reality and dream, dissolve. First seen emerging from the "profondeurs du miroir," *l'autre Ilsée* recalls the white-faced clown of the mirror routine by her extreme pallor and by the oxymoronic "ombre lumineuse" that her other dimension produces and to which she returns at the end of each day (Schwob 130). We are tempted to understand Ilsée's kisses on the cold glass of the mirror and her conversations and irritations with *l'autre Ilsée* as part of a child's rich imaginary existence, but if *l'autre Ilsée* can only raise her dolls at the same time as Ilsée and mouth the same words as Ilsée, she also possesses autonomy from her prototype, striking her hand against the glass in equal frustration whenever the girls fight. She chooses to simultaneously produce Ilsée's gestures, but one can imagine that she could slip up like

Harpo who drops his hat during the *Duck Soup* mirror routine. The narrator confirms *l'autre Ilsée*'s independence from Ilsée when he notes that the former smiles at Ilsée's fiancé and that she displays sadness at Ilsée's absence now that her fiancé occupies all her time. When the fiancé's visits cease, Ilsée accuses *l'autre Ilsée* of running him off, and in anger nails a piece of white linen to the mirror frame, a shroud behind which Ilsée finds only "une ombre blanche" (135). While the reader can attribute this white shadow to a reflection of the cloth's whiteness, Ilsée concludes that *l'autre Ilsée* has withdrawn into the depths of the mirror. The years pass; the lover never returns; and Ilsée grows old. When Ilsée finally removes the cloth, loss of silvering in certain spots makes *l'autre Ilsée* a strange collage of reflecting and non-reflecting glass, a sign perhaps that she would retreat definitively with the passage of even more time and the loss of even more silvering. When elderly Ilsée goes to her bedroom, she discovers that *l'Ilsée du miroir* has crossed over from her milky realm ("la dame du miroir s'est délivrée'); as before, when *l'autre Ilsée* was on the other side of the looking glass, she is in perfect harmony with Ilsée's movements as she lifts her lamp and sits down on the bed (138). For sure, there exists a reading in which Ilsée's reflection functions like an imaginary friend, a symbolic coping mechanism in which her psychological problems are projected onto others, in this case her mirror double. There is also a reading of the ending in which *l'autre Ilsée* is merely a metaphor for the act of dying. In Schwob's tales, however, the commonplace world possesses a bittersweet magic that transforms everyday acts into marvelous moments and time into an eternal childhood.

*

As noted above, using experience of the natural world and knowledge of human social behavior to understand Ilsée's relationship with her mirror double results in a plausible, if conventional, reading of the tale. Indeed, we can explain the incidents in each of the tales discussed in this chapter using the same tools. Tombre is an alcoholic, and the horror that the spectator experiences at his performance comes from his perverse display of real delirium tremens; Rodenbach's protagonist's obsession with mirrors and *l'épouvanté*'s terror before them undeniably signal mental illness; Pierre Lurier of "L'Assasssin nu" and Huysmans's narrator in "Damiens" are the victims of a momentary perceptual confusion caused by bad lighting in the former and by the intermediary state between sleeping and waking in the latter; and, as stated, Schwob's narrator distills Ilsée's life through the metaphor of a mirror relationship.

The clinical eye cannot, however, account for inconsistencies that escape logical explanation. Tombre is not an alcoholic in denial when he revels in the successful application of his aesthetic theory of "zig, zag, paf." *L'ami des miroirs* is not locked inside himself in a narcissistic confirmation of his identity: he sees and seeks not only reflections of himself but catches glimpses of women dashing from one mirror into another. The cheval glass in the drawing room does eerily emit its own light in "L"Araignée de cristal." There are two mirrors in the bedroom in which Huysmans's narrator finds himself, with one reproducing as expected the "images d'ameublement dont elle était pleine" (110). An irritatingly bright reflection off the fireplace flashes in the middle of the mirror, causing him to turn his eyes away to the ceiling and the second, duplicitous mirror. Is this merely a sign of his nervous sensitivity or is this an incongruity reminiscent of the quasi-animate mirror in *l'épouvanté*'s salon? The narrator of "Ilsée" inexplicably notices *l'autre Ilsée*'s sadness when Ilsée is out with her fiancé, an agency and emotion not dependent on the presence of her archetype. Finally, the young domestic worker in "L'Assassin nu" is the spitting image of Pierre Lurier when he was that age. At the sound of what he assumes is his employer crying out, he rushes upstairs, only to fall unconscious on the landing, ostensibly at the sight of Lurier's upper torso protruding through the hole in the door. When the police try to question him later, however, he answers only "par un rire effrayant": the boy had lost his mind (61). Is his life profoundly and irreversibly altered by the horrible scene alone, or does he fall under the spell of the doubling effect? Each story presents a detail that contradicts the comforting conclusions drawn from objective analysis. These tales hardly exhaust the number of Decadent variations on the mirror double from Villiers's android Hadaly in *L'Ève future* (1886) to Rodenbach's actress Jane Scott in *Bruges-la-Morte* (1892).

The Hanlon-Lees formula for producing an experience of ontological vertigo is composed of two parts, one of which is the display of the reality of an object or the humanness of the performer and the other of which is an impossible event happening before one's eyes. This interplay of perspectives results in a flash of desemantization in which protagonists glimpse creative potential in a novel juxtaposition of heretofore unrelated elements. In the mirror routine, one loses one's signature traits as they become detached and are shifted to an objectified version of one's self. Or in the case of Huysmans's narrator in "Damiens," he assumes the features of the assassin. The narrator may have initially had the shock of loss of identity when he sees himself as Damiens, but there is also liberation from a previously limited understanding of the scope of human experience.

Not all of the writers discussed in this chapter had the good fortune to see the Hanlon-Lees. They would build, however, on the aesthetic discoveries of their contemporaries. What those who did attend Hanlon-Lees performances took away was not an aesthetic device that set itself in opposition to the reigning conventions of Naturalist method. On the contrary, Naturalism was essential for establishing the empirical reality of an object or human behavior, only to have its impartial observation contradicted by an inexplicable event. The Decadents did not cultivate illusion so much as explore the possibilities of desemantization, something that Huysmans expressly did in "Paraphrases," the last section of the *Croquis*. In "Cauchemar," the narrator captures the nightmarishly liquid movement from one figure to another in Odilon Redon's paintings. In "L'Ouverture de Tannhäuser," sounds become shapes and colors, and in "Similitudes," images and textures become scents. Zola said in his review of the Hanlon-Lees' *Voyage en Suisse* that the reality presented by the acrobats can only be shown, not written. Huysmans, Richepin, Rodenbach, Rachilde, and Schwob, however, demonstrated that it can be done as long as you are willing to allow that reality to ferry you into the fluidity of uncharted space.

Notes

1 At what was a later stage of their career, the troupe increasingly specialized in acrobatic pantomime rather than in the aerial circus numbers of their early years. It was troupe member Agoust who is credited with the decision to transition from circus acrobatics to pantomime. This was an echo of the incorporation of pantomime into the acrobatic entertainments at Mme Saqui's Spectacle des Acrobates after the authorities granted permission to the rival Théâtre des Funambules in 1813 to add silent harlequinades to their programs as long as only acrobats performed them (Rémy 1500). This permitted both theaters to lengthen the duration of a performance and augment receipts. The results were similar for the Hanlon-Lees. Pantomime facilitated the troupe's move from featured act (usually the headliners) to sole evening's attraction and from contract hires to entrepreneurs. The brothers eventually became producers of touring companies of successful pantomimes, beginning with *Le Voyage en Suisse* (1879) and followed by successful productions like *Fantasma* (1884) and *Superba* (1890).

2 According to Mark Cosdon, the troupe enjoyed a successful engagement during the 1867 *Exposition universelle de Paris* as well ("Appendix A").

3 There is a reversed view of that same poster pasted on the outer side of the establishment's window in Édouard Manet's *Au café, cabaret de Reichshoffen* (1878).

4 Goncourt explicitly cites the Hanlon-Lees as an influence in his preface to *Les Frères Zemganno*. I have not been able to verify any explicit influence on Jean Richepin's *Braves gens* (1886) beyond Tombre's signature "zig, zag, paf!," which can be described as an approximation of the wild flying of the acrobats' bodies through space. Jacques Rancière finds "traces of their performance" in that of Tombre and his act the Happy Zigzags. As for Laforgue's *Pierrot fumiste*, scholars usually identify Willette's panel cartoon of the same name (1882) as an, if not the, inspiration for his pantomime. Laforgue, however, clearly refers to Huysmans and Hennique's pantomime in the first act of *Pierrot fumiste*. Regarding *Pierrot sceptique*, it was written specifically for the Hanlon-Lees, but, as is well known, it was never performed. Instead, it was issued in book form with a book cover and four illustrations by Chéret, the poster artist that Huysmans had praised in his "Salon de 1879" (*Le Voltaire*, 10 June 1879).

5 In "Literature of the Circus," American Townsend Walsh comments in 1914 that in the US, where the circus:

> has grown to colossal proportions, its literature is strangely scant: while in England, France and Germany, where the circus is still conducted on the smallest possible scale, and where people seem to take far less keen an

interest in it than on this side of the Atlantic, there is a special literature of the circus that embraces every form of treatment – historical, romantic, technical and biographical. (84)

Among nineteenth-century efforts to explain "in the colder light of scientific observation," the profession and art of the acrobat are Guillaume Depping's *Merveilles de la force et de l'adresse* (1869), Gaston Escudier's *Les Saltimbanques: leur vie, leurs moeurs* (1875), A. J. Dalsème's *Le Cirque à pied et à cheval* (1888), Hugues Le Roux's *Les Jeux du cirque et la fête foraine* (1889), Henry Frichet's *Le Cirque et les forains* (1898), and Baron de Vaux *Écuyers et écuyères: histoire des cirques d'Europe* (1893) (Stokes 285).

6 Curiously, in a move reminiscent of Banville's suppression of his name in the title of his *Odes funambulesques*, Lesclide's name does not figure anywhere in the *Mémoires et pantomimes des frères Hanlon-Lees*. Contrast this omission with the author's claim to Maurice-Pierre Boyé that it was he, and not Catulle Mendès, who wrote the first volume (*La Demoiselle en or*) of Mendès's *La vie et la mort d'un clown* (Basch 286).

7 While many who write about the circus emphasize spectators' experience as grounded in an awareness of a very real danger to which the acrobat is exposed, Carmeli explains that danger plays a more interesting role in constituting the acrobat as both a real human being and as a being capable of doing the impossible ("Performing" 205). In his discussion of the Cimmaro brothers' high-wire act in Jimmy Brown's circus, he notes that "[t]he public should believe there is a chance of getting to the other end, yet should not believe the effort to be too highly controlled" (Carmeli, "Performing" 205).

8 The drunk routine was for a long time a standard circus act. One version of the act would begin with an inebriated spectator disrupting an acrobatic performance. He would enter the ring and climb the trapeze or tightrope scaffolding, boasting that he could do as well as the acrobats. With each of his clumsy yet stupidly confident efforts, the audience would gasp in fear for his safety. At one point, however, the troublemaking spectator's antics become the assured gymnastics of an expert acrobat, who ends the performance as part of the troupe.

9 We should remember that one of the character traits of Pierrot is a fondness for alcohol. Tombre takes that penchant to excess. Richepin may also have incorporated the English clown into his characterization of Tombre: "Sur sa face enfarinée, le frère de *Punch* a collé sans souci des gradations ou du modelé deux plaques de rouge pur, saignantes, à la façon de plaies ou pommettes vermillonnées trahissannt les longues lampées de gin ou d'old brandy" (Hugounet 192).

10 These were not dwarves at all, but three Irish boys whom the Hanlons had trained to be acrobats (Cosdon 24). The Hanlon Midgets, as they were known, featured with the Hanlon-Lees from 1868 to 1875.

11 "There is a legend, which he [Richepin] has himself encouraged, that there is some gypsy blood in his veins, and his wanderings all about France, when a young man, with a company of nomads, sleeping *à la belle étoile*, or in a caravan, according to the weather, and exhibiting his accomplishments as an athlete at the fairs, for which profession nature has well fashioned him, are a sufficient proof that the vagabond spirit, of which he is proud, is not a vain boast" (Barker 63).

12 It is also possible that Richepin drew from the Hanlon-Lees' *Les Cascades du diable* for Tombre's delirium tremens. The use of the term delirium tremens may belong simply to Lesclide's own interpretation of the pantomime, which, of course, Richepin could very well have read, but in this version, the farce's Pierrot joins a group of people breaking wooden boards over each other's heads and hits one head so hard that "la maison d'en face est prise

du *delirium tremens* et tombe en poussière" (141–42). In Cosdon's version, the activity is a "street fight" and the house "snaps into a series of delirium tremens" (52). Coquelin Cadet, however, does not attempt to make heads or tails of the fantastic scene, simply stating that "il y a un escalier magique et une maison qui s'écroule" (207).

13 Carmeli notes that contemporary British traveling circus companies limit themselves to one dwarf ("From Curiosity" 73). Limiting a circus company to one sole dwarf is in contrast to the practice in fairgrounds up through the nineteenth century of exhibiting entire dwarf families (Carmeli, "From Curiosity" 75).

14 This is, of course, a reference to the philosophy of performatives found in J. L. Austin's *How to Do Things With Words* (1962). For a discussion of how Banville did things with words in the *Odes funambulesques*, see Chapter 2 of this book.

15 It is customary to interpret such a setting as symptomatic of the Decadent's disparagement of all things relative to the dominant bourgeoisie, as one finds in Champsaur's Lulu. In both *Lulu, pantomime en un acte* (1888) and *Lulu, roman clownesque* (1900), Lulu makes humiliation of the fat bourgeois her objective. With *Une soirée en habit noir*, however, it is more accurate to understand that all social settings, from those associated with the petite-bourgeoisie to those of the elite, are fair game for the acrobat's disruptions to cultural codes. Their target is not social class, but all social codes. If the bourgeoisie appears targeted specifically, it is because this is the class that most upholds the "truth" of social codes.

16 This story first appeared in *Le Journal, quotidien, littéraire, artistique et politique* 2433 (27 May 1899).

Works Cited

Banville, Théodore de. *Odes funambulesques, suivies d'un commentaire. Œuvres de Théodore de Banville*. Paris: Alphonse Lemerre, 1892.

Barker, Edward Harrison. *France of the French*. New York: Scribners, 1910.

Basch, Sophie. Introduction [to *Les Frères Zemganno* by Edmond de Goncourt]. *Romans de cirque*. Ed. Sophie Basch. Paris: Robert Laffont, 2002. 273–93.

Baudelaire, Charles. *Œuvres complètes*. Ed. Marcel A. Ruff. Paris: Éditions du Seuil, 1968. 370–78.

Carmeli, Yoram S. "From Curiosity to Prop – A Note on the Changing Cultural Significances of Dwarves' Presentations in Britain." *Journal of Popular Culture* 26.1 (1992): 69–80.

———. "Performing the 'Real' and 'Impossible' in the British Traveling Circus." *Semiotica* 80.3–4 (1990): 193–220.

———. "Wee Pea: The Total Play of the Dwarf in the Circus." *TDR* 33.4 (1989): 128–45.

Coquelin Cadet. *La Vie humoristique*. Paris: Ollendorff, 1883.

Cosdon, Mark. "Appendix A: A Chronological Timeline of the Hanlon Brothers." Online posting 3 February 2019. <http://siupress.siu.edu/sites/default/files/pdf/Chronological%20Outline%20of%20Hanlon%20Brothers%203-12-14.pdf>.

Hugounet, Paul. *Mimes et pierrots*. Paris: Librairie Fischbacher, 1889.

Huysmans, Joris-Karl. *Croquis parisiens. À Vau l'eau. Un dilemme*. 2nd edition. Paris: Plon, 1905.

Jones, Louisa E. *Sad Clowns and Pale Pierrots: Literature and the Popular Comic Arts in 19th-Century France*. Lexington, KY: French Forum, 1984.
Lemaitre, Jules. *Les Contemporains. Études et portraits littéraires, Troisième série*. 2nd edition. Paris: Librairie H. Lecène and H. Oudin, 1887.
Lesclide, Richard. *Mémoires et pantomimes des frères Hanlon Lees*. Paris: Chez Tous Les Libraires, 1879.
Loehr, Joël. "*L'Assommoir* de Zola, Les *Croquis parisiens* de Huysmans: un changement d'optique." *Revue d'histoire de la France* 102 (2002): 211–39.
Noiray, Jacques. "Tristesse de l'acrobate. Création artistique et fraternité dans *Les Frères Zemganno*." *Revue des sciences humaines* 259 (2000): 91–110.
Rachilde. *Le Démon de l'absurde*. Paris: Mercure de France, 1894.
Rancière, Jacques. *Aisthesis: Scenes from the Aesthetic Regime of Art*. Trans. Zakir Paul. London and Brooklyn: Verso, 2011.
Rémy, Tristan. "Le Mime." *Histoire des spectacles*. Ed. Guy Dumur. Paris: Éditions Gallimard, 1965. 1493–1519.
Ricatte, Robert, ed. *Journal. Mémoires de la vie littéraire, I: 1851–1865*. By Edmond and Jules de Goncourt. Paris: Robert Laffont, 1989.
Richepin, Jean. *Braves gens, roman parisien*. Paris: Maurice Dreyfous, 1886.
———. *Les Morts bizarres*. Paris: Decaux, 1876.
Rodenbach, Georges. *Le Rouet des brumes*. Paris: Séguier, 1997.
Schwob, Marcel. *Le Livre de Monelle*. Paris: Léon Chailley, 1894.
Stokes, John. "*Aux Funambules*: Acrobats and Aesthetics." *French Cultural Studies* 3.9 (1992): 277–98.
Sutton, Howard. *The Life and Work of Jean Richepin*. Genève: Librairie Droz; Paris: Librairie Ménard, 1961.
Villiers de l'Isle-Adam, Auguste. *Œuvres complètes*. Ed. Alan Raitt et al. Vol 2. Paris: Éditions Gallimard, 1986.
Walsh, Townsend. "Literature of the Circus." *The Theater. The Magazine for Playgoers* 20.164 (October 1914): 84.
Ziegler, Robert E. "Fantasies of Partial Selves in Rachilde's 'Le Démon de l'absurde.'" *Nineteenth-Century French Studies* 19.1 (Fall 1990): 122–31.
Zola, Émile. *Le Naturalisme au théâtre: les théories et les exemples*. Paris: Charpentier, 1881.

4 1879, Part II

Time and Space and the Hanlon-Lees Effect

Richard Lesclide's liberal transcription of the Hanlon-Lees' account of their formation, professional career, and adventures, accompanied by a magical preface by Banville, served several purposes. On a basic level, it catered to the curiosity of fans who wanted to know more about the troupe who had been the entertainment sensation of Paris in their 1878–79 season. More important, however, the book furnished a particular type of information, functioning less as a faithful biography and as rendering them more approachable (and knowable) than as a narrative reconstitution and continuation of the acrobats' real lives as "objects for display" and, therefore, paradoxically as inaccessible (Carmeli, "Text" 176, 181). In *Mémoires et pantomimes des frères Hanlon Lees*, Lesclide reactivated the strange performance dynamic in which the "real" Hanlon brothers play their own bodies, effectively making objects of themselves, exemplified by the portrait/mirror routine in *Une soirée en habit noir.*

Both Goncourt's novel *Les Frères Zemganno* and Lesclide's *Mémoires* offered readers behind-the-scenes peeks into circus life.[1] Appearing respectively during and just after the Hanlon-Lees season in Paris, Goncourt's novel and Lesclide's pseudo-biography of the troupe had the advantage of being more than just circus literature for the curious. As members of a select group of artists and writers who were familiar with each other's work in some fashion, they were at the forefront of the distillation and dissemination of circus desemantization as an aesthetic device. As both works demonstrated, an acrobat's life is marked by uprootedness: circus troupes travel from one town, country, or continent to the next either in their seasonal tours (a set schedule) or in their quest for paying audiences (a more random itinerary). Constant travel as a job description is also due in great part to the dynamics of an entertainment characterized by materializations of the impossible. The effectiveness of the performance of the impossible depends on townsfolk perceiving acrobats as outside the social order, an observed state that can only be maintained short term. A negative consequence of this necessary condition of marginality, defined by brief stays in towns and no personal ties to townsfolk, historically also made them objects of distrust, resulting in the enactment and enforcement of anti-morality and anti-vagrancy laws and licensing regulations. They were the natural suspects when disorder erupted, a burglary occurred, a murder was committed, or a child disappeared. In those circumstances in which troupes possess the requisite licenses and where the risk of being drummed out of town is slim, however, Carmeli contends that it is through spectators' experience of performance that "the travelers' [i.e., itinerant circus companies] marginality is thus transformed and perceived as an embodiment of unique ontological isolation, epitomizing a temporality out of social time and a spatiality out of relations and meanings" ("Text" 176). On a very basic level, because of their duality (real people playing their own selves), identity and the social-cultural systems associated with the construction of identity are temporarily suspended.

This state of being "out of social time" and "spatially out of relations and meanings," products of general desemantization, pertains as well to acrobats who performed in the permanent circus structures of big cities. Acrobats performing in urban centers built on the perception of their marginality – defined not only by living at the edges of social groups, but also by suspended identities and social-cultural systems – in other ways than encampment in and parades through a town and interaction with small-town folk. The perception of their difference from others was built through posters, interviews with performers, entertainment reviews, and circus literature like Lesclide's *Mémoires*.

Paul Bouissac offers another example of desemantization that places acrobats "out of social time" and "spatially out of relations and meanings" in a third concept of time – the "time of action" (neither linear nor cyclical) – which involves the inception and visualization (feedforward) of a plan and its implementation by means of a tool or apparatus, a concept that reveals that notions of time are social constructs (141).[2] We can infer that this concept affects the concept of space as well, which is determined by the action of the "time of action" having no relation to anything other than the apparatus. These components create a unique universe outside of the everyday order. In addition to general time- and space-suspending desemantization, the figures and protagonists in each of the paintings, stories, and novels discussed in this chapter also employ a tool or apparatus that is specifically designed for a particular action that differs from normal tools in that it has no superfluous components outside of the requirements of a planned action (trapeze scaffolding, swing bars, tightrope equipment, swinging cable, barrel, etc.). This apparatus is removed from the vagaries and accidents of real time since it and the action performed on it enjoy ideal conditions: the act is, as a general rule, always successful (Bouissac 141). The writer and artist spectators of circus acts and Hanlon-Lees pantomimes understood this particular notion of the time and space of action. One finds an example in chapter 56 of Goncourt's *Frères Zemganno*, which he devotes to the plan for an acrobatic trick (comprised of a concept and the feedforward visualization/projected accomplishment) and the apparatus (a trampoline or springboard). Manet's acrobat swings on a trapeze bar in *Un bar aux Folies-Bergère* (1882). Degas's Miss Lala hangs from a cable by her teeth from the rafters of the Cirque Fernando. Huysmans's acrobats work on a trapeze or a swing bar. As for Catulle Mendès's *La Vie et la mort d'un clown*, while the author did not provide the reader with access to the thought processes of his acrobat Aladin during a circus performance, we do witness how he adapts objects in the real world into the "timeless tools" of a gymnastic feat (Bouissac 133). For these writers and artists, this was an aesthetic revelation and liberation.

The Mirror as "Timeless Tool"

In the Hanlon-Lees' *Le Duel*, two white-faced figures in black suits meet in a forest clearing to face off over some undisclosed and probably insignificant insult. In contrast to their witnesses and the attending doctor, the duelists "tremblent abominablement" (Coquelin Cadet 202). To the right of the stage, there is a tombstone, whose inscription differs according to three accounts of the pantomime, with each revealing the aesthetic orientation of the writer/spectator as well as what each took away from the experience. Lesclide, the Naturalist, offers narrative coherence to the best of his abilities, filling in the gaps by describing the tombstone as reading "Ci-gît un homme tué en duel" (150).[3] While clearly receptive to the comical aspect of the entertainment – after all, he transcribed all of the Hanlon-Lees pantomimes of their season – he clearly misunderstood the role of the tombstone as anything beyond being one source of the overall fear affecting the two men. For him, they are afraid of fighting the duel because they are afraid of dying.

There are two possible interpretations of the inscription in Lesclide's version. In the first, the generic "homme" signals that other duelists have lost their lives in defense of their honor. In the second, he anticipates that stone masons will replace the generic reference with the name of the loser of the present encounter. As for Coquelin Cadet's version – "Ci-gît X ..., tué en duel" – we can rule out the "X" of the tradition in which an author either feigns suppressing a name in order to protect the identity of the real-life model for the protagonist or insists that the name is presently unknown but potentially retrievable (202). Both Coquelin Cadet's version and Huysmans's ellipsis ("ci-gît ... tué en duel") offer the tombstone as an "épitaphe-pronostic," an oxymoron that strangely pairs a possible past with a possible future that suspends the clowns in a non-time (Coquelin Cadet 202).

While Coquelin Cadet describes each figure as "un monsieur en habit noir," for Huysmans they are two "pierrots" (Coquelin Cadet 201; Huysmans 21). One "pierrot" is tall and thin, reminiscent of Deburau *père* in illustrations by Bouquet, and the other, "plus ramassé, plus boulot, le nez court, goguenard, la bouche crevant d'un trou rouge le masque blême," suggests the English clown along the lines of the one cited by Baudelaire (probably Tom Matthews) in "De l'essence du rire" (Huysmans, *Croquis* 21).[4] However different in physique, the two pierrots offer yet another variation on the mirror routine. For Bonnet, this is one of many nineteenth-century pantomime scenarios featuring Pierrot in a duel with himself, citing Paul Legrand's *Le Rêve de Pierrot* (173). In that pantomime, Pierrot attempts to commit suicide by shooting his mirror image with a shotgun: he pulls the trigger, but suffers no injuries from the blast.[5] For Bonnet, one consideration in the failure of both Pierrots to fight in *Le Duel* turns on the verb's double application in both a reflexive and a reciprocal sense: according to the context, *se tuer* can mean "to kill each other" (two Pierrots) or "to kill oneself" (one Pierrot and his mirror image, which is technically the same person) (173). This verb illustrates perfectly the desemantization that results from the mirror routine in which the observing human subject establishes his mirror image as an object that is both himself and separate from himself. As Carmeli notes regarding circus performance, the acrobat establishes her humanness (identification with the performer by the spectator) while also "de-realizing" that identity by transforming herself into the object of her play ("Performing" 196). In distancing herself from herself by playing herself (as Tombre did by playing his own real alcoholic delirium tremens), she places herself outside the social-cultural code by revealing its arbitrariness, hence putting in limbo the legitimacy of that code. In doing so, she removes herself from "social time and relations" (Carmeli, "Performing" 209). The distancing in *Le Duel* as presented by the duelists, each of whom is paradoxically the mirror image of the other (there is no prototype, just the type), places them outside of time as represented by the tombstone's inscription's "épitaphe-pronostic" state, to use Coquelin Cadet's words. The situation of being simultaneously in the past *and* in the future is not only paradoxical, it is technically impossible, or so it would seem.

Many of the stories discussed in Chapter 3 reflect this untethered sensation with respect to time. In Rodenbach's "L'Ami des miroirs," the protagonist makes a collection of exceptional mirrors, all purchased for their capacity to return a "sincere" and "truthful" confirmation of his sense of himself (25). The narrator describes mirrors as being waterlike. One looking glass has a faded gold frame like "une couronne de feuilles d'automne" that forms the edge of a well. The other older mirrors, whose glass had turned greenish with age, looked like ornamental ponds in a park (24). The image of watery glass is an oxymoron that announces a fluidity between liquid and solid states and a suspension of reality that projects the protagonist "hors du temps, en voyage dans le passé" (24). This is a past, however, that encompasses not only true past events but also, paradoxically, those of the future that are seen as having already taken place: "Il se voyait dans un recul, tel qu'il serait plus tard, tel qu'il devait apparaître à ses amis, plus vague et pâli par l'absence" (24). In essence, he is dislodged from time by virtue of objectifying his mirror self.

Similarly, in the conclusion of "L'Assassin nu," we may more clearly understand the disturbed and uncommunicative mental state of the boy Pierre at the end by locating him outside of time once he discovers the mutilated body of Lurier stuck in the door separating the bedroom and the landing, an appropriate metaphor for depicting a person poised between two temporal realms. While staking out the Berlots' house, Pierre Lurier had traveled in a flash in time: he reconnected with his past as a young boy in the employ of the Berlots when he saw little Pierre exit the house, and in a perverted feedforward plan he saw himself in the future about to be beheaded under the guillotine (this vision comes true in the sense that the glass of the mirror does sever part of his neck). Ironically, the boy Pierre possibly sees Lurier as himself in the future. Unfortunately for the boy, however, the flash of temporal limbo will last a lifetime. However much he appears an imbecile to the authorities, his dumbness reflects an inability to speak caused by his permanent suspension in time.

Huysmans's narrator in "Damiens" also becomes temporally detached at the moment that he perceives his own face and body as that of the would-be assassin. In that flash of recognition, "mes pensées remontèrent, au travers des âges, jusqu'à cet homme qui avait si puérilement tenté d'exterminer avec une pointe de canif un roi" (*Croquis* 111). He finds himself not only transported in time to that "solennel interrogatoire," but sees himself across that feedforward temporal flash drawn and quartered on the place de la Grève, a detail that does not figure in the print representing the moment of his sentencing (111). This projected vision resembles that of Pierre Lurier when he recognizes himself under the guillotine. He trembles at the disconcerting realization that the terrifying image is a literal confusion of the position of his own body and the expression of his own face with those of Damiens. His trembling forces us to return to the description of the intense shaking of the two Pierrots in the Hanlon-Lees' *Duel*: their uncontrollable and convulsive body movements spring not only from fear, but from finding themselves suspended in a non-time outside of their own bodies.

Edmond de Goncourt's Imperfect Time and *Les Frères Zemganno*

In his fictionalized depiction of the creative collaboration between him and his deceased brother Jules in *Les Frères Zemganno*, Edmond de Goncourt attempts to bridge the gap in time separating them through a novel use of the imperfect tense. This stylistic feature functioned less as a caprice, a "substitut chic du passé simple," contends Jacques Noiray, than as "l'imparfait de la nostalgie, ou mieux encore, celui de la mélancolie" (93–94). In this light, the effort to reconnect somehow with the past is doomed from the outset. This was Goncourt's first solo novelistic effort since Jules's death in 1870, and he intended it to be his last.[6] The book signaled his objective to chronicle their broken partnership, one defined by a style that appeared seamless, as if the work of one person. It would fictionalize – and immortalize – as well their creative process and devotion to aesthetic innovation. An explanation for Goncourt's use of the imperfect is that it is the tense suited to memory in its function as the present of the past. The indefinite time of the imperfect, beginning sometime in a vague past and continuing (forward almost to the present, or backwards? suspended in that moment? in a repetition of habitual activities?), represents, as Noiray points out, a misguided effort to create temporal fluidity. The imperfect is "le signe de l'irrémédiable" (Noiray 94).

Is the story, then, just a sad acrobatic clown tale? Does the decision to depict the magic of their relationship and accomplishments through the figure function merely as a metaphor, or does it play a more central part in this attempt to deceive time?[7] While both Edmond and Jules had always had admiration for the feats of circus performers and the art of pantomime, and while it would not have been unusual for the pair to explore the lives of lowly groups like circus performers, it was unusual for Edmond to entrust acrobats with such a delicate task, however much they were an "aristocratie d'en bas," especially since he found their real world utterly unappetizing (Noiray 97).[8]

The first reference that Goncourt made to the general narrative structure of his project in the *Journal* was on December 27, 1876 (II 721–22). He speaks of transposing the love that he and his brother shared, as well as their intellectual and creative symbiosis, onto the narrative of two clown brothers. The plot turns on the brothers' quest to develop and successfully execute a never before attempted acrobatic trick (in other words, a novel aesthetic discovery). Goncourt situated his tale as accurately as possible in the circus milieu, studying the formation of acrobats and their engagements in itinerant and stationary companies, their work ethic, and their working conditions. He carried out the same rigorous documentation associated with the Goncourt literary aesthetic, extensively interviewing Victor Franconi of the Franconi circus dynasty and director of the Cirque d'Été and the Cirque d'Hiver, Léon Sari, director of the Folies Bergère, and the Hanlon-Lees.[9] Although the idea for a novel memorializing his life of collaboration with Jules predates the interviews with the Hanlon brothers, Goncourt most certainly found the tight family bond of the British acrobats a suitable model for the shaping of his two acrobatic protagonists Gianni and Nello Zemganno, with Gianni standing in for the elder Edmond and Nello standing in for the younger brother Jules.[10]

It is clear from his description of the acrobats' first performance at the Cirque d'Hiver and of the transformation that Nello undergoes before he enters the ring that Goncourt had attentively studied numerous acrobatic acts as well as his own reactions to these acts over the years, had obtained from some performers a detailed account of their physical and mental states during performance (notably, the Hanlon brothers), and had come away with a sophisticated understanding of circus's play of opposites, of the real and the impossible, of social-cultural manipulation as rich avenues of exploration in his development as sole author. Achieving the impossible is an expression that occurs frequently as Gianni strives to come up with a new "tour": "Et l'impossibilité de ce qu'il ambitionnait de tenter, il la demandait grande, presque surhumaine, méprisant *l'infaisable* ordinaire, commun, bas" (*Les Frères* 176).

Acrobats provided a very serviceable model for depicting collaboration and producing aesthetic transcendence. In the brothers' trapeze act, Gianni is the "male" catcher, a position that requires strength, and Nello is the "female" flyer, a position defined by gracefulness. Gianni is also the more pragmatic, technically accomplished, and yet paradoxically more inventive of the pair, while his brother Nello possesses more aesthetic prowess and the mocking talent associated with the clown. If the acrobats served to express every facet of the Goncourt brothers' complex relationship (the depth of their love and respect for each other, their work together, their intellectual and psychological compatibility, etc.), Edmond discovered at some point in the process that they were also tools of aesthetic transformation. If he had intended to say goodbye to his creative life with this novel, the two acrobatic brothers would instead lead Goncourt down a new creative path.

Noiray finds a double meaning in Gianni's quest for and eventual realization of a heretofore unattempted leap: first, it is symbolic of Goncourt's (the Goncourts') devotion to and honing of his (their) art and the aesthetic fruit that he (they) reaped; second, it reunites the brothers by means of a metaphorical apparatus, a "machine à remonter le temps" that restores the unity destroyed with the death of Jules (103–04). Yet, while the Goncourt duo was technically disbanded with Jules's death, the collaborative spirit remained. For example, although *La Fille Élisa* (1877) did not include Jules as co-author, it was for all intents and purposes the fruit of a partnership in which both brothers carried out extensive preparatory work. In creating his circus dyad, Goncourt both reunited the writing team *and* reversed that dynamic by tapping circus desemantization in order to split the one entity in two. If the work that the brothers produced astonished readers by its seamlessness, by the inability of the reader to tease out distinctive evidence of their division of labor, then circus play was the instrument by which Goncourt could break this singular symbiosis into two individuals, with Jules functioning as the objectified, projected image of their creative union.

Goncourt began this process of literary mitosis with revealing the roles each brother played in the creative process: Gianni/Edmond was the idea man and Nello/Jules took care of their signature style.

We find this split or objectification in Goncourt's description of the creative process of each brother exactly mid-way through the novel, a textual barrier that literally brings about a body/mind separation. In their creative union, Nello is the body and Gianni the mind. Nello embodies the objectification that Goncourt strives to achieve in separating himself from his brother. Nello is the mirror image.

For his portrait of Nello, Goncourt seems to have drawn from the Hanlon-Lees, their impassive facial expressions, the dreamlike quality of their performances, and their movements that seem at times to succumb willingly to the momentum of their own bodies. Nello's white face is that of a statue, characterized by immobility, yet paradoxically frozen in "une sorte de dilatation extatique" (*Les Frères* 168). His separation evolves like that of the protagonists of the mirror tales discussed in this and the preceding chapter: looking at himself in the great stable mirror begins the process of objectification. After two or three glances, the mirror sends back "son autre lui-même," an image that divests him of his identity, leaving him in an "état indéfinissable aux sensations fugaces et hétérogènes" (167–68). Nello's awareness of the presence of this other self entails the vague sensation of "une vie fantasque" and "funambulesque" that courses through his veins. He becomes his own object, a "homme-statue" who finds himself paradoxically suspended between gaiety and seriousness, between reality and a dream state, the familiar display of circus performance oppositions (167). For Nello's final performance on the evening of the accident, he designed a costume that communicates his double state. In his leotard "imbriqué de petites écailles d'ablette" (spangles, in essence miniature mirrors), his body becomes "chatoyant et miroitant" (234). And like Tombre in Richepin's *Brave gens*, his limbs express both control (he is the subject producing motion) and absence of control (his body is his own object) as they begin to "se contourner en des arabesques excentriques" (Goncourt, *Les Frères* 167).

As for Gianni, he undergoes a similar split from himself both in performance and in his quest for an impossible trick, one never before attempted. In contrast to Nello whose head is emptied of all thought during performance such that he is nothing more than his reflection in the circus's mirrors, Gianni is lost "[e]n sa vie toute cérébrale" (*Les Frères* 175). His human encasing temporarily becomes a mechanism apart from himself and in whose functions he has no participation since he is mentally transported to a vague other place and time (175). If someone in the "real" world spoke to him, their words "lui arrivaient à voix basse de loin, de bien loin, ou plutôt comme s'il était sorti de son être et qu'il lui fallut pour répondre, le temps d'y rentrer" (175). Both brothers are "perdu[s], enfoncé[s], noyé[s] dans le vague," and it is no wonder that in their ordinary existence they choose to live in an equally indeterminate place that is neither city nor countryside, "dans cette extrémité pauvre de Paris qui se perd et se confond avec la campagne de la banlieue" (175, 177). In Goncourt's use of the term, "le vague" does double duty, referencing both that which is indistinct and that which is faraway. In such a space, signifiers become separated from their signifieds, permitting for their movement to other signifying systems, as in the "conversations" that the brothers have with their violins outside of performance and during their act, the shunting of that metaphorical violin "conversation" to the paradoxically silent communication of normally inanimate objects, the "bavardage, en sourdine, des fleurettes mouillées de rosée avec le rayon de soleil qui la boit sur leurs lèvres humides" (180, 158). The signifiers do not float so much as fall upon new, unexpected analogies.

The mimesis of Goncourt's loving tribute to his brother is the acrobatic springboard for desemantization and the creation of such analogies. His peculiar use of the imperfect tense, on one level intended to abolish the temporal distance between Edmond and Jules in order to reunite them, simultaneously serves to banish Jules to the non-time and non-space of his nightmare near the end of the novel. This acrobat tale does not end in Nello/Jules's death because death has been transformed into a mimetic metaphor for Edmond's complete exorcism and objectification of his brother. In Nello's dream, which transpires in a space that is and is not the circus, where spectators are faceless, he fully merges with or is captured within the mirror, a medium in which things "miroitaient avec les brillants glaceux et cristallins des figures et des sujets gravés dans les miroirs de Venise" (252). If we recall from Chapter 3, the experience of the impossible is necessarily short-lived and takes place in a non-time because it occurs outside of the linear progression of everyday life activities. In his dream, however, Nello gets caught in the timeless "espace infini" of the impossible in which performers, not subject to the laws of gravity, perform continuous somersaults; trapeze scaffolding has no beginning and no end; contortionists twist their bodies like ribbons; a strongman picks up a bus filled with passengers; and an elephant dances light as air on a tightrope (250–52).

As Carmeli notes regarding acrobatic performance, "The mimetic [i]s not there in order to interpret, but to perform a surprise, to communicate discommunication and the break of sense" ("Marginal" 262). The "break of sense" was an aesthetic liberation for Edmond de Goncourt. We need only compare a Goncourt brothers' *Journal* entry from June 2, 1860, to Edmond's description of a rainy evening in Paris in *Les Frères Zemganno*. In 1860, they remark how scenes from life invariably recall works of art: "Voilà un cheval dans une écurie: aussitôt une étude de Géricault vient dans notre cervelle. Un tonnelier frappant sur un tonneau, c'est un dessin à l'encre de Chine de Boissieu, que nous revoyons" (I: 569). Here, the brothers' frame of reference is art, indicative of a coping mechanism when faced with the mundane scenes of everyday life. It also validates their incomparable taste, a discernment that separates them from ordinary people.

In the novel, however, everyday life becomes a source of creative engagement with the outside world resulting here in a blurring of the separation between sky and ground, a pairing of the incompatible elements of fire and water, and a flurry of wind-blown leaves becoming a host of scuttling crabs:

> C'était un jour de la fin d'octobre, pendant lequel il avait plu toute la journée, et à la fin duquel on ne savait pas bien s'il ne pleuvait pas encore, de ces jours d'automne de Paris, où son ciel, sa terre, ses murailles semblent se fonder en eau, et où, à la nuit les lueurs du gaz sur les trottoirs sont comme des flammes promenés sur des rivières. Dans l'allée déserte, aux deux ou trois silhouettes noires noyées dans le lointain aqueux, des feuilles crottées, soulevées par les rafales, accouraient vers les deux frères et tout autour de leurs pieds, les rondes ombres des sièges d'innombrable chaises de fer, projetaient, sur le sol mouillé, l'apparence d'une de ces inquiétantes légions de crabes escaladant le bas d'une page d'un album japonais. (260–61)

The art of others – pieces seen before in books, private collections, exhibitions, and museums – is no longer the only prism through which Goncourt engages with the world; the circus effect of desemantization, of separating signifiers from their signifieds, opens the world to magically beautiful analogies.

Édouard Manet and the Time of Action

Albert Boime attributes Édouard Manet's choice of setting and his deliberate stylistic inconsistencies in *Un bar aux Folies-Bergère* (1882) to nostalgia, a yearning for a time preceding the latter stages of the painter's degenerative syphilis-related paralysis. In this reading, Manet countered the severely diminished mobility and pain of the last few years of his life with wish fulfillment images recalling his days as a *flâneur* of the Parisian landscape (Boime 126). For T. J. Clark, the painting's anomalies point to uncertainties regarding the larger issue of class, with the café/café-concert serving as the symbol of a society in transitional limbo: members of the petite-bourgeoisie who were soon to be absorbed into the class above them found themselves temporarily classless, poised between the working class to which they formerly belonged and the bourgeoisie to which they aspired. Both Boime and Clark locate the tensions of their readings – reluctant but unavoidable withdrawal from the social realm (Boime) and the awkward position of the artist vis-à-vis a social-historical moment of flux (Clark) – on the incongruous relation of the

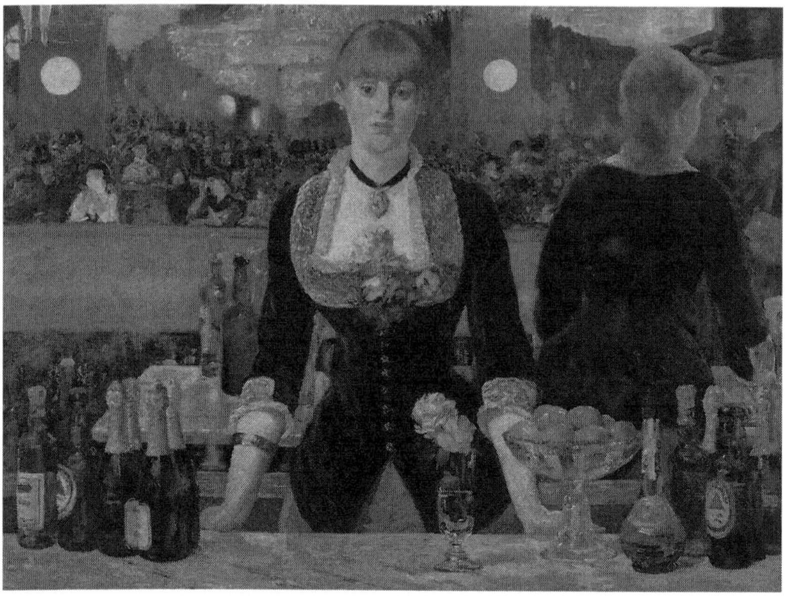

Figure 4.1 Édouard Manet, *Un bar aux Folies-Bergère*, 1882. The Courtauld Institute of Art, London.

barmaid to her mirror image: as "real" woman, she appears detached; as mirror reflection, she leans toward a client in a more inviting fashion. For both, the barmaid represents the co-presence of two incompatible moments or spaces (Figure 4.1).

For Boime, "real" woman and mirror image exist in two different time frames, with the first associated with our direct line view of the "real" barmaid, and the second with the oddly angled reflection, which pertains to the barmaid's fantasy. "This conflation of multiple views in a single compound image could be explained by assuming two separate states of reality depicted simultaneously," Boime explains, with one in "real-time" in which a *flâneur* crosses the field of vision (we do not observe that movement) and a "split-second afterimage" recording his glance at the barmaid (127). In his reading, the barmaid shares in the gentleman's phantasm, since she too "weaves her own fantasy about their imagined encounter" (Boime 127).

In Clark's analysis, the painting depicts simultaneously two different spaces. In addition, he contends that the discrepancy between direct line image and another at an impossible angle was deliberate, since Manet's oil sketch for the painting presents no such perspectival ambiguity. Clark lists three discordant relations. First, if we as viewers are expected to take the position of the gentleman reflected in the mirror, then this necessitates the positing of "*another* space altogether, a quite contrary diagonal," which the painting's composition prevents us from assuming (Clark 250). Second, the "real" woman and her mirror image do not resemble each other: the former, as noted earlier, has a detached air, and the latter is physically inconsistent, with her body being "plumper" and her body language "deferential" (Clark 250). Indeed, one would be tempted to take them as two different women, with the second being an objectified projection of the first. Third, the "real" barmaid looks back at the viewer who, if the reflection is to be trusted, is also technically in the presumed position of the gentleman, and yet, relying on our empirical knowledge of perspective, we are not occupying the same space as he. The result in all three instances is that "doubts about looking accumulate in front of *Un Bar aux Folies-Bergère*," and that "we are left in a kind of suspended relation – to the barmaid, to ourselves as viewers, to the picture itself as a possible unity" (Clark 251).

Both Boime and Clark identify Manet's relation to the Folies Bergère as the source of the painting's peculiarities. For Boime, a physically incapacitated Manet nostalgic, not for a lost brother as in the case of Goncourt, but for his days of mobility, visually compressed the time between the present of immobility and the past of *la flânerie*. For Clark, the entertainment venue, in particular the play of its mirrors, functioned as a distillation of Manet's attitude "towards modern life in Paris" and as a serviceable site for the conflict between that attitude and his "beliefs about painting and vision" (253). Clark's comments about the painting leaving the viewer with doubts, not about *what* she is seeing, but *about* seeing as a social practice and about the viewer's "suspended relation to the picture itself as a possible unity," recall Bouissac's and Carmeli's identification of the way in which circus arts manipulate social-cultural codes. This manipulation results in existential uncertainty, a momentary suspension of the ability of those social-cultural codes to be meaningful as is customarily expected from daily experience. Clark's reference to a "suspended relation" redirects our attention unexpectedly to the incidental, almost inconsequential, figure of the trapeze artist's lower legs in the upper left-hand corner of the painting.

For Boime, the implied athletic vigor of the trapeze artist's legs serves to contrast with the painter's irreparably lost health. Her lower legs do three other things: they record a feature of the cultural landscape, contribute to the painting's "dominant female presence," and counterbalance compositionally the figure of the gentleman (Boime 120, 131). For Clark, the trapezist's lower legs also possess a social-historical value, communicating to the viewer that the Folies Bergère was a swankier establishment in its ability to offer top-tier entertainments such as trapeze acts (244). It was, after all, at the Folies Bergère that the Hanlon-Lees appeared in both 1872 and 1878–79. Through her legs, however, Manet may have acknowledged the acrobat as the source for his deliberate juxtaposition of incompatible perspectives and temporalities, identities (the "real" barmaid and her mirror image), and identifications (the viewer and the gentleman). We find the trapezist in the painting's margins, but she may be at the center of its ambiguity.

There is an earlier painting that also casually includes a reference to acrobats. We find a visual record of the Hanlon-Lees' 1878–79 season in Manet's *Au café* (1878). The outdoor window in the background offers a reverse view of a large water-stained print of Jules Chéret's poster *Folies-Bergère/Do Mi Sol Do/Les Hanlon-Lees.* In 1877, Manet had started a canvas featuring the Reichshoffen café. In 1878, he split the canvas in two, with one half becoming *Au café* and the other *Coin de café-concert* (1879). The Chéret poster figures in the former, with a viewpoint looking out toward the street. A dancer on stage features in the background of the other, an oddly different, if not opposite, orientation from *Au café.* That these two works were once part of the same canvas was discovered when they were placed side by side in preparation for an exhibition of both paintings. An X-ray examination confirmed the relation between them, with *Au café* undergoing less reworking than *Coin de café-concert* in its shift from the external window to the internal stage (Cachin et al. 420) (Figures 4.2 and 4.3).[11]

The two paintings' different viewpoints make the seemingly casual presence of the Chéret poster in Manet's 1878 work more intriguing than serving as just a historical detail from the Paris café scene of the last quarter of the century. This is not just any poster, but one of an acrobatic troupe whose pantomimes were a revelation to their artistic patrons. In *Un bar aux Folies-Bergère*, Albert Boime contends, the painting "questions the very nature of the 'real'" (121). It would perhaps be more precise to state that, beginning with the original Reichshoffen café painting, Manet strove to question the way we are culturally conditioned to see by short-circuiting that system through the display of incompatible elements within the same space and time. With only *Au café* and *Coin de café-concert* as evidence of the existence of an earlier painting, it is their opposed viewpoints that suggest that Manet may have attempted to portray the disorienting experience of an acrobatic act. In *Au café*, in particular, the characters are literally, and I think figuratively as well, underneath the sign/poster of circus desemantization. The conductor of *Do mi sol do* (pantomime and Chéret poster) and the figures in *Au café* and *Coin de café-concert* share impassibility with the barmaid of *Un bar.* The pantomime contrasts the tumultuous activities of the orchestra's members against the total concentration and oblivion of the conductor. The paintings communicate the din of voices, the clinking of beer and alcohol glasses, and the lively music from a packed café/music-hall against the shockingly quiet isolation of its featured employees and patrons. Ten years later, Georges Seurat recreated this disparity in imbuing the highly animated fairground atmosphere with a striking

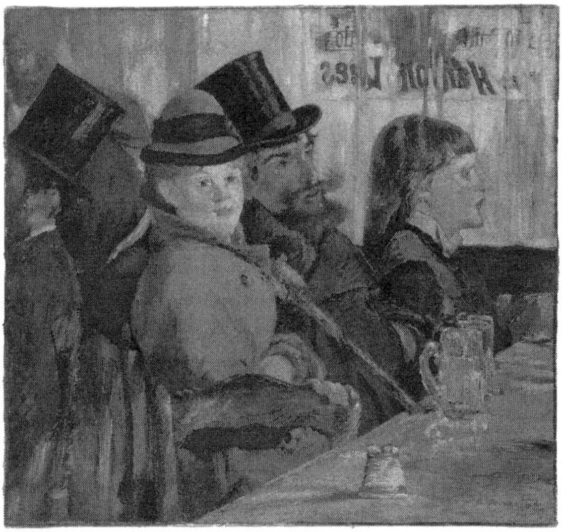

Figure 4.2 Édouard Manet, *Au café*, 1878. Oil on canvas. 78 cm × 84 cm. Inv. no. 1953.3. Oskar Reinhart Collection "Am Römerholz," Winterthur.

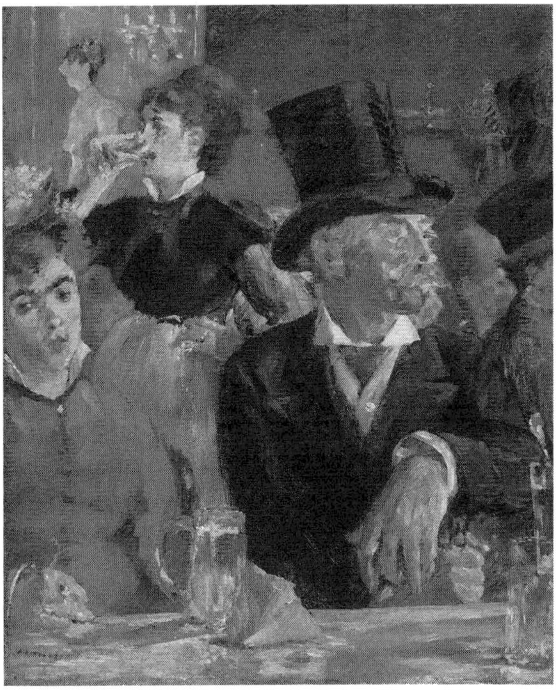

Figure 4.3 Édouard Manet, *Coin de café-concert* (1879). The Walters Collection, London.

stillness in his circus-themed painting, *Parade de cirque* (1889). *Un bar*, however, goes one step farther by extending the discrepancy in its perspectival instability: the viewer, the barmaid, and the gentleman occupy an indeterminate space.

As noted, *Au café*'s activities literally take place under the sign of circus acrobatics, and so too do those in *Un bar aux Folies-Bergère*. The trapezist's foot position on the visibly swinging barre indicates that she is preparing to leap. This is the moment of the mental "time of action" for executing a plan. By preventing the viewer from getting the total experience of the trapezist's trick, Manet shifts her "time of action" capability to the barmaid such that her mirror image functions as a feed-forward visualization of her plan of action to engage in conversation with a client.

Huysmans Travels Through Space and Time at the Folies Bergère

The acrobat is perceived as paradoxically double: she is both real person and objectified version of herself as she acts on or "plays" her performing body, the latter functioning as a manipulation of the social-cultural system (Carmeli, "Performing" 207). In the execution of an impossible physical feat, the only possible explanation for the failure of the social-cultural system's rules to account for what is seen happening (its inability to confirm the accepted ideas regarding daily experience) is that those rules are arbitrary. At the moment that the acrobat's duality manifests itself, signifiers become detached from signifieds, and social time and space cease to obtain. For most circus patrons, desemantization is a source of temporary anxiety. For some artists and writers from 1879, it was a source of creative liberation.

Desemantization and the creation of another space and time occur to varying degrees in two sections of Huysmans's "Les Folies-Bergère en 1879." The narrator of the poems is a spectator of acrobatic acts that provoke uncanny experiences in him. In section I, the narrator glimpses a male acrobat as he hangs by his hands and feet from a barre and begins to make his body spin. At one point he rotates so quickly that, as he succumbs fully to his own momentum, he no longer resembles a human being, his gold-bedizened costume making it appear that this inanimate thing is "crachant des étincelles comme ces soleils d'artifices qui virevoltent, en pétillant, dans une pluie d'or" (Huysmans, *Croquis* 10).[12]

Each section in "Les Folies-Bergère en 1879" seems to correspond to the sequence of numbers in the type of variety show that the venue offered, but it is not certain that this aerial feat took place on the same evening as the one in section IV. What is clear, however, is that what distinguishes the narrator's receptivity to the two acrobatic performances is that in the first, he has just arrived. Bouissac notes regarding the disservice of televised recordings of circus acts that the constant camera cuts and change of perspective create a rupture in the perception of ambiguity: the "very system of the circus [...] requires that a complete act be seen from only one special point of view – whatever it is" (143). Huysmans's narrator's viewing position is partially obstructed by the "créneau formé par deux bouts d'épaules et par deux têtes" (10). If it is to work, the "system of circus" also requires that the spectator be present from the beginning to the end of an act. Huysmans's narrator is sensorially distracted in his survey of all the sights, sounds, and odors of the bustling music-hall, both on and off stage. We must wait for the trapeze act of section IV for him to find himself existentially suspended in time and space.

In section IV, the narrator is present for the total play of the acrobatic number, from the quick setting up of the equipment to the final applause and rapid dismantling of the trapeze. The conditions preparing for the contamination of signifying registers are set well in advance of the entrance of the acrobats onto the stage. As the circus grips assemble the acrobats' net, it swings to and fro and its brass rings clink against the scaffold bars as it unfolds, activating the first auditory impression of "une mer qui joue avec des galets" (*Croquis* 15). The play of electric light that turns the English acrobats' costumes silver-blue, the sound of the words "all right" exchanged throughout the number, the aerial rebound of the lady trapezist after she lets her body drop into the net – she is "comme un poisson qui roule et saute dans un épervier" – are the final elements that activate a visual and olfactory breach in time and space that, for Huysmans's narrator, is a revelation (18). He finds himself suddenly in the Belgian port of Antwerp:

> Et voilà que je songe à Anvers maintenant, au grand port où dans un roulement pareil s'entend le "all right" des marins anglais qui vont prendre le large. C'est ainsi pourtant que les lieux et les choses les plus disparates se rencontrent dans une analogie qui semble bizarre, au premier chef. On évoque dans l'endroit où l'on se trouve les plaisirs de celui où l'on ne se trouve pas. Ça fait tête-bêche, coup double. C'est la courte joie que le présent inspire, déviée à l'instant où elle lasserait et prendrait fin et renouvelée et prolongée en une autre qui, vue au travers du souvenir, devient tout à la fois plus réelle et plus douce. (*Croquis* 18)

Huysmans's narrator describes this remarkable phenomenon as a transfer from one temporally unrelated moment to another (one from the present, the other from an unspecified past) and from one spatially unrelated context to another (a trapeze act at the Folies Bergère, then the port of Antwerp). The expressions "tête-bêche" and "coup double," however, indicate that the semantic register of the music-hall is not eclipsed by that of the port. The sensory signifiers of the music-hall are one half of the "bizarre" analogy for which the port provides the signifieds. The unstable semantic atmosphere provoked by an acrobatic performance detaches the signifiers of the English acrobats' cries of "all right," the sight of their net, the sound of metallic cables against trapeze bars and poles, the rumble of the net as it is refolded at the end of the trick, and the play of stage light on costumes, allowing for their attachment to the signifieds of the seaport with its corresponding sounds of English sailors' voices, the clanging of mast cables, the roll of nets as they make their "bruit de lames qui déferlent," the sight of nets on the boats, and the flickering play of sunlight on the waves and on quivering fish (18).

The detached signifers do not for all that float, but the normal spectrum of analogous semantic registers expands in "bizarre" and unexpected ways. Huysmans was not alone in being struck by an analogy between a circus act and sea-related scenes. In *L'Écuyère* (1882), Octave Mirbeau describes a similar marine effect, but in this passage, the experience belongs not to a spectator but to the *écuyère* Julia Forsell since the "self-referential structure and self-referential condition is performed, conveyed, and experienced" by both acrobat and spectator (Carmeli, "Performing" 206):

> Le cirque, tendu partout de toiles verdâtres, semblait l'entre-pont d'un bateau de pêche énorme, encombré d'engins, de filets ruisselants qui séchaient, avec des tons glauques d'algues marines. Une lumière blonde, tombant des jours de la coupole comme par les hublots du sabord, jetait ci et là des taches vives, accrochant des paillettes aux bosselures des cuivres posés debout à l'orchestre; à l'entrée du couloir d'écurie, les trois becs jaunes d'un lustre allumé barraient le sol d'ombres sales. Des relents nauséeux du fumier poignaient la gorge, pareils à des odeurs fortes de marée. Parfois une ruade sonore dans une stalle éclatait ainsi qu'un coup de mer brusque au bordage, au dehors le roulement des voitures dans l'avenue grondait avec un bruit de vagues profondes. Et on eût dit l'écuyère secouée par un roulis d'océan sur sa selle, quand, déplacé tout à coup, elle ne tanguait pas sous un saut de mouton en saccade. Les sangles gémissait, ainsi que des cables, dans le cliquetis d'acier fin des gourmettes, sous les mâchements du cheval en action, qui s'échauffait, hennissant parfois longuement. (69)

The equestrienne Julia Forsell shares with the spectator of Huysmans's poem the full gamut of sensory details that shift to the signifieds of another semantic register: that of the sea – the green-blue hues, the play of light upon the water, the strong ocean odors, and the rumbling of waves.

It is significant that Huysmans opened his *Croquis parisiens* with "Les Folies-Bergère en 1879," in particular with the poems in which he describes the three acrobatic entertainments (the spinning acrobat, the trapezist couple, and the Hanlon-Lees in *Le Duel*), because they prepare the reader for an optical shift in which "une perspective naturaliste [est] au bord de basculer dans la vision décadente" (Loehr 230). It is in the last section of the *Croquis* ("Paraphrases"), in particular, that the narrator abandons himself fully, as Joël Loehr remarks, to "[des] comparaisons inédites et inattendues entre les réalités les plus disjointes [qui] aboutissent à la rencontre et à la conjunction des contraires que l'oxymore met bord à bord" (236).

Of the three acts, it is the coupling of the trapeze act with marine conditions that has a lasting effect, perhaps marking it as a seminal decadent experience. In Huysmans's *À rebours* (1884), des Esseintes has an architect embed one small dining room within a larger one in his suburban retreat at Fontenay-sur-Roses. The former area resembles a ship's cabin, and the latter, continuing the marine theme, is fitted with portholes, an aquarium, an infusion of the smell of tar, and paraphernalia related to sea travel (itineraries, promotional posters, compasses, binoculars, fishing rods, etc.). In a striking echo, if not a deliberate reprise, of the narrator's flashback to the port of Antwerp in "Les Folies-Bergère en 1879," des Esseintes "se procurait ainsi, en ne bougeant point, les sensations rapides, presque instantanées, d'un voyage au long cours" (105). In contrast to his Antwerp "voyage," however, it is here a question of a flash-forward. That this is the first room in the house described by the narrator situates it within the other aesthetic practices of the novel. Huysmans, the spectator, had glimpsed during a mind-expanding trapeze act the emergence of a breach in the ability of normal sensory examination and analysis to account for everyday experience. Natural and empirical laws momentarily lost currency as he witnessed referential components become detached, displaced, and recombined in ways far beyond the limited scope of the conventional metaphor.

In this seminal novel, Huysmans's return to the marine motif tags it as a springboard for des Esseintes's general manipulation of the real, something that the latter will do with great relish, inventiveness, and humor. General manipulation of the real involves detached signifiers not only in flashbacks but also in flash-forwards, producing new experiences that for all intents and purposes have never taken and do not take place in real time and space.[13] Humor emerges as des Esseintes entertains himself in one activity after another, actively inducing desemantization in the creation of ever more "bizarre" pairings. For example, his mouth organ brings together the very different senses of taste and hearing in a gustatory-musical composition. With his vials of essential oils and boxes of aromatic substances, he can make a ball of styrax usher in the odors of factories (230). He pursues the trapezist Miss Urania for the perceived separation from her natural gender: she becomes visually male in performance. He enters into a relationship with a ventriloquist precisely for her ability to split her voice from her body. And he seeks the incongruous in nature, cultivating one flower whose petals look like veined skin and another for its resemblance to a metal pipe. Like the critical moment at which an acrobat performs the impossible, however, these experiences are necessarily of short duration, and any attempt to prolong the sense of surprise and the existential magic will fail. It is for this reason that des Esseintes must continually move on to the next project, it too doomed to be short-lived. It is for this reason as well that any attempt to read this novel in terms of linear narrative progression is futile. Each action undertaken by the protagonist suspends any potential for meaning in its procession of startling paired opposites. Indeed, the objective is either the discovery or better yet, the creation of "bizarre" analogies that short-circuit meaning. As Starobinski advises regarding an attempt to understand what acrobats do, "[q]u'on ne se hâte donc pas de leur assigner un rôle, une fonction, un sens; il leur faut accorder la licence de n'être rien de plus qu'un jeu insensé" (141).

Edgar Degas's *Miss Lala au Cirque Fernando*

Edgar Degas's *Miss Lala au Cirque Fernando* epitomizes the short-lived quality of acrobatic performance on two levels. In the first, practical considerations determined that with this subject the painter did not work as he normally did in "procédant de la répétition, de la série" (Pencenat 59). Tackling the technical problems of perspective in the circus's domed ceiling proved so challenging that he had to resort to a draughtsman, a state of affairs that might have nipped in the bud any inclination to undertake further paintings on the theme of aerial acrobatics (Pencenat 59). In the second, as Corinne Pencenat remarks, the time of the painting as project is that of "le temps vécu de la *performance*" (59). By this, she refers specifically to acrobatic performance, not theatrical or vocal performance. To take it one step further, her astute interpretation of the painting as portraying the time of the action in the painting – Miss Lala performing the "iron jaw" – connects with Bouissac's "time of action." The "time of action," as I have noted, which ends with the successful use of an apparatus, ushers in not only a temporal conception other than linear and circular time, but another spatial configuration as well, since the space of action is that of the apparatus's peculiar universe, one designed only for the execution of one particular action. It can be wondered if Degas's problems with perspective were complicated not only by perspective proper, but by his perception of and effort to communicate Miss Lala's different relation to the space of her apparatus – the "iron jaw" – as well (Figure 4.4).

Degas was a regular patron of the Cirque Fernando, and the painting reveals a keen sensitivity to the way circus acrobats play with social-cultural signifying systems through the performance of the impossible.

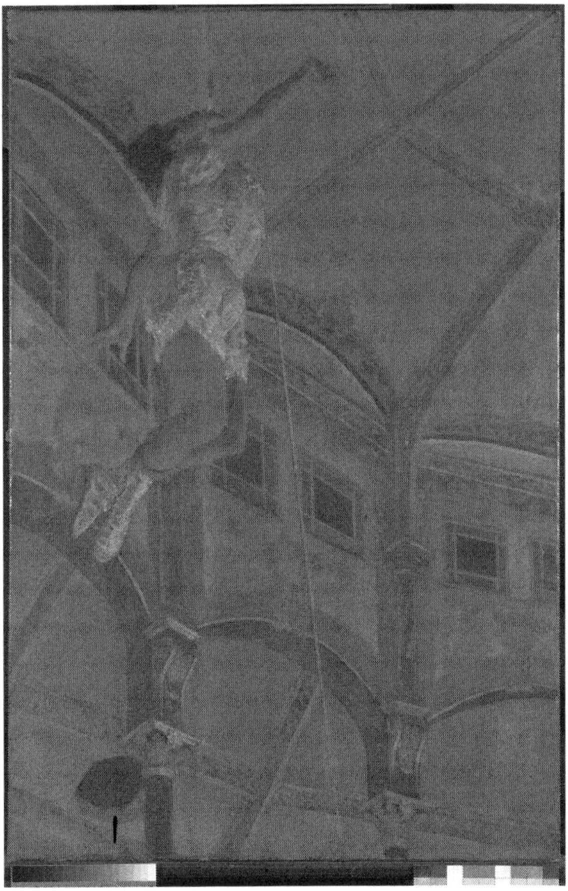

Figure 4.4 Edgar Degas, *Miss Lala au Cirque Fernando* (1879). The National Gallery, London.

With his heightened awareness of the mechanics of acrobatic play, Degas incorporates multiple paradoxical pairings into his work. First, he draws on the way in which the acrobat embodies and forces the audience to acknowledge a duality initiated by the hand wave directed at them, one of which opens her number and the other which "punctuates" its end (Carmeli, "Performing" 202).[14] In the painting, Miss Lala is perhaps about to begin her act, but, in line with my interpretation, it is even more likely she has just come to a stop after her dizzying rotation and will momentarily signal for applause before beginning her descent. Degas literally and figuratively captures her in suspension: she literally hangs by her teeth and she is figuratively in an intermediate state (is she real? is she human?).

The viewer too is suspended between existential states, one that is linked to the everyday real with all its accepted social, natural, and empirical laws, and the other that is outside those systems. Like Huysmans's narrator who remarks in "Les Folies-Bergère en 1879" that the male acrobat who has succumbed to the momentum of his spinning body has become a spiral fireworks display, the audience members find themselves in perceptual and existential limbo, puzzled by Miss Lala's exhibition of both human and inanimate qualities (she is both source of her motion and object of that motion). Among the elements that force spectators to question their certitude regarding their own existential identity is the appearance and disappearance of Miss Lala's racial identity (she was half black, half white). Although some argue for Degas's (and his society's) ambivalent if not downright racist relation to his subject, understood in the context of circus semiotics, Miss Lala's race serves to increase the tension between and aggravate the sense of suspension in all the opposites that her act elicited, including its role in what Richard Thomson calls Degas's humorous "send-up" of "Renaissance and Baroque ceiling painting" (15).[15] "[I]n a format suitable for a mythological, or more specifically, a religious subject such as a Transfiguration or an Assumption," Thomson points out, Degas's pictorial gesture is blasphemous in depicting a "mulatto acrobat whose act consisted of being raised to the ceiling by her teeth" in place of an ascending Virgin (15). For a nineteenth-century spectator, Miss Lala's race would have made her an unlikely candidate for the reverent treatment of an Assumption, and yet, strangely, she is also the most suitable subject for figuring a different kind of transcendence by virtue of the medium's manipulation of the signifying registers of everyday reality.

While realist in depicting accurately the cable of Miss Lala's "iron jaw," Degas's painting places that cable within the space/universe of her apparatus in a way that anticipates the use that Jules Chéret would make of the apparatuses associated with a handful of celebrated lady acrobats beginning in 1880, including the one that he did of Miss Lala at the Folies Bergère. As in Chéret's posters of the aerialists Leona Dare and Emma Jutau, the one featuring Miss Lala includes the accurate details of her tools – her trapeze barre and cannon. These tools, however, seem to materialize suspended in an indeterminate background space that resembles nebula, as if Miss Lala has just emerged from another spatial dimension. We can call this dimension the spaceless space of the apparatus. Or to borrow from Starobinski's description of the acrobatic clown, it is "un autre espace," "un autre univers," "un franchissement des limites du réel" (139). If Degas did not conceptualize Miss Lala's space in terms of a gaseous cloud like Chéret, he did indicate through the play of asymmetry and detailed perspective the space of the acrobat, including her "iron jaw" and its cable as an alternate space. In *L'Art moderne*, Huysmans praised Degas's depiction of "miss Lola, grimpant à la force des dents jusqu'aux combles de la salle Fernando," daring to "faire pencher tout d'un côté le plafond du cirque" (134).[16] In *Degas: The Artist's Mind*, Theodore Reff translates "faire pencher tout d'un côté le plafond du cirque" as "[has made] the ceiling of the Circus incline completely to one side" (180). Reff's reading of Huysmans's comment places emphasis clearly on Degas's technical mastery of perspective. In line with the introduction of the space of the apparatus into the painting, Huysmans marvels rather at the impression that the muscular and powerful Miss Lala is pulling down that ceiling, as the backward motion of her head, her arched back, her bent knees and lifted feet, and the off-center placement of her body within the canvas seem to suggest.

These opposite approaches, one focusing on precise perspective, the other on an alternate spatial dimension, may in reality conform to Degas's aesthetic objective: to execute in a painting the feat of neutralized artistic traditions and conventions through the figure of Miss Lala. She is both symbol and tool of that action. Thomson attributes a perceptual duality to the painting: it is both an "accurate pictorial composition" and an irreverent gesture against conventional artistic practices (15). "[E]mpirical observation" (attention to reproducing the real details of the circus interior, the performer, and her apparatus) served to underpin Degas's "visual witticisms" (the manipulation of those same details to make them produce uncertainty about what one is seeing) (Thomson 15). Thomson cites Degas's reputation as an excellent and entertaining imitator of people as a talent that carried over into the visual puns that he incorporated into his paintings. Mimicry is a "dual" skill that involves "observation" and "accurate repetition of the action" as well as the simultaneous commentary on that action (9). In Miss Lala, Degas found the perfect conduit for transposing a personal duality – being subject (the observer) and object (treating one's body as an object in the repetition of an action) – into a professional aesthetic.

Catulle Mendès and the Urban Landscape as Acrobatic Apparatus

In *La Vie et la mort d'un clown*, Catulle Mendès does more than have his acrobat Aladin bend the ceiling of a circus structure. A stationary circus building like the Cirque Fernando contains the spatial distortion caused by Miss Lala within its walls. The danger of that type of spatial manipulation bleeding into the street is nevertheless always present.[17] Not only is Aladin an id-driven animal, he is also an unpredictable force capable of transforming the features of the urban landscape into apparatuses. The arrangement of urban space – the buildings, sidewalks, streets, bridges, steps, walls, and more – is another social-cultural system that organizes our experience of reality and restricts our movements, and it does so in the name of law and order. More dangerous than the risk of a fall from a trapeze or highwire, Aladin's acrobatic turns threaten the core beliefs of his unofficial spectators – police, hotel guests, witnesses, passersby, and so on – in the presumed inviolability of the systems' proscriptions.[18] Aladin is doubly suspect: not only does society deem that he is a real criminal (he murdered his stepbrother), but also it designates him as "lawless" from the way his tricks neutralize a society's ability to communicate meaning and enforce compliance. The threat of criminality feared by civil authorities in their persecution and prosecution of *funambules* throughout the nineteenth century may refer to real crime, but it also includes how these performers put in question the legitimacy of social-cultural rules. There is a blurring of the distinction "between actual circus travelers, who live in social and political marginality and a performance of marginality," which for travelers involves their existentially disruptive activities both inside and outside the circus tent for the duration of their stay in a town (Carmeli, "Text" 176).

The acrobatic clown Aladin is a force that literally slips out of the grips of the law on repeated occasions throughout the novel, and almost always in his reduction of elements of the urban landscape to apparatuses. In his plans of action, he turns common objects into the tools of an acrobatic performance. In the opening chapter of Mendès's novel, Aladin, who has escaped from prison in Paris and fled to the south of France, comes upon a group of harvesters. Separated from them by a wide and deep trench, he promises to leap across the chasm if they will let him work. To their stupefaction, "[i]l se rapprocha du bord, joignit les pieds, se courba, se redressa, bondit et tomba de l'autre côté si légèrement que pas une motte de terre ne jaillit sous le coup" (Mendès, *La Demoiselle* 4). The trench surrounding the field of crops, a natural configuration probably modified artificially for maximum drainage, becomes the tool in the acrobat's plan for executing his leap. The trench's functionality – drainage – disappears before the strict functionality of the apparatus, which is to facilitate the execution of an impossible leap. The signifiers of the trench – its shape, dimensions, textures, surfaces, and more – become detached and reapplied to the conditions and materials of an aerial circus act: the trench's edge becomes a springboard and its chasm the void below the leaping body, creating a new analogy. Bouissac notes that the apparatus "constructs a universe for the actions which it makes possible by determining their forms, and conversely it comes to full existence as a universe through the action(s) which – so to speak – bring(s) it to life" (141). In other words, while Aladin's plan to leap is dictated by the dimensions, surfaces, and gap of the trench, the trench can only materialize as an apparatus in the performance of the leap.

There are three other escapes that precede Aladin's execution for the murder of his acrobatic "brother" Icare in the circus ring and each involves the spontaneous creation of an apparatus designed to the measures of his plans.[19] The first is Aladin's flight from a band of thieves intent on taking the 100,000 francs that he has won at the roulette table in the German town of Bade. The walls, stairwell, banisters, poles, and light fixtures that figure in the hotel lobby where he is staying become a series of surfaces ideal for the display of impossible acrobatic prowess. The second attempted escape takes place in the near-by town of Ober-Ursel, where Aladin is incarcerated and heavily guarded in a hotel room. He puts his acrobatic talents to the navigation of an intricate chimney flue system. In the third, he leaps from a balcony as if it were a trapeze podium. In this last attempt, however, he takes off on a circus horse. Instead of carrying Aladin away to freedom, the horse brings him back to his point of departure in the completion of the circuit of an equestrian performance. Aladin's plan only involved the balcony from which he leapt. He neither anticipated nor considered that the circus horse had his own plan: to turn whomever rides him into an *écuyer.* He transforms Aladin's escape route into a circus ring and brings the acrobat full circle. If Aladin is ultimately unsuccessful in his objective to flee, it is because there are two circus performers planning and executing at cross purposes.

In the last chapters of the novel, Aladin's criminal potential – his ability to shake literally and figuratively the very building stones of society – is realized fully. The director of la Grande Roquette prison and the chaplain conduct him from the room holding those condemned to die on that day to the Place de la Roquette, which from 1830 to 1974 was the site of Parisian executions. In the preceding chapters, preparations for the execution, from the mobilization of workers, policemen, and municipal officials, identify the space's symbolism as one controlled on that day by the state: workers unload the van transporting the official instrument of death (the guillotine) and set to erecting the scaffold; the policemen, whose duty it is to direct the movement of attendees around the scaffold, establish a barrier between those who form a human wall around the enclosed area (city officials and journalists) and the crowd beyond that human wall; and the police officers who spread themselves out around the square in order to ensure order (Mendès, *La Petite* 344).

The presence of four living walls (policemen) extends the imposing and menacing stature of the two prisons of the place de la Roquette – the Petite Roquette and the Grande Roquette – with each facing into the square. This is a place that welcomes neither commerce nor fraternization (344). The *place* is in the shape of a square, a form repeated in the location of the guillotine "between the four trees" of the square and the square-shaped mass of the scaffold (343, 354). Everything breathes angles, straight lines, order, and symmetry. The guillotine itself is crowned with "l'horrible symétrie de deux hauts madriers" (354). Even within the Grande Roquette, the cells of death row inmates reproduce the "administrative symmetry" of the exterior: they "correspondent bien à toute la bâtisse sociale, correcte et mathémathique" (375).

Buttressing the state's authoritarian spatial organization and mobilization of the square is the church. The ghost of the former convent of the Hospitalières appears in five inlaid paving stones patterned like a cross, comically referred to as "L'Abbaye de Cinq Pierres" or "La chaire de Cinq-Pierres," of which "le bourreau serait une espèce de pape" (Mendès, *La Petite* 343). Even the Berger guillotine's form replicates a miniature cathedral. Here, social and spiritual justice join forces, incarnated in the figures of the director of the prison and the chaplain who accompany Aladin to the scaffold. We would have every reason to believe that the infernal machine of social order will function normally. But something extraordinary happens at the moment of the beginning of the state ritual. Aladin disrupts the spectacle of state punishment as he steps onto the scaffold, wriggles free, leaps into the air, and grips the dull side of the blade "comme un gymnaste fait d'un bâton de trapèze" (*La Petite* 383). The shapes, surfaces, sizes, and functions become neutralized.

As Starobinski notes, the acrobatic clown who erupts into our space brings no meaning with him. Indeed, he is a non-sense. His movements, however, are breathtakingly beautiful and unsettling. The bascule becomes a trampoline, the guillotine becomes a trapeze, the circle of officials become a circus ring and spectators, punishment is nullified by play, and the certainty of death that the blade promised becomes the uncertain danger of the aerial performance. While Aladin is able to perform a complete circus number, he is unable to sustain it beyond a certain critical period of time because the performance of the impossible as real cannot be sustained. With the acrobatic number, since there is no meaning offered to replace the state's message, it must disappear. The danger that the witnesses experience, however, is very real, for the absence of meaning calls attention to the arbitrariness of social-cultural codes.

The Expanding Universe of the Apparatus: The Hanlon-Lees Effect

For the Hanlon brothers, "[l]asting fame came in 1878," Mark Cosdon notes, "when Paris hosted the Exposition Universelle" (*The Hanlon* 53). They were performing perhaps as early as May of that year, a booking that coincided with the opening of the world's fair on May 1 (Cosdon "Appendix A").[20] From that time on, the brothers never failed to coordinate their shows with world and state fairs whenever possible (Cosdon, *Hanlon* 53). This decision was most assuredly motivated by the attendance of enormous crowds. While there was no direct connection between the two events, however, certain facets of the *exposition* undoubtedly boosted and magnified the effect that the Hanlon-Lees had on their audiences.

Although the Hanlon-Lees were not itinerant acrobats in a strict sense, they were associated by profession and peripatetic lifestyle with traveling circuses and fairground attractions. Traveling troupes arrive in caravans, set up tents, have daily contact to varying degrees with townsfolk, all activities that indirectly advertise their shows as well as establish the performers' difference. Indeed, they do more than merely announce their arrival with the hanging of the first posters – they are already performing their own selves (Carmeli, "Performing" 196).

The Hanlon-Lees' engagement at the Folies Bergère lasted 10 months, a few months longer than the *exposition universelle*, which ended on November 10, 1878. There exists an overlapping in the practices of these events: like traveling circuses, preparation for the *exposition* involved the rapid erection of structures and its closing required their quick dismantling. Among the ephemeral buildings of the *exposition*, and perhaps the ones that most impressed themselves on the Parisian imaginary, were the pavilions of the many participating countries.[21]

The national pavilion exhibitions were constructed by workers from their respective countries, an activity that put cultural difference on display, producing a *dépaysement* – the French word captures both its literal meaning as a change in physical place and its figurative as a feeling of disorientation – in Parisian onlookers. Something happens, for example, to the Chinese and Indian construction workers building pavilions in their national style, to the Algerian potters throwing pots, and the Japanese farmers – all customary activities – once they no longer ply their trades nor wear their dress unconsciously but also perform their culture and themselves for onlookers, even if this is merely out of an awareness of being observed.

Featured technological advances of the likes of Thomas Edison's electric street lights, megaphone, and phonograph, and Alexander Graham Bell's telephone materialized in the setting of a modern *féerie* – steel, glass, cement, and temporary building materials like plaster of Paris – amazing visitors with an array of impossible inventions that had become unimaginably yet clearly possible. There is but one step from the confusion of sensations caused by the transitory and dizzying urban exhibition to those caused by the equally fleeting and vertiginous performances of the Hanlon-Lees. The separation between outside (the city) and inside (the Hanlon-Lees at the Folies Bergère) becomes blurred. The marvelous city in an extravagant state of display (the Paris "exhibition"), removed from everyday time and space by that display and the very ephemerality of its structures (quickly erected and just as quickly disassembled), mimics the labor of staging a circus sojourn that prepares spectators for an experience of existential desemantization inside the tent (Carmeli, "Performing" 197).

In the fluidity between inside (the Hanlon-Lees) and outside (the *exposition*), the universe of the apparatus expands to encompass the entire city. In Villiers's *chronique* "Les Hanlon Lees," the London cityscape offers its many features as familiar apparatuses for the brothers, with their "accessoires" being roofs, underground tunnels, iron park fencing, boats, water gutters, and building ledges (739). In the universe of the apparatus, one is outside of everyday time and spatial relations, capable of moving in a flash between cities. Banville had remarked that we are witnesses to the proof that the Price brothers "jouent et se désarticulent le même soir à Paris et à Marseille" (289). "[J]'imagine," he adds, "qu'ils sautent de l'une à l'autre de ces villes, grâce à leurs bonds prodigieux" (290). Like the Prices, the Hanlon-Lees are everywhere at once, "la tête à vingt lucarnes à la fois, par un miracle d'ubiquité" (739).[22]

Their antics in Villiers's *chronique* make them doubly criminal. Detectives are in pursuit of them because they have kidnapped a young woman. They are also criminals like Mendès's Aladin because their performance of the impossible places them outside the purview of law and order. Such a performance is accompanied by a "bouffée de gratuité [qui] oblige à reconsidérer tout ce qui passait pour nécessaire" (Starobinski 142–43). Whenever the "real" law tries literally to capture them, which is also the moment in which the social-cultural order tries to absorb them, they volatilize into "une nouvelle région de l'être," a region we can liken to the cloud that Chéret will situate in the background of his depictions of celebrated lady acrobats, and from which they emerge (Starobinski 140).

Notes

1 Prior to 1879, only one book in France examined the world of acrobats, and this only tangentially in its perceived relation to sports: Guillaume Depping's *Merveilles de la force et de l'adresse.* This is an excellent resource and went through several editions (1869, 1871, 1878, and 1886), but it cast its net wide, appealing primarily to sports enthusiasts (boxing and wrestling, rifle and pistol shooting, slingshot, archery, discus throwing, dressage and horse racing, running, swimming, diving, skating, javelin, and even boomerang throwing), only including the circus skills of tightrope dancing and acrobatics. Both organized sports and circus became disciplines during the nineteenth century, but despite superficial similarities (equestrian exercises and dressage, high-wire and high beam balancing routines, tumbling and gymnastics, for example), they function differently. Sports belong to a recognized order, governed by rules, competition, and the obtaining of results (Carmeli, "Marginal" 258). Circus skills play with the rules of social-cultural systems.

2 Guy Ritchie's *Sherlock Holmes* (2009) provides excellent examples of the concept of the "time of action," particularly in the bare hands fight sequence, which serves in this particular instance to link the great detective's analytical skills less with expert observation than with the conception of a plan, a feedforward visualization of that plan, and an action that carries it out. The action takes place in two times. In the first, Ritchie shows Sherlock as he conceives his plan in slow motion, with a voice-over detailing each projected step and expected result. Sherlock uses his opponent as an apparatus whose every physical feature and movement (action and reaction to Sherlock's slaps and punches) he has mathematically accounted for. In the second, Ritchie

presents Sherlock executing his plan to perfection. In the plan sequence, slow motion is the visual equivalent of non-time. In the execution sequence, real time comes into play, but is not for all that more "real." It does not dismiss the feedforward version as purely imaginary. These are two enactments of the same action.

3 Although Lesclide describes the pantomime as "une étude réaliste," the realism breaks down for him with the arrival of the harvesters (147). "Pourquoi ces moissonneurs? Parce que" (151). In the absence of a narrative motivation for the harvesters, he gives them a structural function: "[c]e sont des moissonneurs de transition" (151).

4 Richepin's Tombre offers a similar aesthetic battle between old and new Pierrot, between the teachings of the mime Louis Rouffe (1849–85), who was mentor to Séverin, and his own more modern method of "zig, zag, paf!"

5 He does not die, first, because the mirror image is not an objectified version of Pierrot, and second, because the action takes place during a dream. This pantomime, whose scenario is charming, nevertheless adheres to conventional narrative and to the empirical laws of nature.

6 In the early stages, Goncourt calls the novel the work "avec lequel je rêve de faire mes adieux à l'imagination" (*Journal* 721). He wrote, of course, two more novels after *Les Frères Zemganno*: *La Faustin* (1882) and *Chérie* (1884).

7 Goncourt compared his profession to that of acrobats from an April 6, 1878, *Journal* entry ("nous, nos tours, ce sont nos livres!"), an obvious reflection of his immersion in the circus world as he worked on *Les Frères Zemganno*. His equation of writers' work to that of acrobats, however, goes back to at least 1859, when the brothers commented that they had given up the theater, whose actors "pretend" to have talent, for the circus, where acrobatic talent is "un fait" (II 774; I 491).

8 Just one example of the Goncourts' attraction to the figure of the clown/acrobat is Anatole Bazoche, who revises his allegorical painting by replacing the Christ figure with Pierrot in *Manette Salomon* (1867).

9 While Sari was not a specialist in circus acrobats and pantomime in the true sense of the word, when he took over the direction of the Folies Bergère in 1871, he "booked internationally popular circus and vaudeville entertainers" (Boime 122). He had knowledge of the kind of sundry details – booking acts, organization of a program, and so on – that Goncourt would have found useful in creating a feeling of authenticity regarding the engagement of circus talent. Katherine Ashley notes that the "accuracy of the circus details is attested to by the many letters, both of praise and of information, that Goncourt received regarding specific circus issues" (91).

10 Contrary to Sophie Basch's assertion, Goncourt probably did not turn to the Hanlon-Volta troupe for inspiration, however much these acrobats preferred "devoir leur succès non à une mise en scène luxueuse, mais à leur seul talent" (Basch 278; Strehly 186). If the Zemgannos strove to rise above the strength and skill of the average acrobat, they paid equal attention to the aesthetic presentation of their act. Their whimsical production at the Cirque d'Hiver has all the markings of the English Price brothers who, like the Zemgannos, played violins during their performances. Goncourt's great friend Banville gives a charming portrait of "Les Clowns Price" in his *Lanterne magique* (1883):

> Coiffés de toupets feu et bleu faïence, tachetés de chrome et d'écarlate, vêtus de maillots où tantôt flambent Orion et Sirius, où d'autres fois brille une Lyre absurde, ils s'envolent dans les airs, se prennent, se mêlent,

retombent sur le front l'un de l'autre, deviennent un monstre à deux têtes, jouent du violon au milieu de tout cela, s'effacent comme des fantômes, reparaissent étincelants de paillettes et d'astres; puis, de nouveau, sont lancés, flèches vivantes, par je ne sais quel arc invisible; et ces adolescents aux visages de Deburau-Apollon flânent violemment dans l'éther, comme des oiseaux, avec le sérieux d'une satisfaction enfantine. Parfois, – nous l'avons tous vu, – ils jouent et se désarticulent le même soir à Paris et à Marseille; j'imagine qu'ils sautent de l'une à l'autre de ces villes, grâce à leurs bonds prodigieux. Des réalistes expliquent cette ubiquité des Price en prétendant qu'ils sont quatre au lieu de deux; mais je hais ces transformations bourgeoises des faits surnaturels! Ajoutez que nos deux clowns sont peintres, musiciens, gentlemen accomplis, et qu'ils lisent dans son propre idiôme… qui? le poète des poètes, Homère! (289–90)

Like the Price brothers, the Zemgannos produce the total play of oppositions, immersing the spectacle's atmosphere in "du clair-obscur" and producing an "aigre enchantement" (Goncourt, *Les Frères* 141, 158). In performance, Nello is no less omnipresent in the performance space than the Price brothers and the Hanlon-Lees. In Banville's portrait, spectators speculate that there must be four Price brothers instead of two (the only possible explanation for their ubiquity); in Goncourt's, spectators glimpse only a flash ("éblouissement") (*Les Frères* 156). On a side note, Banville's claim that the Price brothers could read Homer in Ancient Greek echoes other writers' desire to make celebrated acrobats members of a true "aristocratie d'en bas" by attributing a solid cultural formation to them (Noiray 97). According to Hugues Le Roux, the Volta brothers also read "fort bien l'*Iliade* en grec" (196). And Villiers's Hanlon Lees, pursued by the police for kidnapping a young woman, sit casually on park benches "[à] deviser des brûlantes questions sociales" (740). This seems more likely a conceit on the part of these writers than a boast on the part of the acrobats.

11 The poster played an important role in the dating of the second work since several art critics and scholars had attributed its completion to 1877 (Cachin et al. 420).

12 "In the case of the trapeze performer, the swinging movement is experienced by the public as initiated at the beginning of her routine, but the high point of the performance is when the performer who initiated the movement and sustains it is simultaneously subjected to its 'independent' momentum" (Carmeli, "Performing" 200).

13 My use of the term flash-forward is not to be confused with the plot device in which a narrator has knowledge of events that will take place in a characters' future.

14 "Like the posture that engages the whole body, this gesture [hand wave], too contains an ambiguity. It indicates an ending, communicating the accomplishment of a routine and a demand for applause. […] However, at the same time, the hand gesture is, as we have observed earlier, also part of the routine itself – a part of the final stretch of the arm in the completion of a body form. Unlike the situation of an actor who turns to the public after the curtain falls and rises again, closure having been established, performance and performer, text and context clearly separated, in circus the hand gesture is not only part of the performance itself, but also its ending, its framing. It indicates, points at, and is being indicated by itself. The performer is both performing and communicating about his performance." (Carmeli 210)

15 For discussions of Miss Lala's race, see Smalls; and Marilyn R. Brown, "'Miss La La's' Teeth: Reflections on Degas and 'Race,'" *The Art Bulletin* 89.4 (2007): 738–65.

16 The register for the 1879 Impressionist Exhibition lists an incorrect title for the painting, which explains why Huysmans calls the performer Miss Lola (Smalls 377).

17 Traveling circuses that set up tents in a town, conduct pre-performance parades through the streets, and interact in some fashion with the townsfolk in the carrying out of "normal" activities (buying groceries, going to bars or cafés, washing clothes, etc.) act on, and transform temporarily, the givens of the structural configuration of the elements of the town.

18 Mendès never situates Aladin in a professional circus act. All of his acrobatic feats occur in the context of his status as a fugitive from justice.

19 It is interesting to note that the protagonists of Goncourt's *Les Frères Zemganno* and Mendès's *La Vie et la mort d'un clown* feature a "brother" who falls from a trapeze. In an echo perhaps of the dueling Pierrots of Couture and Gérôme in 1857, one can wonder if Mendès had gotten wind of the subject of Goncourt's novel in 1878. Did he mischievously have his Aladin kill off the brother that Goncourt could not, beginning his own novel in the aftermath of that accident?

20 Cosdon does not indicate the venue for the brothers' May performances.

21 While some were reconstructed at and/or incorporated later into other sites and structures – for example, the Indian, the Swedish, and the Norwegian pavilions were relocated to the Parc de Bécon in Courbevoie – most were dismantled at the end of the fair (Ageorges 68).

22 Banville, too, uses the word "ubiquity" in his description of the Price brothers: "Des réalistes expliquent cette ubiquité des Price en prétendant qu'ils sont quatre au lieu de deux" (289).

Works Cited

Ageorges, Sylvan. *Sur les traces des expositions universelles. 1855 Paris 1937.* Paris: Parigramme, 2006.

Ashley, Katherine. *Edmond de Goncourt and the Novel: Naturalism and Decadence.* Amsterdam and New York: Rodopi, 2005.

Banville, Théodore de. *La Lanterne magique. Camées parisiens. La Comédie française.* Paris: G. Charpentier, 1883.

Basch, Sophie. Introduction [to *Les Frères Zemganno* by Edmond de Goncourt]. *Romans de cirque.* Ed. Sophie Basch. Paris: Éditions Robert Laffont, 2002. 273–93.

Boime, Albert. "Manet's *Bar at the Folies-Bergère* as an Allegory of Nostalgia." *Textual Intersections: Literature, History and the Arts in Nineteenth-Century Europe.* Ed. Rachael Langford. Amsterdam and New York: Rodopi, 2009. 119–39.

Bonnet, Gilles. *La Pantomime noire, 1836–1896.* Paris: Hermann, 2014.

Bouissac, Paul. "The Timeless Tools of Time: Circus Performance Revisited." *Communication & Cognition* 14.2/3 (1981): 133–52.

Cachin, Françoise, Charles S. Moffett, and Juliet Wilson Bareau. *Manet, 1832–1833.* New York: The Metropolitan Museum of Art and Harry N. Abrams, 1983.

Carmeli, Yoram S. "Marginal Body and Bourgeois Cosmology: The British Acrobat in Reference to Sport." *International Journal of Comparative Sociology* 37.3 (1996): 252–73.

———. "Performing the 'Real' and 'Impossible' in the British Traveling Circus." *Semiotica* 80.3–4 (1990): 193–220.

———. "Text, Traces, and the Reification of Totality: The Case of Popular Circus Literature." Special Issue of *New Literary History* 25.1 (1994): 175–205.
Clark, T. J. *The Painting of Modern Life: Paris in the Art of Manet and His Followers*. Princeton, NJ: Princeton UP, 1984.
Coquelin Cadet. *La Vie humoristique*. Paris: Ollendorff, 1883.
Cosdon, Mark. "Appendix A: A Chronological Timeline of the Hanlon Brothers." Online posting. 3 February 2019. <http://siupress.siu.edu/sites/default/files/pdf/Chronological%20Outline%20of%20Hanlon%20Brothers%203-12-14.pdf>
———. *The Hanlon Brothers from Daredevil Acrobats to Spectacle Pantomime, 1833–1931*. Carbondale and Edwardsville: Southern Illinois UP, 2009.
Goncourt, Edmond and Jules de. *Journal*. Vol. I. *Mémoires de la vie littéraire I, 1851–1865*. Ed. Robert Ricatte. Paris: Robert Laffont, 1989.
———. *Journal*. Vol. II. *Mémoires de la vie littéraire II, 1866–1886*. Ed. Robert Ricatte. Paris: Robert Laffont, 1989.
Goncourt, Edmond de. *Les Frères Zemganno*. Fleuron. Paris-Geneva: Éditions Slatkine, 1996.
Huysmans, Joris-Karl. *À rebours*. Ed. Marc Fumaroli. Paris: Gallimard, 1977.
———. *Croquis parisiens. À Vau l'eau. Un dilemme*. 2nd edition. Paris: Plon, 1905.
———. *L'Art moderne*. 2nd edition. Paris: Stock, 1903.
Le Roux, Hugues. *Les Jeux du cirque et la vie foraine*. Paris: Plon, 1889.
Lesclide, Richard. *Mémoires et pantomimes des frères Hanlon Lees*. Paris: Chez Tous Les Libraires, 1879.
Loehr, Joël. "*L'Assommoir* de Zola, Les *Croquis parisiens* de Huysmans: un changement d'optique." *Revue d'histoire de la France* 102 (2002): 211–39.
Mendès, Catulle. *La Demoiselle en or*. Paris: Dentu, 1879. Vol. 1 of *La Vie et la mort d'un clown*.
———. *La Petite Impératrice*. Paris: Bibliothèque-Charpentier, 1907. Vol. 2 of *La Vie et la mort d'un clown*.
Mirbeau, Octave (under the pseudonym Alain Bauquenne). *L'Écuyère*. Ed. Pierre Michel. Angers: Éditions du Boucher and the Société Octave Mirbeau, 1993. <http://www.leboucher.com/pdf/mirbeau/mirbeau-ecuyere.pdf>
Noiray, Jacques. "Tristesse de l'acrobate. Création artistique et fraternité dans *Les Frères Zemganno*." *Revue des Sciences Humaines* 259 (July–September 2000): 91–110.
Pencenat, Corinne. "Étude de tableau: *Miss Lala au Cirque Fernando* de Degas." *Beaux-arts Magazine* 55 (1988): 58–59.
Reff, Theodore. *Degas: The Artist's Mind*. New York: The Metropolitan Museum of Art and Harper & Row, 1976.
Rodenbach, Georges. *Le Rouet des brumes*. Paris: Séguier, 1997.
Smalls, James. "'Race' as Spectacle in Late-Nineteenth-Century French Art and Popular Culture." *French Historical Studies* 26.2 (2003): 351–82.
Starobinski, Jean. *Portrait de l'artiste en saltimbanque*. Geneva: Editions d'Art Albert Skira, 1970.
Strehly, Georges. *L'Acrobatie et les acrobates*. Paris: Librairie S. Zlatin, 1977.
Thomson, Richard. "Notes on Degas's Sense of Humour." *Degas 1834–1984*. Ed. Richard Kendall. Manchester: Department of Art and Design, Manchester Polytechnic, 1985. 9–18.
Villiers de l'Isle-Adam. *Œuvres complètes*. Ed. Alan Raitt et al. Vol 2. Paris: Éditions Gallimard, 1986.

5 The Paradox of the Lady Acrobat

If women in Decadent literature and art are often tormentors, the female acrobat should be ideally positioned as one of these "persécutrices idéales" (Starobinski 45). In her form-fitting spangled costume which catches and reflects the play of light as she flies through the air during a performance, she dazzles with her beauty, grace, physical perfection, and perceived nudity. She also disturbs in the exhibition of a very troubling strength associated with masculinity.

Félicien Champsaur's Lulu from *Lulu, roman clownesque* (1901) is a female body behind which "se cache en fait une virilité agressive et dangereuse" (Starobinski 52).[1] Lulu's target is not her pseudo-Decadent lover, however, but the stereotypical fat cat capitalist who is the moral and aesthetic enemy of all artists. Accompanied by her pet pig and circus apparatus Rambô, she makes sport of the Baron de Motschild, leading the besotted banker to think that she will give herself to him. She does, however, offer herself fully to the novel's worthy artist, Georges Decroix, who enjoys vicariously the comeuppance of the baron and, by extension – since he is symbolic – all members of his reviled class.

Champsaur's privileging of the female acrobat never involves, however, her ability to push spectators into the abyss that has engulfed their comforting social-cultural assumptions. The *écuyère* Miss Io from *Miss America* (1885), for example, is just one conquest in an impressive collection of the protagonist's lovers: "l'horizontale de marque, l'acrobate, la tragédienne, la danseuse, les bourgeoises, les mondaines, les divas d'opérette" (184). In performance in *Dinah Samuel* (1882), Miss Io never reaches the point of presenting a troubling duality. His Patrice Montclar is too distracted by other women among the spectators to pay anything but a passing attention to what is happening in the ring. When he does, Montclar notes only the evidence of her corporeity: in the beginning stages of her act her breasts are "moites," become "de plus en plus humides," until the end of her act when her entire body is "suant" (*Dinah Samuel* 261–62, 264). While he clearly recognized the importance of the acrobat in the modern aesthetic of the 1880s and 1890s, Champsaur did not understand that the acrobat was often an instrumental tool in that aesthetic, and thus his circus heroines possess no other power than that of an erotic titillation capable of distracting an aesthete bored with the usual amorous fare.[2]

Jones conceives of a "Beastly Couple" as the Decadent updating of the traditional Bourgeois-Artist rivalry in which the "artist's rival and opponent may be either the pig-like man of wealth and power [...] or the courtesan *femme fatale* – or both" (129). Lulu's performing pig constitutes a stand-in for the repulsive but wealthy financier in this dynamic. In her act, whenever she would soften her cruel treatment toward the pig, "le cochon renaissait et odieux, parce que Riche, – il était gras, – il s'imposait, laid, dégoûtant, ignoble, immonde, riche enfin" (72).

Goncourt's La Tompkins in *Les Frères Zemganno* establishes herself as such a rival for Nello, a man whose body she examines in a perverse desire mixed "avec un peu de l'attention marchande d'un oeil d'eunuque noir achetant à un marché d'esclaves" (204). She is both a fabulously wealthy American pig and a *femme fatale*. Unaccustomed to being refused the whims that her vast fortune permits her and mercilessly taunted by the object of her acquisitive gaze, she takes her revenge by orchestrating the accident that shatters the acrobat's legs and, in doing so, destroys his brilliant future (204).

La Tompkins is the novel's tool of fate, however, not a tool of aesthetic discovery. She is an example of the anti-acrobat, whose defiant and willful ambition to "faire de l'impossible, du surhumain, des choses défendues par la nature et par Dieu" is the antithesis of the acrobat who performatively executes an impossible physical action that short-circuits the ability of the social order to obtain (193). She willfully breaks laws; she does not reveal the arbitrary nature of laws. If she is the source of a suspension of meaning, it is because the disorder is within her: her capriciousness contains "un brin de déraison, de folie, d'*insenséisme*" (193).

The majority of lady acrobats in literature and art of the last quarter of the nineteenth century are not *femmes fatales*. The lady acrobat possesses "un immense pouvoir de métamorphose, associé à son agilité" that springs from the unsettling doubling associated with all acrobats during the performance of the impossible: their real selves play their own bodies, provoking a momentary suspension of the accepted truth of spectators' beliefs about the world in which they live (Starobinski 52). More so than their male counterparts, female acrobats evince gender confusion because their sex is on display in a way that men's bodies are not.

Ironically, prejudices about women's bodies existed even within the circus profession where there should have been ostensibly no question regarding female athletic accomplishment. The Volta brothers, for example, express revulsion at the sight of the female body, citing its natural functions as evidence of its unsuitability for exhibition: women's hips "débordent la ligne tombante des épaules, écrasent les jambes courtes, brisent la proportion" (Le Roux 199). In addition to aesthetic disharmony, they find that women's lower and wider hips weigh them down, proof of women's predominant reproductive function, and hence making them unfit for the soaring flight of the aerialist.[3]

The journalist Le Roux initially accuses the Voltas of a jealousy caused by the ignorance of spectators regarding acrobatic skills: the seeming nudity of female acrobats draws greater applause than the superior gymnastic talent of men. Le Roux accepts the brothers' denial of resentment, supporting their conclusions with a reference to the historical practice of Ancient Greeks to sequester women in gynaeceums. Le Roux equates women's apartments in Antiquity with the modern home, the domain which nurtures their "destination naturelle d'épouse, de mère et de nourrice" (199).

Le Roux voiced the doubts and concerns of many men. The intensity of those social-cultural assumptions about what a woman's body can and cannot do evidently pressed themselves uncomfortably upon the male spectators as they watched female acrobats execute feats of remarkable strength and skill. When those accomplishments effectively short-circuited the validity of their convictions regarding the natural place of women and the permissible spaces within which they could operate, the doubling effect became more than playfully threatening.

Because the acrobat, as Starobinski notes, is an "absence de signification," she functions to "nie[r] tous les systèmes d'affirmation préexistants" (143). There is a desire, nevertheless, in many of the aesthetes who frequent the circus to account in some fashion for the "sentiment difficile à définir" described by des Esseintes (Huysmans, *À rebours* 210). There is an attempt to tease out even the merest wisp of meaning. For some, this entails an effort to resolve the ambiguity of the circus experience by making the lady acrobat "speak," an endeavor destined to end in disappointment, with the self-fulfilling confirmation that she is, like all women, just another "maîtresse ordinaire" (Huysmans, *À rebours* 212).

The Performative Silence of the Lady Acrobat

Characteristic of a circus performance, acrobats rarely utter words beyond expressing "un 'all right' [qui] traverse la salle" just before the lady acrobat leaps from the trapeze bar to her partner (Huysmans, *Croquis* 17). This "all right" serves a dual purpose. To use J. L. Austin's distinctions, the statement is constative because it represents the result of an assessment of the present conditions; the catcher is ready, the synchronization of the swinging bars is set, and the lady acrobat can leap. The "all right" also has a performative function, because it changes, however temporarily, spectator reality. It is at this moment that all the disruptive elements that the acrobats have set in place come together, subsumed in the performance of the impossible.

In nineteenth-century France, the lady acrobat's silence is demonstrably more disturbing than her male counterpart's because of assumptions about the moral and social function of the female body, and about what it is capable of doing. Representative of this position is the male spectator of the tightrope dancer Miss Jessica in Jean Lorrain's short piece "L'Acrobate."[4] The conditions for existential confusion present themselves at the moment that Lorrain perceives Jessica as "un grand oiseau bleu baigné de rayons de lunes" (202). As she "oscille endormie, dans l'espace, sur un invisible fil de fer," her swaying becomes a catalyst for a troubling mixture of emotions (202). The male spectator quivers out of apprehension that she could fall as well as from perverse pleasure as he ogles "l'offrande de sa nudité quasi divine" (202). He projects onto her a paralyzing fear of falling while she executes her number, a projection that bounces back, reflected by "le brillanté de son maillot soyeux" (202). Lorrain, interpreter and spokesperson of the male spectator's reaction, makes Jessica's silent body express "la souffrance et les appréhensions qui doivent [la] torturer" (203). During her aerial suspension in the void, Lorrain attempts to pull her down, tying her destiny to Shylock's daughter in Shakespeare's *The Merchant of Venice* and in Edmond Haraucourt's *Shylock* (1889) and holding her symbolically captive in 'l'éternelle faiblesse féminine et l'éternelle souffrance féminine" (Lorrain 203).

Des Esseintes, too, will end by reducing his lady acrobat to the presumed failings of her sex. He desires the gender-shifting Miss Urania because he anticipates that she will be able to induce a gender shift within him. He tries to impart meaning to her "sourire immuable et fixe" by placing his own thoughts, and by extension scripted words, on "les lèvres inconscientes de la femme" (Huysmans, *À rebours* 211). To his disappointment, a self-fulfilling prophecy makes real contact with Miss Urania reveal that she "possédait le caquet et la coquetterie des filles entichées de balivernes" (212). What kills his desire for her is precisely her "caquet," her prattling that returns her to the feminine, destroying all hopes for experiencing within himself "[d]es impressions de féminité, de faiblesse, de quasi-protection achetée, de peur même [...]; l'illusion n'était plus possible" (212). Language, however, is unable to account for the paradox of the lady acrobat because it deals in certainties, in things and situations that can be identified. Des Esseintes's error is in seeking transcendent conversation with a figure that in performance exists in a different space and time and that is by necessity outside of language.

It is therefore telling that, after Miss Urania, he turns immediately to a substitute for the desemantization that he seeks to force into everyday reality. That replacement is a specialist in matters of disembodied speech: a ventriloquist. To prevent her from uttering feminine blather, however, he provides the script. By throwing her voice – in essence, detaching it from her body – she is able to partially replicate the tearing of signifier from signified. The first stage of his relations with her centers on having her make a black marble sphinx and a chimera statuette recite passages from Flaubert's *La Tentation de Saint Antoine*. In this way, he maintains an ambiguous state: the objects are perceived as curiously both inanimate and lifelike. This scripting has the virtue of controlling for the appearance of the dreaded feminine jabbering, something that he was unable to avoid in Miss Urania. The ventriloquist's desemantization effect, however, is a one-sided illusion, not a real manifestation of the impossible. If des Esseintes perceived earlier that Miss Urania had become distinctly male at a crucial point in her act, he was equally aware that she remained distinctly female: she attached the markers of masculinity to her feminine body. Since both acrobat and spectator are involved in the tearing apart of signifier from signified, des Esseintes had the "impression que lui-même se féminisait" (211). Without the ventriloquist being able to participate, however, she soon bores of des Esseintes's game. As for him, he has to seek elsewhere the thrilling ambiguous state that liberates him from the numbing torture of everyday reality.

Gustave Kahn: *Le Cirque solaire*

Count Franz, the protagonist of Gustave Kahn's *Le Cirque solaire* (1898), is more fortunate than des Esseintes. He emerges from his debilitating decadent neurasthenia – he has extreme sensitivity to sounds and light, he is lethargic, and lacks all appetite – with the arrival of the Cirque Cramer and its star attraction, the *écuyère* Lorely, in the town of Oelsborn in Bohemia. Lorely's very entrance into town in the circus parade prepares Franz's separation from the neurasthenia and premature old age attached to his body.

As Carmeli notes regarding small travelling circuses, even the action of setting up tents upon a circus's arrival puts on display for townsfolk the very disconcerting duality of acrobats: they look like we do, eat, walk, and talk like us, and yet they are different, and not just because they come from somewhere else and dress oddly. Acrobats play themselves from the moment that they arrive. They carry heavy metal poles as if they were as light as feathers; they parade dangerous or abnormally large animals around their encampment as if they were domesticated; and each ambiguous display during the troupe's stay in town builds on the last such that at the moment of a performance, we as spectators undergo an existential upheaval because our inability to place their actions neatly in a function associated with our established social order ends by putting that order in suspension. The arrival of the Cirque Cramer effects a wondrous transformation not only on Franz but on Kahn's narrative style as well: fragmented, impressionistic perceptions of the town of Oelsborn, its people, and the circus personnel result in passages of extraordinary sensory beauty (sounds, aromas, colors, shapes, and textures), erasing the line between poetry and prose.[5]

So great is the transformation in Franz that he literally runs away with the circus. Over the span of a year spent with Lorely, however, Franz, who misunderstands the source of the paradox of the acrobat, relentlessly and unsuccessfully attempts to have Lorely renounce her profession and independence to live with him at his château. While he is hardly disillusioned like des Esseintes in his interactions with the real woman Lorely, it becomes clear that he is completely deaf to her words. His tour with the circus comes to an end following the troupe's engagement in London at the Athenaeum with a show of Barnum-like proportions and extravagance. When he finds a life-size publicity cut-out of her body in their hotel room, he reacts in disgust, dismissing it as typical of the crass commercialization associated with American culture. He fails to recognize, however, that the dummy participates in the process of semantic rupture that was the source of his liberation from his own body.

As with des Esseintes, who seeks a substitute vehicle for the sensation of desemantization, Franz counters his disappointment at the cardboard Lorely by wandering into a tavern in Whitechapel where he meets a man who may or may not be Jack the Ripper. There, Franz sees "Jack" tend to the local poor as a charitable physician, examining them and prescribing medicine. "Jack" also sketches portraits of the tavern patrons, portraits that are disturbingly deformed versions of their originals. "Jack" produces a disturbing duality like Lorely: he is both benevolent physician *and* brutally surgical mutilator; he is both a scientific student of the milieu that he frequents *and* unfaithful documenter of that milieu through his distorting portraits; he is a man of fine literary formation with a particular fondness for Baudelaire *and* an animal capable of savage violence. When he offers to escort Franz out of Whitechapel, the latter wisely refuses. While Jack does offer Franz a sense of danger that approximates the existential uncertainty experienced during an acrobatic trick, that path leads only to another kind of liberation: death.

Édouard Rod: *La Chute de Miss Topsy*

Like Kahn's Franz, Édouard Rod's André Frémy depends on the lady acrobat's ability to reproduce, if not sustain indefinitely, an invigorating "flash of freedom" (Tait 9). In *La Chute de Miss Topsy* (1882), Frémy, the ambivalent courter of the *écuyère* Miss Topsy, experiences extreme agitation in watching the evolutions of a rehearsal that will be her last. In an example of the phenomenon of desemantization being shared by both performer and spectator, Frémy's very being literally hangs in the balance: if Miss Topsy falls as she did six weeks before, he too will fall, which for him would promise him a fate akin to death.

In discussing the high-wire feats of Philippe Petit, perhaps most famous for his walk between the twin towers of the World Trade Center in 1974, Peta Tait describes the execution of his walks as "flash[es] of freedom," as acts of defiance against "natural and social laws, and the law *per se*" (9).[6] Flashes of freedom at the circus pull him, like Count Franz, temporarily out of his own neurasthenic debilitation. In one evening spent at the circus, his eyes discover a familiar face among the spectators: Antonia, "une actrice des Variétés," with whom he had had a love affair but who abandoned him when he had depleted his inheritance money (35). Like Huysmans's narrator in "Les Folies-Bergère en 1879," Frémy undergoes the sensation of "tête-bêche," with the hazy atmosphere of the circus ("la buée lumineuse du gaz") opening a breach in perception in which present and past intermingle (Huysmans 18; Rod, *La Chute* 35). Frémy finds himself mentally and sensorially transported to Antonia's "boudoir si parfumé," where he relives "toutes les douceurs de ses caresses" (35).

The circus promises to make real the glimpse of the impossible. Miss Topsy possesses the requisite signs of biological superiority, "de la vigueur, de la grâce, de l'adresse, de la bravoure" (42). Her feet appear to barely touch the rose embroidery of her saddle board. She is seemingly a supernatural, magical being: "on eût dit un grand papillon léger" (41). When she leaps, "elle semblait suspendue dans le vide" (41). Bits of paper from the hoops through which she leaps remain "attachés à ses épaules ainsi que de petites ailes," turning her into a winged fairy-like creature, as *écuyères* were often represented in illustrations throughout the first half of the nineteenth century (41).

Miss Topsy's entrance serves to activate semantic detachment for Frémy. When she enters the circus ring, she is aristocratic in the seemingly luxurious fabric of her dress, in her powdered hair, her pink cheeks and lips, and in her porcelain white skin, which creates an unexpected analogy with "les bergères Pompadour en porcelaine de Saxe" (39). The Columbine of the *commedia dell'arte* pantomime tradition that Miss Topsy's general physical appearance recalls initiates a transition into the semantic register of eighteenth-century Rococo art depicting figures and scenes from a *fête galante*. So complete is the impression that when Frémy leaves the attraction, he persuades his friend Pellard to accompany him to the pricey enchanted garden of the Bal Mabille, which serves to extend the *fête galante* code initiated at the circus. He goes there to admire the beauty and elegant toilettes of the demimondaines who stroll around like creatures from another time under the entrancing garden's lights, and to take one home for the night.

On another evening at the circus, the sound of English words exchanged during numbers by the troupe's multiple English acrobats prompts Frémy to prolong the semantic markers of Englishness. He goes to an English tavern to get mind-numblingly drunk on "plusieurs pintes de stout," anticipating des Esseintes simulated trip to London by way of an English tavern in Paris in *À rebours* (65). Like des Esseintes as well, Frémy is unable to sustain the magic of the entrancing analogies that the circus awakens in him.

When Miss Topsy is absent from the circus for six weeks due to her fall, and afterwards when she considers leaving the circus to lead an ordinary existence as a shop girl, the aura surrounding her life in and outside the ring begins to volatilize irreparably. Frémy cannot conceive of her quitting the circus to take up "un métier banal et moins dangereux" (118). He had already experienced disappointment at her ordinary appearance when he was first seated next to her in the performers' section of the stands. In her "modeste toilette de ville, elle lui restait indifférente: c'était une femme quelconque" (52). During those moments when he is away from the circus, he doubts that he loves her, only to feel, at the familiar sound of the music of her number announcing her entrance into the ring, that "spasme" and the powerful emotions that pull him out of his "indolence habituelle," giving him "une plus grande force de vivre" (108). Seeing her once again in the ring, all doubt disappears, and he finds her literally "transfigurée," another person entirely (54). "Le fait est," the narrator tells us, "qu'il ne l'aimait jamais autant qu'aux moments, trop courts à son gré, où il la voyait tourbillonner, dans son frais costume de ballerine, sur le cheval lancé, aux sons du quadrille toujours le même" (83–84). Like Baudelaire's Samuel Cramer, who rejects La Fanfarlo when she offers her nude body to him, insisting that she put her Columbine costume back on, Frémy wants only Miss Topsy "dans la piste, Topsy seule, vêtue de rose, vêtue de noir, vêtue de bleu, souple et gracieuse" (86).

Miss Topsy understands, albeit instinctively, the nature of her hold on Frémy. Upon her return to the circus after her hiatus, Miss Topsy senses that her relationship with him can survive only if she can recreate her "total" circus persona:

> elle y mettrait deux fois son âme; elle s'efforcerait de paraître plus souple encore dans ses envolements, de si bien oublier son cheval qu'elle pût ressembler à une fée aérienne, capricieuse, voltigeant dans l'espace dont elle est souveraine comme un nuage, comme une fantaisie de poète. (140)

By sitting in the stands with Miss Topsy and engaging her in conversation, Frémy complicates the moment of communication during the execution of her number for both of them. Instead of being a mere acknowledgment of him as a spectator among many, she actively looks for his face, deliberately seeks to connect with his eyes, abstracts him from the "masse compacte, houleuse" that is the audience, and short-circuits her real-acrobat-playing-an-acrobat, leaving only the ordinary relation of real acrobat (Eva) to real spectator (Frémy) (43). It is the search for his face in the crowd that led to her fall in the ring: she experienced a physical, not an existential, vertigo. When she returns to the circus for rehearsal after her convalescence, she makes the additional error of asking for Frémy's emotional support. For his part, Frémy, too, errs in attending the rehearsal on which he senses that his own future depends. That the event is a rehearsal and not a performance signals that the already weakened circus persona "Miss Topsy" will be unable to create a "flash of freedom." They both fall, not into a semantic void, but into the real.

Even more than her male partner, the lady acrobat embodies a troubling hybridity: in performance, she is simultaneously and irresolvably male *and* female, strong *and* weak, corrupt *and* chaste, victimizer *and* victim, suspended between life *and* death. The lady acrobat who facilitates male liberation from the prison-house of the real is by necessity silent and inaccessible. In wanting to make the lady acrobat speak, these protagonists induce the self-fulfilling prophecy of the presumed emptiness of women's speech.

The Lady Acrobat Breaches Space and Time

For adolescents, the flash of liberty glimpsed while watching the lady acrobat in performance – a sensation often infused with the confusing desires of their own budding sexuality – makes them seek her out in an attempt to recreate, if not sustain indefinitely, the attraction's magical reality. In contrast to those aesthetes who would script her body in order to force it to convey meaning, adolescents ultimately understand and seek precisely the very lack of meaning that the lady acrobat promises. Like a fairy, she emerges into our reality "d'un autre espace, d'un autre univers" at the moment of her leap when she overcomes an impossible obstacle, and just as quickly disappears (Starobinski 139). The adolescent dreams of following her into that neutral space where violent slaps are also gentle caresses and an equestrienne is unproblematically both mother and lover.

Since playful mischief against narrative conventions and perceptual blurring are characteristics of the Decadent aesthetic, it is no wonder that some Decadent works and works that flirt with that aesthetic offer children as willing navigators of this ambiguous state. Rod's "Les Knie" (*Nouvelles romandes* 1890) and Jules Laforgue's *Stéphane Vassiliew* (1881) offer adolescents for whom the circus is a marvelous homeland to which they strive to return.[7] The lady acrobat figures prominently in their decision: she is mother, lover, and otherworldly being capable of executing the wonderous feat of returning the adolescent to a lost state of innocence and bliss.

For many adolescents, the conditions making possible a manipulation of and a breach in social-cultural signifying systems create the phenomenon that Huysmans's narrator in "Les Folies-Bergère en 1879" calls "tête-bêche, coup double" (18). Like Huysmans's narrator who finds himself transported to the port of Antwerp when the signifiers for every aspect of the trapeze act that he is watching (the clanging of cables, the verbal exchange of "all right," the sight of nets, shimmering costumes, physical flight, etc.) are shunted onto the signifieds of a harbor setting, the young protagonists of Rod's and Laforgue's tales use this portal to effect their own flight. The lady acrobat both literally and figuratively emerges as the vehicle facilitating the crossing over into an alternate space and time.

Édouard Rod: "Les Knie"

Édouard Rod's short story "Les Knie" tells of the arrival of a German traveling circus in a small Swiss town and describes the effect of that arrival on a local boy who has reached the critical age where he is receptive to circus magic.[8] The circus had been coming annually for some time, and while the boy's older friend Marius remembers the troupe, the boy has no recollection of them.

While some citizens often find the presence of a circus in their town disruptive to social order, others embrace the liberating potential of transgressive bodies that defy all natural (aerialists, wild animal tamers, contortionists) and social rules (misbehaving clowns). And some just like to ogle in this first glimpse of the female physique in flesh-colored tights and tight-fitting leotards, like Marius. The young narrator's experience is richer.

The townsfolk see the Knie as "pas des saltimbanques commes les autres, mais de très braves gens, tout à fait comme il faut" (198). The Knie widow is "très respectable" (199). One Knie daughter is "aussi distinguée que n'importe quelle demoiselle de la ville" (199). The Swiss townsfolk especially appreciate the troupe for their hard work and the pride that they take in their productions, echoes of the town's own work ethic. The Knies are fundamentally unlike the townsfolk, however. Like most traveling circuses, they put to good use the physical exhibition of their industriousness in the mounting and later dismantling of their tent, putting their bodies on display as a prelude to the marvelous abilities of those same bodies in the ring. The narrator describes the two Knie sons, Louis and Charles, as handsome and elegant, with one even possessing feminine features, traits that serve to enhance uncannily the contrast of their extraordinary physical strength as well as to imbue them with existential ambiguity. Living paradoxes, these dandies "maniaient des poutres comme des badines" (199).

These incongruities, to quote Carmeli, render the townsfolk's "own boundaries ambiguous" ("Performing" 197). The narrator of "Les Knie" embraces this liminal ambiguity, which fully materializes at the moment that he sees Louis and Edwige Knie performing a number dressed "en costumes bleu de ciel pailletés d'argent" (Rod 205). For the boy, "ce fut un enchantement" (205). In the unrelenting feverish state in which he finds himself during the Knies' three-week stay, he creates "une sorte de vie artificielle où je confondais les danseuses de corde, les Croisés et les Infidèles" of Torquato Tasso's *La Jérusalem délivrée*, and with the assistance of Marius, he lays siege to the circus tent, which had become the Holy City, and comes to the aid of Erminia/Edwige Knie (209).[9] What is significant in the boy's "vie artificielle" is the metonymical shift that facilitates the slipping from the categories of one register to those of another. The circus creates a rich sensory play of bizarre analogies, opening the semantic floodgates separating signifying registers, and permitting his favorite characters from Tasso to come alive. The bloody nose that he gets in a scuffle with the youngest Knie, for example, becomes Tancredi's wounds with Edwige Knie as Erminia tending to them (211–12).

A pivotal event occurs when the unnamed young narrator is present at what he perceives as a near accident. As Charles Knie prepares to walk along a rope stretched across the public square, the narrator remarks the pallor of his face. Both Charles and his family who look on seem to experience the anguish of "un danger réel, immédiat" as they must certainly recall their great-uncle, "le frère du fondateur de la dynastie, – qui s'était fracassé dans une chute affreuse" (214–15). Like the spectators watching Miss Jessica in Lorrain's "L'Acrobate," the narrator manufactures fear for the Knies: perhaps that very day will be the one on which Louis or Charles Knie, or both, die in a fall from the tightrope. He is also aware that, while the Knies may very well be afraid, aerialists often incorporate an "error" or failure into their number. During the evolutions preceding his brother's act, Charles "feignait adroitement de perdre l'équilibre," partially in an attempt to enhance the spectator's sense of his ability to overcome danger but primarily as proof, first, of the realness of the event and, then, of his unlikeness to ordinary humans (217; Carmeli 213). In that moment, Charles is impossibly both real person and stripped of his realness in the staging of an error.

The spectators in the square below believe, however, that they risk losing one of their own since Marius has the honor of being in the wheelbarrow that Louis Knie balances as he pushes it across the tightrope. Marius realizes every child's dream of figuring in a circus act only to make what we are made to believe is the near fatal error of looking over the edge of the wheelbarrow before the completion of the number. It is at this moment of redressing the "error" that desemantization manifests itself. The narrator undergoes feelings of ambivalence, defined by an intense anguish that he finds both painful *and* pleasurable: painful because he fears that his friend will fall; pleasurable because Edwige Knie strokes his hair and squeezes his hand as she supposedly "anxiously" watches her brother's efforts to correct the imbalance provoked by Marius. The narrator's psyche finds itself suspended in this moment of heightened awareness in the marvelous makeshift circus space of the town square tower. A prolonged instant of powerful emotions pulls him in two impossibly different directions (intense anxiety and awakened desire).

Accordingly, when the Knie leave town to continue their tour in Italy, he wistfully "pensait aux pays lointains, aux pays inconnus, aux pays merveilleux où les bons saltimbanques dresseraient leurs tentes et tendraient la grande corde ..." (223). He promises himself as well that upon their return the following year, he will join them.

Jules Laforgue: *Stéphane Vassiliew*

Jules Laforgue's novella *Stéphane Vassiliew* is the story of an eleven-year-old boy of Russian descent who arrives as a new student at a boarding school in Tarbes and who dies there five years later after a failed attempt to actually follow a circus to Toulouse.[10] Having gone with his school to the circus, he is dazzled by the performance of the Hungarian equestrienne Wilma, a girl with orange skin and dark, bottomless eyes, a crown of tinkling sequins, and copper earrings and anklets that are like 100 tiny mirrors.

Laforgue drew upon literary sources in the development of his characters, as notes Mireille Dottin-Orsini, an action that one could easily interpret as representative of a young writer still in the grips of powerful precursors as he tries to find his style and his own idiosyncratic themes. Among them was Goncourt's *Les Frères Zemganno*. His Stéphane recalls nominally the Bohemian mother of the acrobatic brothers, Stépanida, but Laforgue endowed the acrobat Wilma with her dark and mysterious nature as well (Dottin-Orsini 16–18). Perhaps more tellingly regarding the influential literary intertexts in the novella, Dottin-Orsini finds, too, that the characters prefigure some of the mythic figures and recurring themes in Laforgue's *Moralités imaginaires* (1887). Stéphane anticipates that work's Hamlet, whose crushing boredom he shares.[11] His Wilma possesses the seductive talents of Gustave Flaubert's Salomé in *Hérodias* (1877), with the latter's intoxicating contortions becoming Wilma's sensually powerful transposition of Hungarian folk dance into equestrian acrobatics. Stéphane's delicate and often injured feet follow not so subtly in the etymological shadow of Oedipus, whose name means "swollen foot," making the novella also an origin story (Dottin-Orsini 18–19). The intensity of the emotions that stir Stéphane at the sound of the Magyar music – ostensibly reminiscent of his boyhood and homeland – becomes an oedipal tale of reuniting with his absent mother, for whom he will call out before he dies at the novella's conclusion.

Accompanying these literary precursors is the semi-autobiographical experience of the young writer himself, who suffered during his own years in boarding school in Tarbes, and who, like Stéphane, went to the circus with his fellow boarders or else drew upon his own subsequent avid patronage of the entertainment. This was an event whose arrival most certainly woke him "de sa léthargie" and perhaps opened him to "les mystères de la femme," as it does his Stéphane (Dottin-Orsini 18–19). More important, however, it was the beacon showing the path to a manipulation of language (and imagery) that would be "plus clownesque" and infinitely more original (*Œuvres* I: 821).

Laforgue's tale is much more than an attempt to weave the dominant figures of his period's imaginary into his tale as part of a literary apprenticeship, however. In light of what he would do with the figure of Pierrot in his poems and in the pantomime *Pierrot fumiste* (1882), and with Hamlet and Salomé among the handful of "legends" in his *Moralités légendaires*, these figures are equally part and parcel of his method of capturing aesthetically their timelessness through circus desemantization. While the doubling which Laforgue's protagonist and troubling equestrienne assume can reflect the faltering steps of a literary apprentice, setting the narrative turning point in a circus and around a circus acrobat equally suggests a writer trying his hands at replicating the way in which the acrobat forces apart signifiers from signifieds. The singularizing traits of his Wilma seem to refract like light hitting the spangles of her costume as she rides around the ring: she is circus equestrienne, but she is also dangerously seductive Salomé *and* nurturing mother. Correspondingly, Stéphane is a boy on the brink of manhood *and* a young boy crying for a maternal touch. He is aristocratic in his physique and luxuries, but wild and bohemian by temperament and, according to the narrator, past lifestyle.

On school walks in fields, he would sit apart from the others, lost in nostalgic dreams of the nomadic past with which the narrator endows him, recalling "les marches au matin dans la rosée et le soleil, les haltes aux heures lourdes de midi, les campements par les nuits scintillantes ou paisiblement innondées de clair de lune, la vie errante, la vie libre!" (37–38). One has difficulty reconciling the frail boy that the narrator describes with the one whose younger years were perhaps spent in a robust ambulatory existence. Yet the inconsistencies suggest a boy who has been ejected from another space and time, one that he confuses with that foggy vapor into which the Hanlons disappeared in Villiers's fantastic tribute, and one to which he seeks to return. He finds a reprieve from the monotony of boarding school life and perhaps even a semblance of a return in the summer when he wanders the fields alone, losing himself "dans l'oubli de la fatigue et parfois, aux heures lourdes, dans un vague état de non-être" (53). In a bleeding of his own being into the natural life surrounding him, "son être s'éteignait, se dispersait à travers la nature" and "il rêvait qu'il s'éparpillait dans le bruissement infini des feuillages" (57). How long he remained in this state is impossible to determine because "il n'y avait plus d'heures" (57).

The use of the imperfect tense throughout the novella communicates effectively both the mind-numbing routine of a child's life in a boarding school and the suspended state of his summer reveries. This was perhaps a deliberate reversal of the use of the imperfect in Goncourt's *Les Frères Zemganno.* Goncourt made the imperfect do the work of compressing the time between the past and the present in order to reunite with his brother. In an unusual use of the perfect tense, Laforgue appropriates the properties of the time of action described by Bouissac, employing it so as to effect Stéphane's momentary return to his lost paradise, and by extension his absent mother. It is this suspension of time, expressed through a flash use of the perfect tense, that Stéphane experiences in watching Wilma perform and which he seeks to replicate, and perhaps eternalize, in his decision to follow her and the circus to Toulouse.

In the beginning of her act, Wilma carries out "les exercices ordinaires, troua des cerceaux de papier frisé que lui tendait un clown grotesque, exécuta plusieurs sauts" (69). A breach in space and time erupts suddenly in an inexplicable pairing of routine equestrian acrobatics with a "danse magyare" that Wilma performs incredibly while straddling two horses (68). In a bizarre analogy in line with the "trip" to Antwerp by Huysmans's narrator in "Les Folies-Bergère en 1879," Wilma transports Stéphane to another place and time. She is both equestrienne executing acrobatic tricks and Hungarian folk dancer performing a brisk, energetic, indeed ecstatic dance. Laforgue enjoins the reader to address this incongruency through the peculiar practice of Hungarian folk dance. It is a traditional form celebrated paradoxically for how it involves an unusual degree of individuality and improvisation. This performance model, based on the interplay of convention and striking originality, anticipates Laforgue's application of it in his poetry and in his *Moralités légendaires.*

In a description of the execution of the impossible – a "danse troublante et compliquée" performed while Wilma is still working on two cantering horses – Stéphane falls into a state of "vertige délicieux" and at the end loses consciousness (70). His feverish state while in the school infirmary is one explanation for his "délire plein d'incohérences bizarres," but it also points to a boy still caught in the nebulous space of the equestrienne's breach between two different temporal and spatial domains (72). It is to that time and space that Stéphane strove to return when he ran away to the circus.

Not of this World

The poster designer Jules Chéret incorporated the cloudy breach into the backgrounds of depictions of lady aerialists in the early 1880s. While the posters depicting male acrobats from 1775 to 1885 share most features with their female colleagues – simple design, vibrant colors, sense of rapid motion, perceptual blurring of verticality and horizontality – it was in the representations of the latter that the artist most fully captured the visual sensation of being out of social time and space. If there is a gendered separation that begins in 1880 with the poster of Miss Lala at the Folies Bergère, it is probably due to Degas's *Miss Lala au Cirque Fernando*, which the artist would have seen at the fourth *Exposition des peintres impressionnistes* in 1879. The painting must have struck Chéret in similar ways that it did Huysmans, who commented that Degas's Miss Lala looks as if she is pulling down the circus dome with her famous iron jaw. Coming on the heels of Degas's painting, Chéret's poster for Miss Lala presents an aerialist not only suspended in the air, ostensibly caught at the high point of her number, but one who, in playing her body, derealizes it by harmonizing the shapes created by her arms and legs with the piece's graphic components. There was but one step to the conceptualization of the artist's trademark *chérette*, who, like the lady acrobat, "mostly appeared in a void" and whose "legs were freed from carrying her weight" such that she "hover[s] restlessly against the background" (Verhagen 103).[12]

In a self-portrait by Chéret from the late 1870s, one finds items that he chose to place strategically in the composition: a dead clown, a gun, and a skull. Having been unable to locate the painting, I am unable to comment on the status of the clown, whether it is indeed dead or whether, as the describer calls it, it is an "unusual variation on the theme of the sad clown" (Collins 206n246). The presence of a dead clown or just a sleeping Pierrot may suggest that Chéret, 15 percent of whose work was devoted to circus events, identified symbolically in some way with the clown, particularly the sad clown. The posters representing circus performers from the 1875 to 1885 period, however, suggest that he did not, a situation further confirmed by all the carefree clowns that often accompany his myriad radiant *chérettes* in the last decade of the century. Instead, his privileging of circus imagery points to a unique aesthetic that he drew from acrobatic performance, one in which the lady acrobat plays a pivotal role.

There have been several books and exhibitions in the past fifteen years celebrating and highlighting the prominence of acrobats and clowns in Chéret's posters. For some, these posters serve as documents of the historical place of the circus among late nineteenth-century entertainments. For others, they serve to show Chéret's influence and the influence of the modern poster in general on academic art, on Georges Seurat, in particular. None, however, explores the nature of Chéret's own relationship to acrobats and clowns, an association which exceeded the dictates of the commissions that he received.

Circus posters belong among the colored examples that Chéret saw first in London before setting up his printing business in Paris in 1866. This example, understood in conjunction with the rise of the entertainment, can in part explain why circus posters would become "l'une de ses spécialités" (Le Men and Bargiel 12). Another factor to consider is the reality of poster production: after all, Chéret's business was advertising, and clients play a big role in determining the content and often even the composition of a poster. Advertising for circuses and music-halls featuring acrobatic numbers would by necessity have called for representations of clowns and acrobats. The 1870s and 1880s correspond to Chéret's advertising campaigns for the Folies Bergère, the Hippodrome, and the Cirque d'Hiver. The circus proper (and the music-hall, which offered circus-related entertainments) represented a significant portion of his clientele; so, naturally he designed a lot of posters with clowns and acrobats. His variety show clients, whether circus or music-hall, were new to the modern poster as an advertising medium, a practice that producers of commercial products were slow to adopt. While the entertainments were not new, there was no tradition to which Chéret's clients would have wished him to conform, giving him the latitude to develop his own professional inclinations as well as to explore his own personal style.

Chéret's professional proclivities took into account effective advertising methods, of which a great concern was poster legibility. The poster of the last half of the nineteenth century was primarily destined for the street and it needed to attract the attention of the passer-by. This imperative necessitated a movement away from superfluous or distracting detail, the use of attractive colors, and the compression of the illusion of depth toward a flatter plane, focusing on a dominant central or framing figure. We discern Chéret's novel approach to these entertainment commissions in the difference between posters advertising theatrical events, as in the one for Offenbach's *Orphée aux enfers* (1866) or the one for *La Biche au bois* (1866) and those for *Tertulia* (1868 or 1871) featuring the face of the mime Paul Legrand and for the burlesque troupe of Lydia Thompson in *Faust!* (1869). The posters for the theaters offer a plethora of details and more muted colors, whereas the ones for burlesque and pantomime are stripped of superfluous figures, offer vibrant colors, compress the space, and further flatten the figures on the paper (Figure 5.1).

The figures for both *Tertulia* and *Faust! Lydia Thompson* also represented an important step in the conception of Chéret's aesthetic. Performances by the mime Paul Legrand and the burlesquer Lydia Thompson created in the designer an experience that he sought to transpose graphically to his posters. Simplicity in design may have been dictated by a client's pocketbook, and it may also have been determined by the emerging standards of effective advertising, but these factors do not fully account for the evidence that Chéret tapped into the code of the marvelous world of circus and circus-related performance.

Baudelaire in "De l'essence du rire" and Carmeli have isolated the primary element of the aesthetic of acrobatics in vertigo. Vertigo comes in several forms. First, Baudelaire refers to the vertigo that is created during

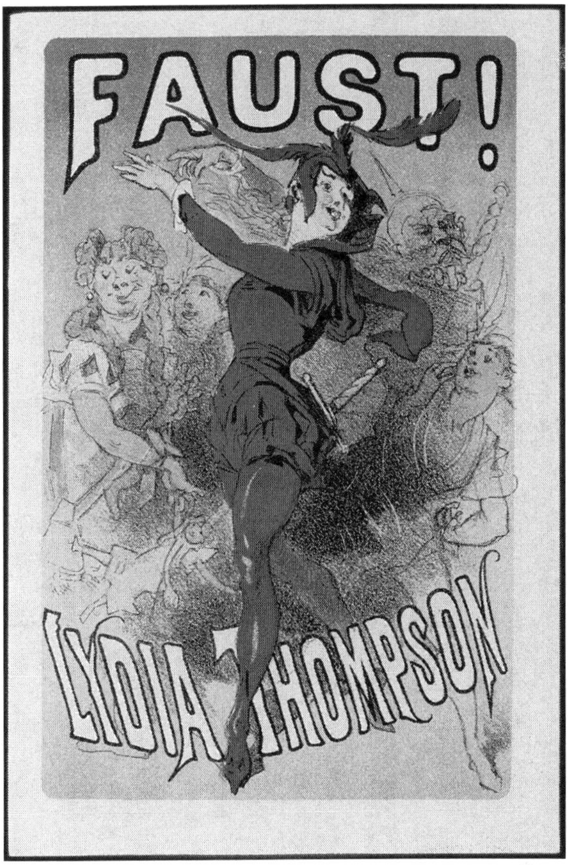

Figure 5.1 Jules Chéret, *Faust! Lydia Thompson.* Bibliothèque nationale de France, Paris.

an acrobatic pantomime performance. This is not the vertigo of the aerialist executing a leap, one associated with dizzying heights. For Baudelaire, it occurs rather at the moment that the fairy waves her wand. This sensation arises, as well, in his description of a decapitated pantomimist who retrieves his rolling head and pops it into his pocket. For Carmeli as well, vertigo is in essence a momentary existential crisis in which one's understanding and acceptance of the world is put into question by that which occurs within the space of the acrobat. This begins not with the wave of a fairy wand but with the wave of the acrobat's hand at the beginning and end of a number (202).

The graphic genesis of this vertigo manifested itself as early as the Chéret poster for the burlesquer Lydia Thompson, who introduced a variation on the burlesque format in the late 1860s. Before it became associated with striptease in the US, it was a variety show based on parody with song, pantomime, and acrobatics. In the parody component, Lydia Thompson and her blondes played the male roles, and in doing so disturbed viewers by the spectacle of their legs in flesh-colored tights and their incongruous impersonation of masculinity (Allen 25). This element she shared with lady acrobats, who also wore flesh-colored tights and executed feats of strength not deemed to be within the capacities of their bodies. The American critic Richard Grant White described Thompson's type of burlesque as "monstrous," but he was quick to add that he did not mean "wicked, disgusting, or hateful, but monstrously incongruous and unnatural" (qtd. in Allen 25). "Its system," he concluded, "is a defiance of system" (qtd. in Allen 25). In this respect, Thompson shared this "defiance of system" with the acrobatic clown, who, as Starobinski reminds us, "nie tous les systèmes d'affirmation préexistants" (143).

Lydia Thompson possessed an "awarishness," to use the term coined by Robert C. Allen in *Horrible Prettiness*, which feminist scholars rightly interpret as a confidence and appropriation of her sexuality, but which lends itself here to an apprehension of her status as a body double: she played a role *and* addressed her audience directly, erasing the distance that would have occurred had she lost herself in the role that she was playing, and as a consequence, instilled in her viewers a discomfort that prevented them from innocently ogling her very visibly feminine physique. In the poster, Chéret translated this "awarishness" in an incarnation of Thompson that seems to jump out at the viewer.

The concept of the body double is another component of the vertigo that Chéret drew from this entertainer and later more fully from acrobats and clowns. She was doubly a body double: first, her performance maintained both the distance of a persona (the role that she was playing) and the absence of distance (she brazenly broke the theatrical fourth wall by addressing the audience as herself), and, second, dressed like a man, she strutted across the stage with masculine swagger, and uttered or sang lines that convention associated with men. A contemporary of the critic White, William Dean Howells, wrote of burlesquers that "though they were not like men, [they] were in most things as unlike women, and seemed creatures of an alien sex, parodying both" (qtd. in Allen 25). In his inability to identify what they were, Howells resorted to the idea of an alien sex in which both sexes are irresolvably present, an echo of the trapezist Miss Urania in *À rebours* who becomes irreconcilably both male and female in flight.

Chéret was able to more graphically realize the body double in his lady acrobat posters in the early 1880s, an evolution influenced undoubtedly by a viewing of Degas's painting of Miss Lala. What distinguishes the acrobat from the burlesquer is the weightlessness of a body in flight, and it is this weightlessness that signals the third facet of Chéret's aesthetic vertigo. In these posters, Miss Lala (1880), Emma

Jutau (1880), and Leona Dare (1883) defy gravity. Chéret endows these figures with the illusion of movement through the air, de-emphasizing visual reference to the nature of their acts, minimizing Emma Jutau's cable, Miss Lala's trapeze bar, and Leona Dare's rope. Chéret was able to translate the experience of existential vertigo, body doubling, and weightlessness into a designing technique that Bradford Collins calls the "ambivalent approach," which he explains as offering a confusing reading (103–04). Two possible readings exist in the same space, with neither cancelling the other. Leona Dare, for example, is simultaneously perceived vertically and diagonally: she is vertically and visibly "locked between the words of her name," but she is also paradoxically "swinging from right to left," as is directionally evident in her flying hair (Collins 99) (Figures 5.2–5.4).

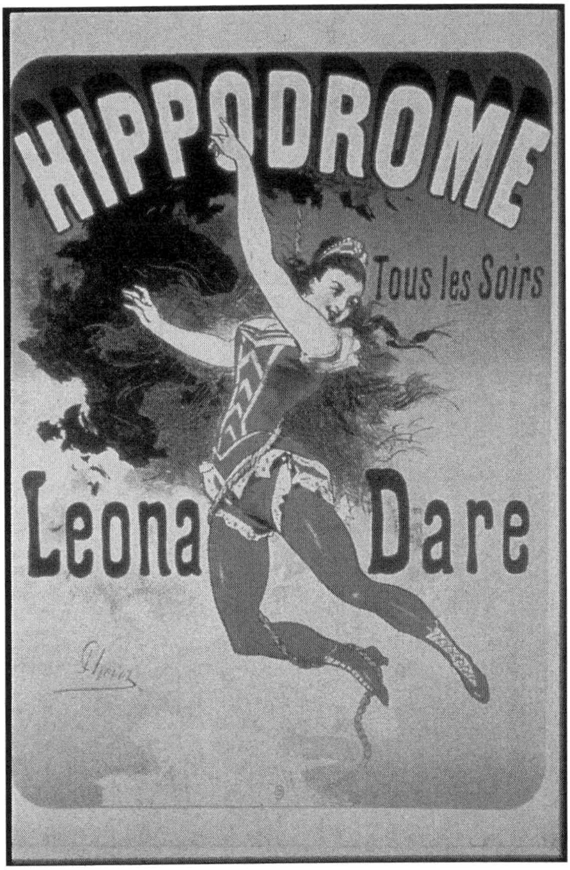

Figure 5.2 Jules Chéret, *Hippodrome. Tous les soirs. Léona Dare* (1883). Bibliothèque nationale de France, Paris.

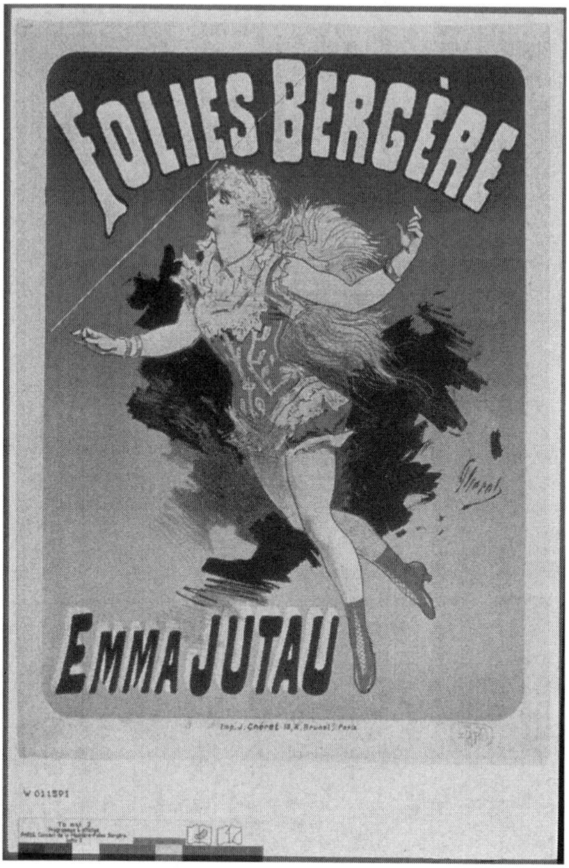

Figure 5.3 Jules Chéret, *Folies-Bergère. Emma Jutau* (1880). Bibliothèque nationale de France, Paris.

Such a conception of weightlessness in an indeterminate space is absent in the representation of male acrobats in Chéret's *L'Horloge. Les Frères Leopold* (1877). In his *L'Horloge. Champs-Elysées. Les Frères Leopold* (1877), while the brothers are not gravity bound, their gymnastic horizontal bar is, with the artist indicating clearly an apparatus firmly anchored to the floor. While a shapeless black chasm forms behind these acrobats in flight, it does not provoke the sensation that it is a portal through which the brothers will access another space and time dimension.[13] In Chéret's 1876 poster for *Cirque d'Hiver. L'Homme obus* as well, the white "ground" through which the human projectile flies is not a breach in space, but the billowing smoke produced by the

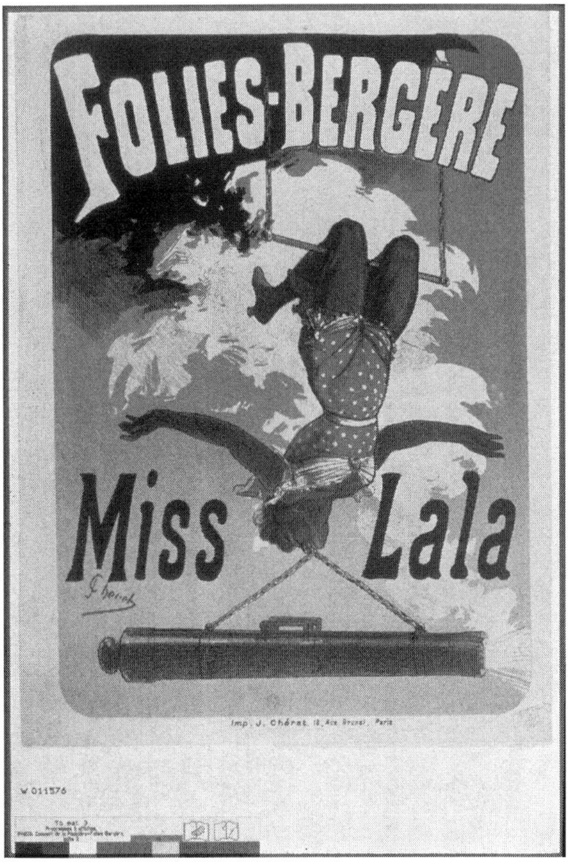

Figure 5.4 Jules Chéret, *Folies-Bergère, Miss Lala* (1880). Bibliothèque nationale de France, Paris.

cannon. This latter poster contextualizes the male acrobat in a circus filled with spectators, whose upturned heads encode and confirm the act as impossibly wondrous. This body is associated with "l'exploit physique": it accomplishes a feat that is "magique" and provokes intense fear and anxiety during the acrobatic number and wonderment and relief at its successful execution (Pencenat 83). While these are superior beings, we do not perceive them falling toward the viewer like astronauts upon re-entry.

In the posters depicting Miss Lala, Leona Dare, and Emma Jutau, one sees the lady acrobat at the moment that she emerges from the "ground" – that amorphous dark mass characterized by Chéret's shapeless brushwork. They have not yet completely penetrated into our realm, however much they seem to be springing toward us. They are still part of the dark unknown. The details that would allow us to perceive the acrobatic body as distinct from the amorphous mass do not fully materialize. Indeed, it becomes clear that they could just as easily be sucked back into the nebulous space from whence they come. Emma Jutau's costume is still part of the mass, Leona Dare's hair is still part of the lettering, and Miss Lala's arms seem to take form from out of the white smokiness. Weightlessness in empty space is integral to the viewer's apprehension of this moment: she is both corporeity and ethereality, a body double, a state incompletely expressed in the poster of Lydia Thompson and one fully realized with the lady aerialists (Figures 5.5–5.7).

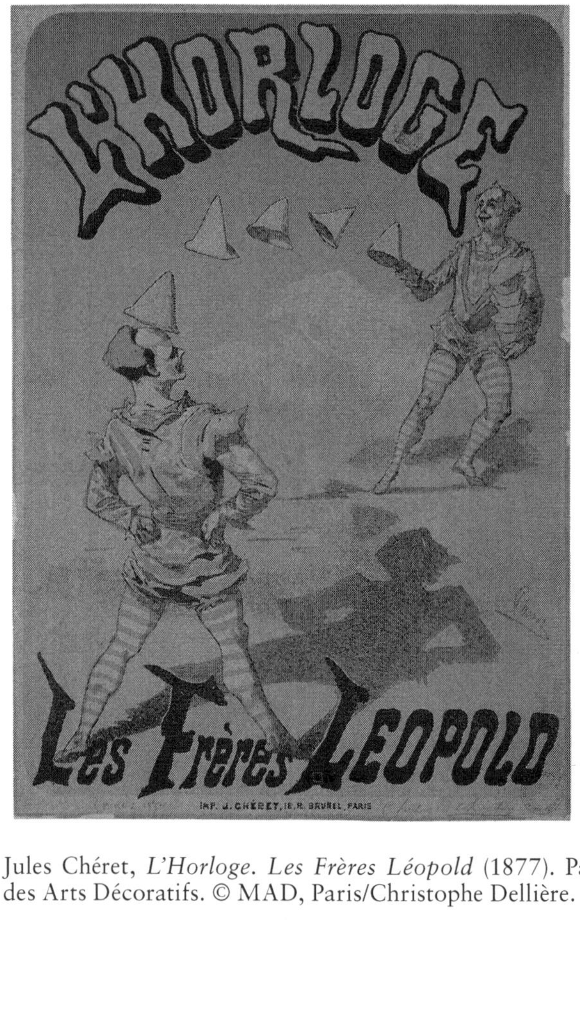

Figure 5.5 Jules Chéret, *L'Horloge. Les Frères Léopold* (1877). Paris, musée des Arts Décoratifs. © MAD, Paris/Christophe Dellière.

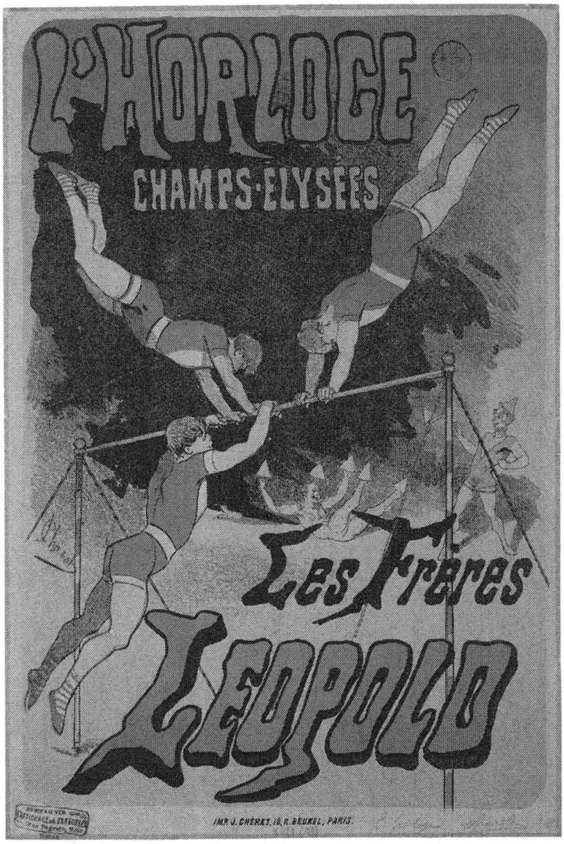

Figure 5.6 Jules Chéret, *L'Horloge. Champs-Elysées. Les Frères Léopold* (1877). Paris, musée des Arts Décoratifs. © MAD, Paris/Christophe Dellière.

While there were illustrators and designers that presented one or two of the elements found in Chéret's posters, none, however, tapped all of them – that element being the vertigo caused by a body double, ambivalent readings, and weightlessness. One designer, Émile Lévy, came very close with *Nouveau Cirque. Miss Géraldine* (n.d.). The rest of his and Charles Lévy's circus-related poster work, however, followed a conventional model of the depiction of an act. The vertigo represented in the bulk of these circus-related posters offers simply the graphic dramatization of a life in balance: a tamer faces a ferocious lion; the tightrope walker executes a backward flip; the trapezist leaps out, ostensibly into the hands of a catcher; a human cannonball is propelled into the air.

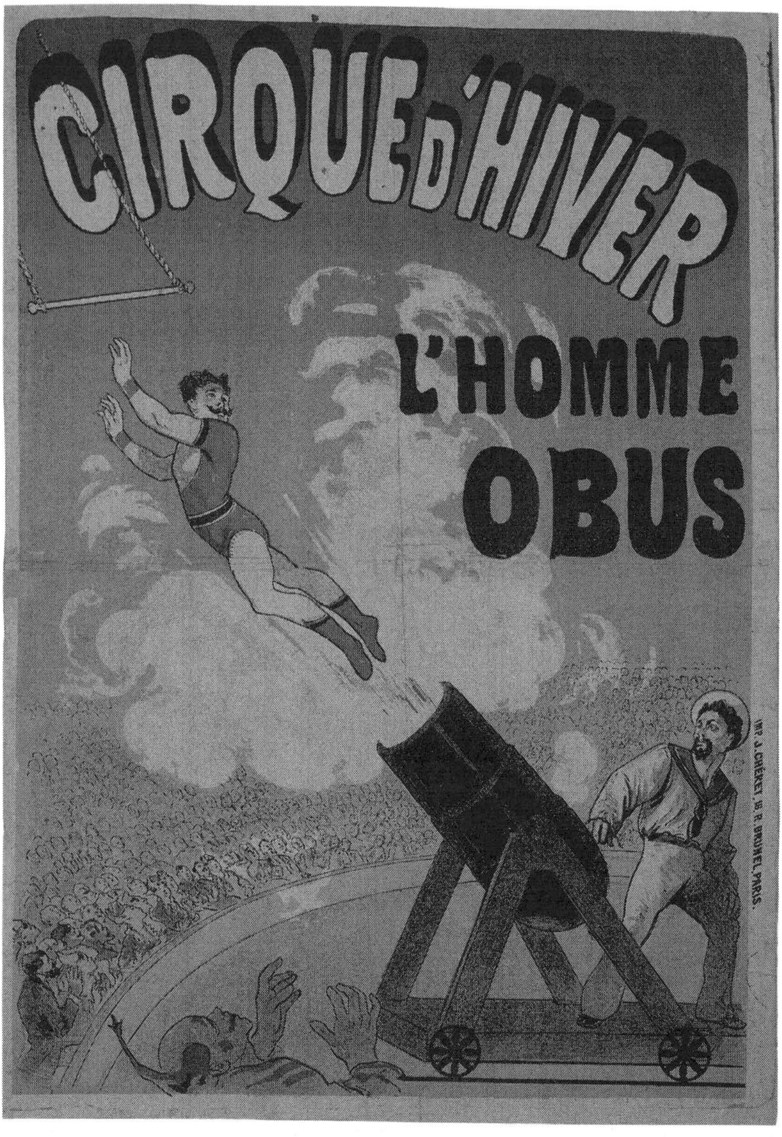

Figure 5.7 Jules Chéret, *Cirque d'Hiver. L'Homme obus* (1876). Paris, musée des Arts Décoratifs. © MAD, Paris/Christophe Dellière

Their lives could be over in one moment of inattention, one misstep, one miscalculation. That kind of poster represents either the successive stages of a number or its central breathtaking moment within the contextualized setting of the circus (Figure 5.8).

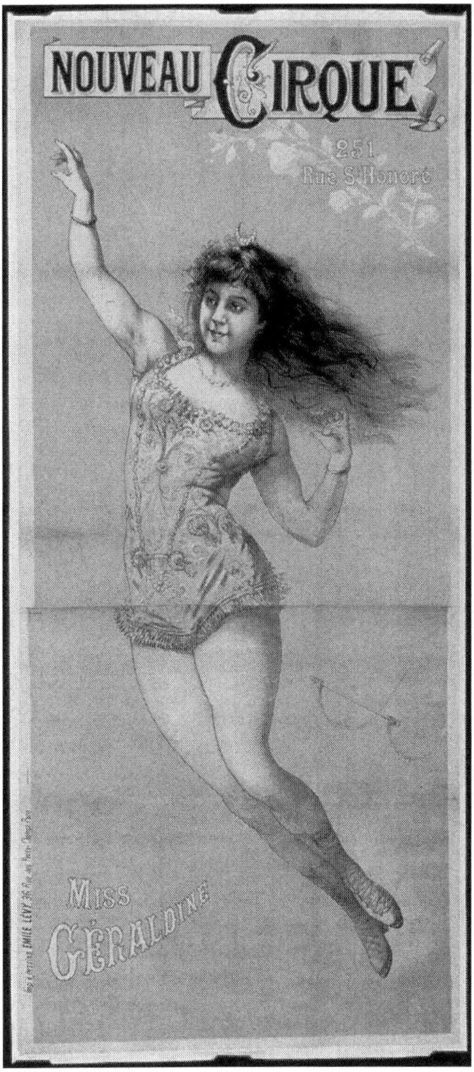

Figure 5.8 Émile Lévy, *Nouveau Cirque. Miss Géraldine*, (n.d.). Bibliothèque nationale de France, Paris.

The circus poster of the type inspired by Chéret, however, represents not a life-death contest, but the paradox of the lady acrobat, a paradox that he extended subsequently to all of his acrobats. Beginning in the 1880s, the *écuyère* and/or her horse jump into our realm, clowns tumble, and aerialists fly weightlessly into our space in these posters. Their bodies enter the frame with a leap as if emerging impossibly from another world. The most imaginative circus poster from the last quarter of the nineteenth century, one capturing and expressing the spirit of aesthetic exploration associated with the era's finest writers and artists, was by Jules Chéret. He tapped the circus's symbolic richness and its non-sense – that inconceivable co-presence of both performer and the body with which she is working – through her sudden appearance from an inchoate world.

Chéret was able to translate graphically, indeed, to encode visually and with great efficiency the system of circus performance, a template that lead to the evolution of his lady acrobat into the *chérette* as the defining figure of his posters in the 1890s. The *chérette* is the distillation of all the lady acrobats of the earlier posters – her weightless suspension, her seemingly vertiginous movement, her problematic identity and unreality, and her ethereal beauty in both face and body. Without the lady acrobats, there would never have been a *chérette*.

Notes

1 Many of Champsaur's characters float from one work to another. Lulu first appeared as a simple courtesan in his short story collection *L'Amant des danseuses* (1888); as a minor character in his first pantomime *Les Éreintés de la vie, pantomime en un acte* (1888), performed the same year at the amateur Cirque Molier; and as the title character of his second pantomime *Lulu, pantomime en un acte* (1888), also performed the same year at the Nouveau Cirque.

2 Champsaur liked to promote himself as the innovator of a modern aesthetic; he had, however, the reputation for the theft of ideas. In a May 22, 1889, article in *Le Moderniste illustré*, Julien Leclercq quotes Charles Cros's exhortation to his companions upon seeing Champsaur enter the brasserie where they were congregated: "Voici Champsaur, Messieurs, rentrons nos idées" (58). There is another version of this anecdote of which Émile Goudeau is the author: "Rentrons nos idées! Voilà Champsaur!" (24).

3 It is interesting to note that the page arrangement of Le Roux's interview with the Volta brothers in *Les Jeux du cirque* features one Jules Garnier illustration depicting a Volta in a handstand atop a horizontal bar and another of Miss Lala in a standing position, gripping a hanging rope. This pairing occurs on the same page where the Voltas compare the bodies of male and female acrobats ("ce poids de la vie, ce poids de l'amour que la femme porte dans ses flancs, l'homme le soutient sur ses épaules"), with their disparagement of women here playing out in the illustrations themselves: a Volta deploys the beauty of his upper body strength against a grounded Miss Lala, whose race is added to her already dismissed sex (199).

4 "L'Acrobate" figured in the series *Une Femme par jour* published in *L'Écho de Paris*. It appeared on December 15, 1890.

5 In a review of the novel, Léon Blum remarked on the strange balance that Kahn achieved in a story that is on the one hand "lucide, transparent, cristallin, mais qui s'envelope et s'embrume de légende et de rêve" (qtd. in Basch 490). He wonders, "Est-ce une aventure ou un songe?" (490).

6 The literal manipulation of social codes had very real percussions since the authorities often arrested Petit after his public strolls in the ether.

7 I discuss two other novels featuring children who dream of running away with the circus in Chapter 7: Octave Mirbeau's *Sébastien Roch* (1888) and *L'Abbé Jules* (1890).

8 The Knies are a real circus dynasty that began with Friedrich Knie, a doctor's son, in the first decade of the nineteenth century in Austria. He fell in love with an equestrienne for whom he abandoned his studies and, taking a liking to the profession, some time later formed his own circus. The Knie circus performed in Austria, Germany, and Switzerland. In 1886, Ludwig and Charles Knie applied for Swiss citizenship and the troupe eventually made Rapperswil, Switzerland, its home base.

9 Hedwig/Edwige Knie is apparently the invention of Rod, since no such name exists in the Knie lineage.

10 The manuscript for *Stéphane Vassiliew* was discovered among Paul Bourget's papers (Dottin-Orsini 18–19). It was dated 1881 when Laforgue was twenty-one. It was not published, however, until 1945.

11 Many of the characters in *Moralités légendaires* suffer from ennui. I discuss Laforgue's *Moralités légendaires* (1887) in Chapter 6.

12 Verhagen compares her to an actress, but she most fully captures the paradox of the lady acrobat, whom one contemporary critic described as having no soul (105). Lacking individuality corresponds to the derealization of the acrobat that occurs during performance (Carmeli 199).

13 Both Leopold brothers' posters offer, however, an alternate version of the irresolvable co-presence of graphic elements. In the poster of Leona Dare, there is a sense of lateral movement, but in this instance, it is not paired with vertical stasis but rather with depth. In the same space, one perceives movement in depth and lateral displacement. In addition, the same depth is undermined by the surface relation of the clown in back to the "plane of the letters" (Collins 103).

Works Cited

Allen, Robert. C. *Horrible Prettiness: Burlesque and American Culture.* Chapel Hill and London: U of North Carolina P, 1996.

Basch, Sophie. Introduction [to *Les Frères Zemganno* by Edmond de Goncourt]. *Romans de cirque.* Paris: Éditions Robert Laffont, 2002. 273–93.

Carmeli, Yoram. "Performing the 'Real' and the 'Impossible' in the British Traveling Circus." *Semiotica* 80.3 (1990): 193–220.

Champsaur, Félicien. *Dinah Samuel.* Ed. Jean de Palacio. Paris: Séguier, 1999.

———. *Miss America.* Paris: Ollendorff, 1885.

Collins, Bradford Ray, Jr. *Jules Chéret and the Nineteenth-Century Poster.* PhD Yale University, 1980.

Dottin-Orsini, Mireille. "Stéphane V. ou Œdipe au pensionnat." *Stéphane Vassiliew.* By Jules Laforgue. Ed. Mireille Dottin-Orsini. Toulouse: Éditions Ombres, 1996. 9–25.

Goudeau, Émile. *Dix ans de bohème/Émile Goudeau, suivi de Les Hirsutes/de Léo Trézenik.* Eds. Michel Golfier, Jean-Didier Wagneur, and Patrick Ramseyer. Seyssel: Champ Vallon, 2000.

Huysmans, Joris-Karl. *À rebours.* Ed. Marc Fumaroli. Paris: Gallimard, 1977.

———. *Croquis parisiens, À vau-l'eau, Un dilemme.* 3rd edition. Paris: Plon, 1908.

Jones, Louisa E. *Sad Clowns and Pale Pierrots: Literature and the Popular Comic Arts in 19th-Century France.* Lexington, KY: French Forum, 1984.

Laforgue, Jules. *Œuvres complètes. Tome Premier, 1860–1883.* Eds. Jean-Louis Debauve, Daniel Grojnowski, Pascal Pia, and Pierre-Olivier Walzer. 3 vols. Lausanne: L'Age d'Homme, 1986.

———. *Stéphane Vassiliew.* Ed. Mireille Dottin-Orsini. Toulouse: Éditions Ombres, 1996.

Leclercq, Julien. "Pompon-Champsaur." *Le Moderniste illustré: numéros 1 à 23, 6 avril 1889–28 septembre 1889.* Geneva: Slatkin Reprints, 1971.

Le Men, Ségolène, and Réjane Bargiel. "L'Art de Jules Chéret, côté rue et côté salon." *La Belle Époque de Jules Chéret: de l'affiche au décor.* Eds. Réjane Bargiel and Ségolène Le Men. Paris: Les Arts Décoratifs/BNF, 2010. 10–33.

Le Roux, Hugues. *Les Jeux du cirque et la vie foraine.* Paris: Plon, 1889.

Lorrain, Jean. "L'Acrobate." *Une femme par jour.* Ed. Michel Désbruères. Saint-Cyr-sur-Loire: Christian Perot, 1983. 202–03.

Pencenat, Corine. *Du Théâtre au cirque du monde: une dramaturgie du hasard dans les arts en action.* Paris: L'Harmattan, 2012.

Rod, Édouard. *La Chute de Miss Topsy.* Brussels: Kistemaeckers, 1882.

———. "Les Knie." *Nouvelles romandes.* Paris: Perrin, 1891. 195–223.

Tait, Peta. "Circus Bodies Defy the Risk of Falling." Keynote Address. Fabulous Risk Conference. University of Wollongong and Australian Canadian Studies Centre, 1–3 December 2006. 14 July 2019 <https://semioticon.com/virtuals/circus/circus%20bodies.pdf>.

Starobinski, Jean. *Portrait de l'artiste en saltimbanque.* Geneva: Editions d'Art Albert Skira, 1970.

Verhagen, Marcus. "The Poster in *Fin-de-Siècle* Paris: 'That Mobile and Degenerate Art'." *Cinema and the Invention of Modern Life.* Eds. Leo Charney and Vanessa Schwartz. Berkeley, London, Los Angeles: U of California P, 1995. 103–29.

6 The Poetics of Pantomime and Circus, Part I

Jules Laforgue

The two nineteenth-century writers most associated with the *funambule* are Théodore de Banville and Jules Laforgue. Both poets adapted the practices of pantomime clowning and circus acrobatics in a manipulation of verbal and stylistic desemantization. In *Odes funambulesques*, Banville made the joyful and rhythmic refrains of old poetic forms take on new relevance by mischievously celebrating otherwise minor and forgettable contemporary Parisian personalities. This was not mere parody, nor was Banville just clowning around. He masterfully neutralized and left in suspension the power, authority, and bite of these personages by detaching their distinctive traits and reattaching them to other objects and figures in the creation of surprisingly refreshing analogies. For his part, Laforgue eschewed commonplace metaphor in his recourse to the figures of legend, myth, and literature. He uncoupled the defining moral and physical attributes from their origin tales and playfully joined them to the familiar fates of other unrelated characters, characters seemingly protected from mischievous tampering, living in houses where their portraits and actions never evolve. In *Pierrot fumiste*, the space of desemantization is where the artist, writer, and poet tap into a sixth sense. He locates this sixth sense first and foremost in a *funambulesque* humor, whose disconcerting yet exhilarating play of opposites in words and imagery produces original analogies of a wholly modern stamp. *Pierrot fumiste* is the manifesto of this modern art; *Moralités légendaires* is its masterpiece.

Pierrot's Decadent Sense of Humor: *Pierrot Fumiste*

Jules Laforgue's *Pierrot fumiste* was not published until 1897, eleven years after his death. This version, based on the manuscript entrusted to Félix Fénéon, is perhaps not the definitive one that Laforgue was in the process of "[remettre] au net" at the same time as he was completing *Les Complaintes* (1885), as he wrote in a letter to his friend Charles Henry on July 27, 1883 (*Œuvres* I: 832). The first two "tableaux" are dialogued, whereas the last one remains in narrative form and contains a recapitulation of the first tableau. Laforgue composed his pantomime during the same period in which he was working on his poetry collection *Les Complaintes*, of which three feature Pierrot: "Complainte de Lord Pierrot" and "Autre Complainte de Lord Pierrot," which are dialogues, and "Complainte des Noces de Pierrot," whose title more literally describes the pantomime's context, if it does not capture its mechanics. The relation between the poems and the pantomime is particularly strong here, given that Laforgue often worked simultaneously in different genres. For example, the last of his three theatrical works, the *Concile féerique* (1886), has been called a dismantling of his unpublished/unfinished collection of poems, *Des fleurs de bonne volonté* (1890). Laforgue's pantomime can perhaps be viewed less as a dismantling than as a generic transposition. In one sense, this "multi-généricité" reflects the diversity of *l'expression fumiste* of the Chat noir, where "chansons, saynètes, monologues, plaisanteries, récits, poèmes se succèdent" (Dousteyssier-Khose 153). But it does not quite explain the temptation to work simultaneously in multiple genres. Jean Cocteau's classification of the genres in which he worked as "poésie, poésie de roman, poésie de théâtre, poésie critique, poésie graphique, poésie cinématographique" may offer another approach to Laforgue's generic explorations (237–38). For Cocteau, every genre was, in essence, a sub-genre of poetry. Much the same can be said of Laforgue: his *Concile féerique* is an example of *poésie-théâtre*, his *Pierrot fumiste* an example of *poésie-pantomime*, and his *Moralités légendaires* (1887) an example of *poésie-nouvelle*. That there is a strong echo effect uniting *Les Complaintes* and *Pierrot fumiste* reflects, therefore, not only that Laforgue was working on both during the same period, but also that these works sprang from the same lyrical preoccupations, which can be described as the quest for new rhythms and new meanings in the direct confrontation of different voices, tones, and registers within the same verse or sentence, depending on the genre at play. *Pierrot fumiste* participates fully in this practice.

The juxtaposition of voices, tones, and registers in the *Complaintes* and in *Pierrot fumiste* exceeds a playful toying with words and points to the greater aesthetic ambition of producing a new kind of meaning from non-sense. The Pierrot of "Complainte de Lord Pierrot" claims that "Le semblable, c'est le contraire," a state of contradiction reflective of the pantomime's method of operating (*Œuvres* II 585). Not quite the figure of soulful sensitivity often associated with fin-de-siècle Pierrot, Laforgue's looks back, in many respects, to earlier characterizations: he is a mass of emotional contrasts and inappropriate behavior. He stuns those around him with his unpredictable actions and reactions: he shouts when he should speak tenderly to his new bride (faulty *sens de la mesure*); he rubs his stomach as if having had a satisfied meal after kissing lovingly her feet (malfunctioning *sens de la perception*); he abandons a night full of sensual potential to devote his intellectual energies to reading the galley proofs of his historical study of mosaics, hardly so engaging a subject as to trump the heat of passion (energies used in the *mauvais sens*). Laforgue's Pierrot is a clown incapable of conducting himself according to accepted social norms: he buys the latest issue of the *Pornographe illustré* and makes the wedding party wait as he reads it; he runs to the flower market of la Madeleine to buy violets, flowers associated with funerals, not to offer them to his new wife, as one would expect from his spontaneous gesture, but to Madame Ventre, the paperwoman (faulty *sens des convenances*). He misinterprets a beggar's plea to have pity on a man with five young children ("j'ai cinq enfants en bas âge ...") as an insulting reference to his "impuissance notoire" (*faux sens*) (*Œuvres* I: 500). On his wedding night, Pierrot, seemingly in the throes of desire for his flesh-and-blood wife, sublimates that desire into a highly developed aesthetic sense, switching semantic registers and transforming her flesh into statuesque alabaster, and himself into a figure of Decadent impotence. The universe of sense and the senses, as the poet comments in "Complainte de Lord Pierrot," is definitely upside-down.

Laforgue's adoption of the persona of Pierrot in the poems of the *Complaintes* and *L'Imitation de Notre Dame de la lune* is generally described as a sad clown mask behind which the poet hides a profound ennui. Pierrot serves perhaps more as the embodiment of the poet's aesthetic practice. In a frequently quoted sentence from a letter to his sister, he expresses his confidence that he "possède ma langue d'une façon plus minutieuse, plus clownesque," a metaphorical reference to the nineteenth-century acrobatic clown's way of playing with cultural codes in an atmosphere of total creative freedom (*Œuvres* I: 821).[1] It also captures the impression of the clown as a mirthful figure in perpetual motion and mutation. Near the end of the same letter, Laforgue allies his poetic method with the clown's instability, with his inexplicable reversals, when he states that the "destinée d'un artiste est de s'enthousiasmer et se dégoûter d'idéaux succcssifs" (*Œuvres* I: 822). Pierrot, man of startling contrasts, is one minute a fool, in the next not a fool. He is servile and rebellious, indolent and frenetically active. He is a character for whom unpredictability and change are a way of life. His traits and actions are anchored in a tradition that is nevertheless in constant evolution, with each interpreter – Jean-Gaspard Deburau, his son Charles, Paul Legrand, Louis Rouffe, Séverin – adapting him to the contours of his own physique and personality. He is Pierrot dressed in both white (his traditional color and the one that he wears in *Pierrot fumiste*) and black (the color associated with the modern urban uniform). It is from a position of great respect for accepted forms and practices (pantomime, but by extension, poetry) that emerges a courteous irreverence that pushes those forms and practices to their absolute limits. While Pierrot may indeed be a persona – albeit, a protean persona – he is first and foremost an aesthetic mode of conduct. His aim is not to destroy, but to create "de l'original à tout prix" (*Œuvres* I: 821).

In his pantomime, Laforgue taps into the stock repertoire of Pierrot, the *lazzi,* which include physical jokes and gestures as well as banter. The reader of the pantomime brings a certain knowledge of and expectations concerning Pierrot's past actions, and hence a certain competence to the construction of his character and the actions in which he is involved. The actualization of the stereotype creates echoes with all the Pierrots of the reader's past experience, whether from the stage, the fairground, graphic arts, or advertising. Laforgue's use of the stereotype, in a much broader sense, is a template that both informs and mediates the entire dense network of literary relations and influences within the pantomime. This shortcut manner of communicating, prepared by the example of the *lazzi,* is the key for deciphering and appreciating Laforgue's pantomime.

Pierrot's Well-Known Impotence

Pierrot fumiste dips in the well of parodic intertextuality, a strategy of citation that recontextualizes and transforms the words of a precursor: he deliberately invokes words, lines, themes, and images from the works of other authors as well as from his own in the creation of a teeming constellation of associations, all the rich layers of which are sometimes exasperatingly difficult to follow, isolate, and decipher. Given the degree of knowledge and cultivation required for a reading of *Pierrot fumiste,* it is no wonder that Laforgue came to the realization that his theatrical piece was probably "injouable où à jouer entre amis" (*Œuvres* I: 810).

Scene III of the second tableau of *Pierrot fumiste* offers a rich and rewarding challenge to decoding. A brief summary of the pantomime is perhaps in order to contextualize the scene in question. It is Pierrot's wedding day to Colombinette at the Église de la Madeleine. On their wedding night, Colombinette's mother explains to her daughter what to expect during the course of the night. She tearfully attempts to steel her daughter to the act of nuptial consummation: "Mon pauv' chat! du courage!" (*Œuvres* I: 506). With the departure of the mother and the arrival of Pierrot in the bedroom, however, Colombinette has little to fear: there is a lot of kissing, but, alas, little lovemaking. Pierrot resists performing his husbandly duties, out of concern, he explains, for emotionally overwhelming his bride any further. But every night over the next few months passes in the same fashion, with Pierrot not fulfilling his conjugal duties. An exasperated Colombinette seeks the help of her mother, who first sends a doctor to look into any physical impediments, and when Pierrot refuses to cooperate, she and the doctor pursue a "procès en séparation" (*Œuvres* I: 512). Once again, Pierrot refuses to submit to a medical examination and, subsequently, he loses the case. On his last night as a husband, contrary to his custom, he brutally ravishes his soon-to-be ex-wife, packs his bags, and leaves on a train for Cairo, dancing in each train station along the way.

In the preceding scene, Pierrot has just torn himself away from a highly aestheticized admiration of the purity, the whiteness of Colombinette's skin, which he compares to traditional poetic equivalents of beauty in whiteness: "Lys! ivoire! satin! neige, épiderme de la femme aimée! Albâtre" (*Œuvres* I: 508). In this series of ideals of whiteness, reminiscent of so much nineteenth-century poetry (Gautier, Baudelaire, Leconte de Lisle, and Laforgue, himself) and as such bordering on cliché, Pierrot has ironically included the very thing to which he was comparing Colombinette's skin and using, as was his habit in his poetry, a not particularly poetic term: "épiderme de la femme aimée." With the inclusion of this term, Pierrot's stance as reverent admirer reverts to his role as prankster, throwing in the element that shocks because it is both discordant and unexpected. This is not just the voice of an adoring husband, but several voices (aesthetic and clinical) that contradict the putative pull of the carnal senses and condemn him to inaction: the reader hears the voice of the poet ("Lys," "ivoire," "satin," "neige," "albâtre"), the scientist/doctor ("épiderme de la femme aimé"), and the sculptor ("albâtre"). Accordingly, Pierrot turns away.

Scene III is a short monologue which could be subtitled "(Im)Potent Pierrot," since it neither answers the question in the first scene of the first *tableau* ("est-ce une allusion à mon impuissance notoire?") nor confirms the overpowering desire of which Pierrot seemed to be in the grips. To distract himself from the insistent call of the senses *and* from his inability to follow through caused by the proliferation of benumbing analytical perspectives, he proposes to recite Nicolas Boileau's *Ode sur la prise de Namur* (1693). The implication is that this ode in the pindaric style is the equivalent of a cold shower as well as being an ideal aid for putting one to sleep. It is tempting to think that Boileau's ode was simply one of those dry and uninspired pieces that were the core educational texts drummed into young students' minds, never forgotten, always mocked. This seems unlikely since history has treated it as generally a "détestable" use of the form (Vapereau 1499). Pierrot notes, however, that there may be "des vertus insoupçonnées" in this ode, with unexpected relevance to his present state (Laforgue, *Œuvres* I: 509). The reference to Boileau's ode opens onto other semantic registers that repeat in myriad ways the same message – that of Pierrot's "impuissance notoire." But first, the ode has a historical role that is important less in what it did for French poetry than in what it did for English parody of stiff French poetry, most notably Matthew Prior's "An English Ballad on the taking of Namur by the King of Great Britain" (1695). Laforgue taps this vein of parody to remind the reader of the piece's intent.

It is from here that it becomes increasingly clear that the pantomime is indeed "injouable" since this scene requires a rather particularized knowledge of literary history and has very little to do with theatrical performance. Boileau, Pierrot states, was a eunuch. The claim that Boileau was a eunuch is an allusion to the correspondence between Claude Brossette and Boileau, in which Brossette repeats a comment made by someone that this latter person attributed to Boileau, which he, Brossette, does not understand at all:

> Voici un bon mot qu'on vous attribue: mais comme la personne qui me l'a rapporté n'en sait pas les circonstances, il m'est impossible de le bien tourner si vous n'y mettez la main: *Bertaud n'auroit pas cru avoir obligation à M. Racine, pour l'avoir loué sur le Théâtre.* Vous compariez, dit-on, Bertaud, Musicien de chez le Roi, avec Atys: parce que Bertaud étoit Eunuque. Mais je ne vois pas bien encore toute la force de cette plaisanterie: et même je ne conçois pas pourquoi M. Racine se trouve placé là, puisque c'étoit M. Quinault qui avoit fait l'Opéra d'Atys. Tout cela, encore une fois, a besoin d'explication, car je n'y comprends rien. (*Correspondance* 254)

Laforgue seizes this bit of non-sense and puts it to sensible use in his pantomime. The economy of this reference within the pantomime is primarily to juxtapose the notion of impotence with Pierrot's reluctance to make love to his wife because she is too much like a work of art. In Brossette's letter, it is Bertaud, not Boileau, who was said to be a eunuch. And Quinault's opera *Atys* has as its subject the consort of the Cybele in Greek mythology whose priests were eunuchs and who mutilated/castrated himself out of love for her. These two references to impotence compel the reader to return to the very site of Boileau's ode – Namur and the 1692 battle – which carries potentially a third allusion to diminished virility, this time Laurence Sterne's *Tristram Shandy*, which features Uncle Toby, who injured his groin in the very same Siege of Namur and who has built a replica of the battle in his garden, which he shows to the Widow Wadman, who herself tries to find out the extent of Uncle Toby's injury before she agrees to marry him. Like the Widow Wadman, Colombinette "se perdait en conjonctures: Ne pouvait-il pas? quoi donc?" (Laforgue, *Œuvres* I: 511). The subtext of Pierrot's monologue is the repetition of castration and groin injuries, which repeatedly contradicts the theme of aesthetic sublimation in which Pierrot refuses to profane beauty. This subtext, which in essence begins in a deliberate misquote, itself based on a misunderstanding, implies that there is a hidden bit of information, namely a real physical impediment to Pierrot fulfilling his duties as a husband.

And yet the next series of references disclaims the putative reasons for Pierrot's abstention. Before launching into his recitation of Boileau's ode, Pierrot takes one more look at his sleeping beauty of a wife and, this time, rather than idealize her, dismisses her as being just like all other women, diverting his aesthetic examination of her to philosophical concerns. "Nous les [women] voyons toutes à travers les vieilles lunettes de la mère Maïa," claims Pierrot, invoking the Hindu mythological concept of maya (illusion), in which Laforgue substitutes ordinary old glasses for the veils of ignorance: the moment when one thinks one perceives reality/truth with one's senses, it has already vanished (*Œuvres* I: 509). As for the illusion to which Pierrot alludes, it destroys the reader's certainty that the preceding information points without a doubt to his impotence. The tangible reason for Pierrot's reluctance to consummate his marriage, revealed in a series of references beginning with Boileau's ode, is suddenly controverted.

The last section of the internal monologue subsequently becomes part of an associative train, first phonetic – the vowel in the last syllable of Maïa becomes phonetically Mayeux – then referential, most likely a reference to the hunchbacked character created by Traviès in 1832. Mayeux possessed all the flaws of the bourgeoisie under Louis-Philippe. He became a stock character for illustrators and caricaturists like Cham, Daumier, and Grandville, and entered so quickly the popular imagination – much like Frédérick Lemaitre's Robert Macaire – that he mutated into the two standard characters of the Carnaval de Paris known as "les deux Mayeux," a duality that mocks the preceding duality caused by the veil of maya. In moving from Hindu mythology (Maïa) to caricature (Mayeux), Laforgue brings Pierrot and the transgressive mechanics of farce back into play. The laughable and self-important Mayeux initiates another offshoot association that returns the meaning back to the ridiculously stuffy Boileau and his ode to the taking of Namur by Louis XIV, only to set off Pierrot's recollection of a train ride in Belgium with stops in Mons and the infamous Namur, reminding Pierrot of a terrific meal that he had on that trip. After all, Pierrot's desires as a stock character in the first half of the nineteenth century "turn more towards food than sex" (Jones 22).[2] Before the reader takes this version as the final interpretation, both of the strange workings of Pierrot's mind *and* of his reticence to bed his wife, he recalls another memorable event of this trip to complicate matters even further: "J'ai même eu à Namur une aventure ruisselante de croustillance, d'épatance" (Laforgue, *Œuvres* I: 509). This adventure ostensibly brings full circle the role of Namur, which served to explain Pierrot's reluctance to make love to his wife as the result of impotence, but instead presents a Pierrot as an eager eater *and* as virile in lovemaking.[3] The adventure is juicy ("ruisselante") – whether literally a meal or figuratively a dalliance with a woman – and deliciously crunchy or sexually naughty ("croustillante"). Lest the reader think that Pierrot will resolve the co-presence of the two meanings (impotence and virility), the monologue is finished off with a clown's somersault, a reminder that in the topsy-turvy world of pantomime two contradictory images can exist simultaneously in the same space.

Lord Pierrot in "Complainte de Lord Pierrot," "[j]ongl[e] avec les entités," much like the Pierrot of scene III. The stanza ends much like scene III, as well, with the paradoxical conclusion that "Le semblable, c'est le contraire" (Laforgue, *Œuvres* II: 585). Accordingly, if Lord "Pierrot s'agite," his action is irresolvably countered by passivity for "Tout le mène." Both Lord Pierrot and Pierrot *fumiste*, bundles of contradictions, prefigure Laforgue's Hamlet in the *Moralités légendaires*, who describes himself as an "homme d'action," but who is in reality, as Michele Hannoosh notes, a "parodic victim of the late nineteenth-century paralysis of will" (75). Like the Pierrot who ends a dreamlike reverie with a somersault out of scene III, Hamlet, who awaits the passing of Ophelia's funeral cortege in the cemetery, is roused from his thoughts, and his "premier mouvement de penseur" is to "singer à ravir le clown réveillé par un coup de mailloche à grosse caisse dans le dos" (*Œuvres* II: 392). The black-suited intellectual is inexplicably also a buffoon in a white blouse. Lord Pierrot and Pierrot *fumiste* dress in white, Laforgue's Hamlet in black, but the presence of white in his *univers pierrotique*, in his "univers … à l'envers," always invokes black and vice versa.

White Pierrot/Black Pierrot

Laforgue adopted the title of his pantomime from that of an illustration by Willette in *Le Chat noir* (March 18, 1882), in which Willette introduced his black-suited Pierrot in a silent comic strip (the journal's first) in six *tableaux*. Pierrot sits down to eat his dinner when the iconic black cat of the Chat noir steals his roast duck or chicken. Chasing after the cat with a shovel, Pierrot enters the next frame (stage left), swings in wild abandon, and accidentally flattens the head of an unsuspecting man, seated, smoking his pipe, and reading the newspaper. As Pierrot continues in pursuit of the black cat (stage right), the stunned man is left holding the shovel. A maid enters with a tray of food (stage left), only to be woefully struck by her shovel-faced employer (Figure 6.1).

The wordless comic strip form was relatively new for the French in the early 1880s. Through the strips of Willette and Steinlen, "the Histoire sans paroles, became a trademark of the [Chat noir]," the publication of the *fumistes* until 1895 (Kunzle 5). With his hero's source in pantomime, Willette is able to quickly activate Pierrot's well-known traits and expand the range of his typical gestures and expressions to include contemporary ones. He also imbues his Pierrot with some *fumiste* ambiguity. He revives the physical slapstick that appealed to pantomime's popular audiences in the first part of the century with an appetite-driven, calamity-prone Pierrot, but the accidental victim of his shovel in the chain of violence is a figure belonging to the established order. David Kunzle identifies the man smoking a pipe as he reads the newspaper as perhaps Pierrot's landlord, but more precisely, the *fumiste* side of Pierrot's personality seems to attack a general category of persons, and not so inadvertently, namely a respectable and productive member of society, the bourgeois (201).

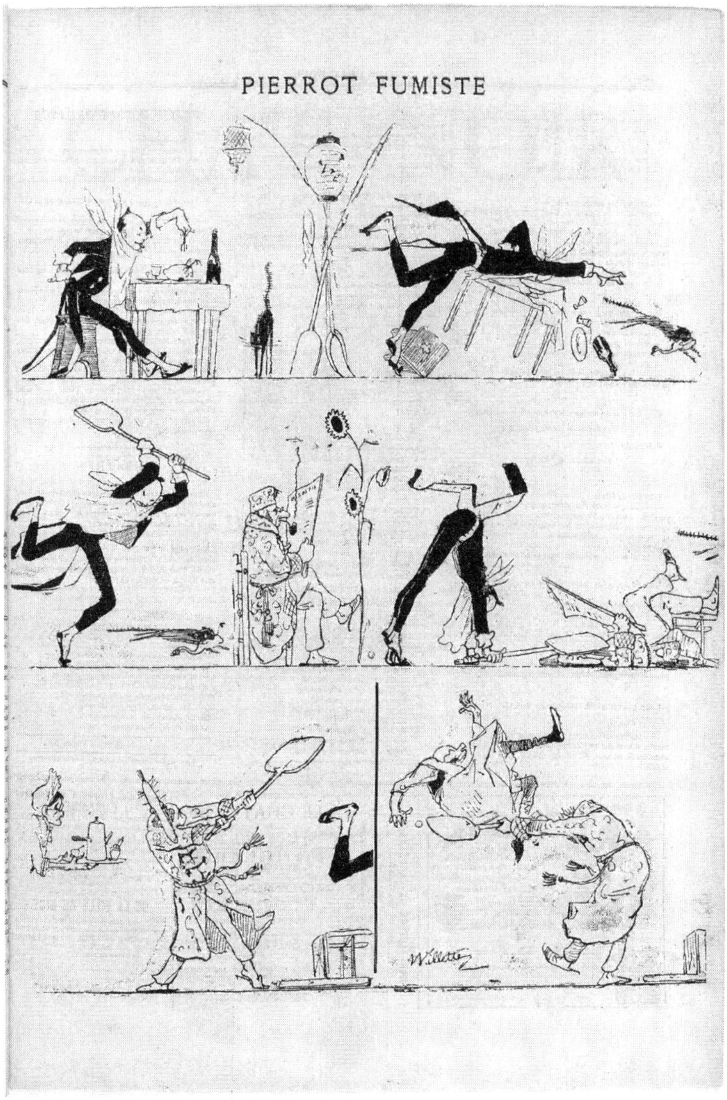

Figure 6.1 Willette, "Pierrot fumiste," *Le Chat noir* (25 March 1882). Bibliothèque nationale de France, Paris.

Like much illustration from the period, Willette's non-captioned, "silent," comic strips possessed their own narrative quality, stealing the ability to narrate from the written word. Kunzle describes the role of the viewer of the silent comic strip as one that encourages seeing over understanding, sensation over intellection: "You are meant to see, experience, empathize, rather than merely understand" (8). With *Pierrot fumiste*, Laforgue adopts not only the *fumiste* strategy of the *blague*, but more particularly the comic strip's (and, by extension, illustration's) ability to create an experience with no referent in real life. The image of the shovel-faced bourgeois, like the circus clown, defies all the rules governing life and survives on paper that which no flesh-and-blood human could. Laforgue followed Willette's lead by capitalizing on familiarity with the traits of his stock character to animate his topsy-turvy world, but more important, he brought to his pantomime "le vertige." Catherine Dousteyssier-Khose describes *fumistes* as "[c]es clowns et bouffons modernes [qui] vont cultiver le rire jusquà l'absurde, au vertige. Le rire fumiste est un rire essentiellement ambigu et brouillé qui hésite entre intégration et subversion de la ou des normes" (151). Laforgue's "vertige" is *fumiste*, but it is perhaps even more that about which Baudelaire spoke in "De l'essence du rire" (377). It is a different space and "une existence nouvelle" where extraordinary things happen, where a character's face is visibly flattened with a shovel (the comic strip page) and where clowns are struck by a volley of kicks, punches, and slaps, and paradoxically never retaliate in anger or vindictiveness (the circus ring and *commedia* pantomime).

Laforgue does not just appropriate Willette's comic strip's title, he puts it to use in the symbolic economy of his pantomime and engages its methods. But if Laforgue's Pierrot is *fumiste*, he is first *sceptique*. The spirited movement that one perceives in Willette's comic strip owes much to the poster designs of Jules Chéret, in particular his illustrations for Hennique and Huysmans's pantomime *Pierrot sceptique* from 1881. Motion is the signature trait of Chéret's illustrations of Pierrot, a trait for which he was celebrated. Laforgue was an early fan of *Pierrot sceptique* and would have been keenly aware of the stylistic resemblances between the two artists' visual interpretation of the stock figure. Like Chéret's Pierrot, Willette's is dressed in a form-fitting black suit. Like Chéret's Pierrot, Willette's is characterized by frantic movement and, in the first *tableau*, in the sowing of general mayhem. Willette and Chéret's graphic versions of Pierrot exude a sense of the delirious motion of billiard balls careening against others, and propelled by their own momentum, they thrust the other balls into motion as well. If the general idea of the associative references to two graphic artists was intended to lead the reader to Hennique and Huysmans's pantomime, Laforgue does not for all that abandon them once she arrives at that reference. In the co-presence of contradictory images and expressions, Laforgue seeks to sustain this seeming communicative instability in the same space. His Pierrot dresses in the traditional white that initially recalls the white costume of interpreters like Jean-Gaspard and Charles Deburau, Louis Rouffe, Paul Legrand, and Séverin. But in summoning to the reader's mind the images of Willette's and Chéret's black-suited Pierrot in the construction of his pantomimic universe, the Pierrot dressed in white continually invokes these two graphic precursors dressed in black (Figures 6.2 and 6.3).

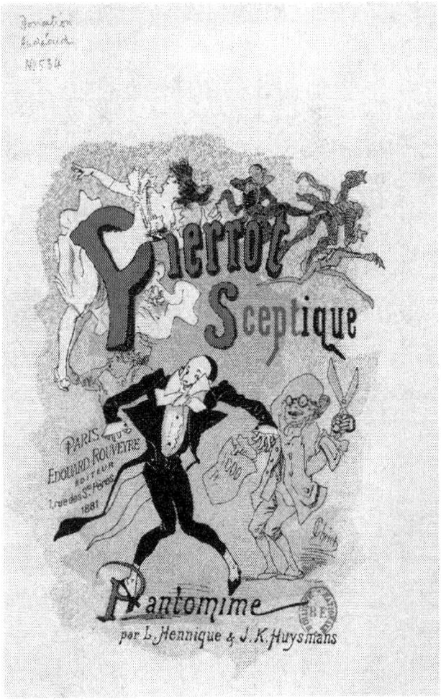

Figure 6.2 Jules Chéret, book cover. Léon Hennique and J. K. Huysmans, *Pierrot sceptique*. Paris: Édouard Rouveyre, 1881. Bibliothèque nationale de France, Paris.

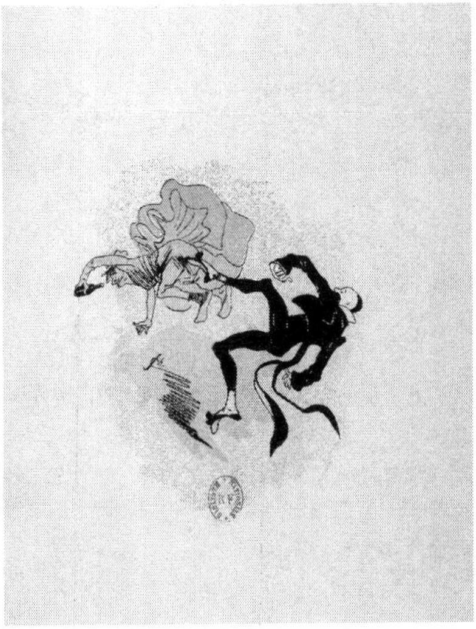

Figure 6.3 Jules Chéret. Léon Hennique and J. K. Huysmans, *Pierrot sceptique*. Paris: Édouard Rouveyre, 1881. Bibliothèque nationale de France, Paris.

Hennique and Huysmans's work operates doubly under the sign of black. The pantomime opens with the funeral wake of Mme Pierrot. Laforgue, whose pantomime opens with Pierrot and his new bride Colombinette leaving church, refers explicitly to the Huysmanian setting by having mortuary workers nailing up black wedding hangings that carry the newlyweds' initials; hearses await the party leaving the church; and the wedding party itself is either leaving for Watteau's Cythera for a celebration of the couple's love or for Baudelaire's where they would find "un pendu déjà mûr" being picked at by vultures (117). The event is both *fête galante* and funeral. This is an upside-down world in which Pierrot is both "poète très lyrique et boursier," where beggars are well off and where the clichéd honest poor are born of dishonest parents (Laforgue, *Œuvres* I: 499).

Pierrot's Sixth Sense

In her work on Laforgue's *Moralités légendaires*, Michele Hannoosh defines the author's parody as uniquely decadent in that it both mocks and reaffirms the conventions of Decadence. A similar strategy emerges in *Pierrot fumiste*. His ambition is less to destroy formidable predecessors (revered or reviled) and literary practices than to engage them in the creation of a new *sens* from *nonsens*. His written activation of pantomime's strategies and modes of conduct through prankish citation and nonsensical word play becomes the counterpart of the comic strip, the poster, and the caricature, resulting in verbal gestures, or graphic words, or even *gestes d'esprit*. This state, which exists only on paper, on the pantomime stage, or in the mind, recalls Baudelaire's description in "De l'essence du rire" of the vertigo created by the wave of a magic wand in a pantomime and the ushering in of a magical space where characters are badly beaten and then stand up as if nothing has happened, where a clown is beheaded and then gropes for his head to pop it into his excessively large pocket. It is a realm where words and images can co-exist with their opposites, where contradictions remain unresolved.

Laforgue embraces the confusion of meanings: Pierrot's repeated cooings to his bride, whom he calls endearingly "Colombinette de mes sens," make clear his deliberate inclusion in the same space of *sens* as meaning (generally indicative of the higher faculties of intellect, but here of the aesthetic) and *sens* as bodily sense (here, lustful pleasure). Roger Pearson suggests that the unresolved co-existence of two meanings in the same poetic space may point to an effort to access a sixth sense which closes the "gap between the sensual and the conceptual."[4] In his art criticism about genius, Laforgue seems to address the concept of a sixth sense in art (*Œuvres* II: 78–79). He identifies genius in whatever the medium precisely in the closure of a gap between the "sensual and the conceptual," but the sensual has a much larger scope than just the traditional five senses. It includes, first and foremost, a sense of humor but embraces as well a potentially endless list of "senses": the sense of meaning, the moral sense, good or bad sense, *faux-sens*, the sense of reality, of ridicule, of propriety, of direction, of entitlement, and more.

Circus Poetics: *Moralités légendaires*

Jules Laforgue's name and work most readily suggest the figure of Pierrot to those familiar with *Les Complaintes* and *L'Imitation de Notre Dame la Lune* (1886). Indeed, Philippe Bonnefis asserts that Pierrot is everywhere present in Laforgue's poetry and prose. "[Q]ue Pierrot soit ou non nommément mentionné," the reader invariably "stumbles over" the character – his "trébuchements," as Bonnefis puts it, deliberately capturing Pierrot's origins in those physical genres of pantomime and farce (74). In this light, Hamlet, another figure frequently associated with Laforgue, becomes merely another incarnation of Pierrot. If, as Bonnefis argues, "la moindre parole suppose ici qu'un Pierrot l'ait prononcée," what can the reader draw from Laforgue's claim in an 1883 letter to his sister that "je possède ma langue d'une façon plus minutieuse, plus clownesque" (Bonnefis 74; Laforgue, *Œuvres* I: 821)? In contrast to Bonnefis's emphasis on the spoken word (*parole*), on Pierrot's status as "celui qui aura dit ce qui est dit" (74), Laforgue's use of the word "langue" indicates the creation of his own system, which he defines specifically as "clownesque," not "pierrotique." In other words, he had appropriated the methods of the clown – the greater category to which Pierrot belongs – in the development of a new aesthetic style and approach. Nowhere is the presence of such a practice more evident than in Laforgue's *Moralités légendaires* (1887), in which one finds characters in an existential confusion caused by the simultaneous attribution of dissimilar traits. In an earlier version of the collection, Laforgue had once proposed as a title "Vieux canevas, âmes du jour," a title promising such an unusual joining of incompatible elements – the timeless and the present day – in the same textual space. If Laforgue abandoned that title, he did not abandon the approach that grounded it.

In *Les Complaintes*, Laforgue had already taken pleasure in fusing unlike words in the "couples impossibles" of his *mots-valise* (*Œuvres* II: 720). In his *Moralités légendaires*, he extends this practice beyond lexically improbable pairings to the existential conceptualization of his characters and their narratives. He does so in a space designated literally and figuratively for the purpose of such balancing acts: the circus ring. In their introduction to *Moralités légendaires*, Daniel Grojnowski and Henri Scepi describe the profusion of intertexts, the "collage" of quotes emanating from a multiplicity of competing sources, the disconcerting presence of vocabulary belonging to different, often non-literary, linguistic registers as operating in an "espace culturel" (12, 38). They refer, obviously, to a figurative space that houses all of the work's interacting components. Laforgue's *Moralités légendaires* also allows for the perception of a textual space not unlike that of the circus ring in the way that it promotes a "metacultural discourse" (Bouissac 8). At the circus, Bouissac notes, the elements constituting a shared community's cultural experience are "combined differently in the system of the circus than in the corresponding everyday instances" (8). Similarly, the shared cultural capital of the *Moralités légendaires* is, first, as the tales' titles attest, figures of legend and myth, and, second, figures from literature, music, art, and popular culture. Laforgue selects traits and actions associated with a figure's legend and brings them together in an unlikely pairing with those reminiscent of another narratively dissimilar figure, also drawn from the same cultural pool.

Some novellas in the *Moralités légendaires* possess only one or two circus-related adjectives ("funambules"), nouns ("cirque"), or expressions ("Jocrisse à la foire") (Laforgue 200, 101, 104). Others feature circus numbers (the clown act in "Salomé" and Persée's dressage routine "en amazone" within an invisible circus ring) (Laforgue, *Moralités* 170). Yet the appearance of circus vocabulary, even in the pieces that either were not included in the volume ("Les Deux Pigeons") or were perhaps lost or never developed ("Corinne au Cap Misène"), indicates that these words, expressions, and references are not to be passed over as mere reflections of Laforgue's continuing allegorical identification with the figure of the clown.[5] Laforgue selected the circus words, expressions, and references so as to connect the *nouvelles* and their parodic objective in as important and unexpected a fashion as the collection's theme of tales built "sur vieux canevas" (*Œuvres* II: 852). Like his Pierrot poems, which put into question "normal distinctions and classifications," Laforgue's circus references signal a borrowing from the strategies deployed by the acrobatic clown at his/her entrance into the circus ring, an entrance that Jean Starobinski has described as a "jeu insensé" that has the power to negate "tous les systèmes d'affirmation préexistants" (King 249; Starobinski 141, 143).[6]

The acrobatic clown is in his/her essence a figure capable of supporting seemingly unsustainable contradictions. Robert Storey describes Pierrot as possessing, on the one hand, "stupidity," "ingenuousness," "timidity," "gullibility," and "submissiveness," and, on the other hand, "poise," "audacity," "bluster," "superciliousness," "preoccupation," and "industry" (31). The paradox of the acrobatic clown's "jeu insensé" unfolds in a space – the circus ring – that encourages the playful liberation of signifiers from their conventionally accepted signifieds and their incongruous recombination with unexpected and unlikely partners. In Laforgue's *Moralités légendaires*, the circus clown or acrobat becomes a metonymy of the circus ring as an aesthetic and semantic space in which the impossible occurs, in which unexpected reversals happen and representational incompatibilities are sustained. In this respect, Laforgue went beyond identifying with the figure of the clown. He understood the fundamentally paradoxical nature of the acrobatic clown and his/her performance as simultaneously real and staged, and he adapted this paradox to the equally paradoxical blend of the parodic and the creative objectives of each *moralité*: he establishes an irreverent relation to a precursor and authoritative text, yet presents his own use of that material as original. Like Banville and Charles Baudelaire before him, he recognized in the peculiar dynamics of the circus performance the construction of a space outside of time in which semantic categories become fluid, and he endowed the textual space within his tales with similar capabilities.

Carmeli identifies the entrance of the acrobat into the circus ring as a blurring of real life and performance that unsettles spectators by its ambiguity. Emblematic of this ambiguity, contends Carmeli, is the moment in which the acrobat waves his/her hand to the audience: the waving is done by a person who establishes a real communication with the audience and goes on to execute a real acrobatic feat, but the real person is also a fictional construct who will perform a circus number that has been rigorously rehearsed (199). The feat takes place in real time, and yet the danger that heightens one's sense of the reality of the moment is complicated by its rehearsed nature. The hand wave is also the gesture that signals the successful completion of an acrobatic action, the final one of which is not to be confused with the bow of the actor before an audience (Carmeli 202). The actor's bow presents to the audience the real person who just minutes before played a character: actor and character never occupy the same existential space. The acrobat's hand wave, however, offers no such resolution because the real and the staged remain ambiguously present in the same person at the same moment.[7] While the acrobat's wave of the hand signals a transition into another state of being, the new state is neither clearly one nor clearly another but paradoxically double.

In his discussion of pantomime in the English and in the *commedia dell'arte* tradition in "De l'Essence du rire," Baudelaire defines the artist much in the same way that Carmeli does the acrobat: he must be an "être double," a being "à la fois soi et un autre" (378). This *dédoublement* occurs when the fairy "promène avec un geste mystérieux et plein d'autorité sa baguette dans les airs" (Baudelaire 377). At that very moment, Baudelaire adds, "le vertige est entré, le vertige circule dans l'air; on respire le vertige" (377). When "le vertige est entré," incompatible events take place. In this rarefied atmosphere, the clowns who wave their arms like windmills are perceived to be windmills. If they leap over each other with great ease, it is because they are no longer constrained by the limits of gravity. If they strike each other with great force, they do so without malice and visibly without suffering physical harm. Locating the state of vertigo in the waving of the fairy wand is appropriate in that, while the common experience of vertigo may involve some form of aerial acrobatics or balancing, vertigo is experienced by acrobats and spectators alike and it exists at all moments and in every corner of the ring during a performance. Laforgue's strategically placed circus vocabulary in the *Moralités légendaires* generally appears at the defining moment of his version of the legend or myth, but the presence of circus vertigo is palpable from beginning to end. Vertigo suspends the characters in an existential disequilibrium where they are simultaneously and irresolvably both themselves and another: Hamlet and Pierrot, Ruth and Jocrisse, Lohengrin and *écuyer de cirque*, Salomé and tightrope dancer, Persée and *écuyère de haute école*, Andromède and *écuyère de panneau*, Syrinx and acrobat, Pan and clown.

Hamlet and Pierrot

Starobinski sees in the choice of the circus as the source of nineteenth-century allegories of the artist the sign of the "déclin des sources traditionnelles d'inspiration" (14). He finds the rediscovery of Shakespeare in France, not in an environment of sacralized productions of his plays, but through the "bouffon" in the Shakespearean mold of early nineteenth-century popular entertainments, particularly those mixing "le merveilleux et l'acrobatie" (20). In his famous article "Shakespeare aux Funambules," Théophile Gautier did perhaps the most to rehabilitate the Shakespearean fool in his description of the Pierrot of the celebrated Théâtre des Funambules pantomimist, Jean-Gaspard Deburau, as "un autre Hamlet" (Starobinski 20). But Deburau was hardly the first acrobat in France to draw upon the Shakespearean fool. As he was only five years old in 1816, Gautier could not have known about the English acrobatic clown Little Wheal, famous for his sequential somersaults, who staged in France a circus pantomime called *Hamlet*, a production that was followed not long afterwards by *Hamlet, pantomime tragique en trois actes* at the Cirque Olympique (Forrest 23n8). Hamlet had arrived in France through the circus entrance.

While Laforgue himself is often discussed as a Hamletic figure, his Hamlet from the *Moralités* owes much to the character's popular genealogy in nineteenth-century France, with Laforgue's own earlier (uncompleted and unpublished) contribution being his *Pierrot fumiste*.[8] If Laforgue's Hamlet is a decadent hero unable to stir himself into action, this trait owes as much to the Pierrot of farce as it does to Shakespeare's conception of him.

The first paragraph of the introductory tale, "Hamlet, ou les suites de la piété filiale," presents to the reader the young prince who, when looking out the window of his tower, could "faire des ronds dans l'eau, dans l'eau, autant dire dans le ciel" (Laforgue, *Moralités* 59). Grojnowski and Scepi interpret the last words "dans le ciel" as a correction of "dans l'eau," with Laforgue deliberately reorienting the glance of this man lost in his thoughts as he moves from the contemplation of lowly water to the lofty sky as if toward "un idéal improbable" (220n2). But, as Michele Hannoosh notes, this opening sentence also marks the space as that of the clown Pierrot by being an autocitation of Laforgue's poem "Locutions des Pierrots, XVI" from *L'Imitation de Notre-Dame la Lune* (*Œuvres* I: 241n12).

> Je ne suis qu'un viveur lunaire
> Qui fait des ronds dans les bassins,
> Et cela, sans autre dessein
> Que devenir un légendaire. (*Œuvres* II: 97)

In the topsy-turvy space of the *moralité*, it is difficult to distinguish between the water and the sky. This ambiguity finds an echo in the blurring of interior and exterior in the dozen landscapes of the Jutland peninsula covering the walls of Hamlet's tower suite: they reproduce the very views just outside his windows.

There are two implicit hypotexts to the indeterminate atmosphere that Laforgue creates in these opening pages of the tale: Banville's comments on his "Le Saut du tremplin" (*Odes funambulesques*), in which the acrobat leaps ever higher into the "gouffre d'en haut," and Baudelaire's appropriately titled "Le Gouffre," for whose narrator "tout est abîme" ("en haut" as well as "en bas") and whose mind is "toujours du vertige hanté" (Banville 225; Baudelaire 88). With "Hamlet," Laforgue introduces the dichotomy of the two abysses that define the destinies of all of the tales' heroes and heroines.

The moment of what can be described as circus "vertige" occurs in "Hamlet" at the cemetery in between the burials of Polonius and Ophélie when Hamlet achieves the dual state described by Baudelaire. He learns from one of the gravediggers that he is the half brother of Yorick, the court jester, and son of the same gypsy fortune-teller mother. He is Shakespeare's Hamlet, whose tale will end in his death, but he is also clown, and accordingly, when the second gravedigger announces the arrival of Ophélie's funeral cortege, he finds himself fighting against the impulse to "singer à ravir le clown réveillé, par un coup de mailloche à grosse caisse" (*Moralités* 77). Due to this doubling effect, Hamlet's famous monologue addressed to the skull of Yorick becomes a rambling, incoherent soliloquy on the meaning of life and death. Hamlet's clown reflex announces a "moment de vide," to borrow the expression that Grojnowski and Scepi used to describe the incompatibility between what is expected and what actually happens in the tale (49). It is a moment of non-sense. The double nature of the space itself – it is both stage and real world – is maintained up to the end as Hamlet and Kate prepare to run away to Paris. Hamlet stops at the cemetery on the pretext of picking "une simple fleur en papier" for Kate, an appropriate gift from a clown (*Moralités* 87). It is here too, however, that Laërtes stabs Hamlet in the heart with, as Laforgue makes clear, "un poignard vrai" (88).

The ending of the tale in Hamlet's inevitable death returns the reader to the double abysses posed in the opening pages. Here, the "gouffre" toward which Shakespeare's Hamlet aspires is that "d'en haut" but that toward which Hamlet the clown is dragged is that "d'en bas."

Ruth and Jocrisse

An earlier version of the second *moralité*, "Le Miracle des roses," describes the landscape surrounding the tale's spa town as "un cirque de collines boisées" (Laforgue, *Œuvres* II: 523n1). While this "cirque" describes a hollow carved by glacial erosion into the hillside, the word does double duty by marking the geological arena as a circus space as well. This interpretation is supported by the subsequent description of the waltz heard in the Casino in the second paragraph: "L'air – avec l'effet en sourdine – de l'équilibriste sur la tête au trapeze" (*Œuvres* II: 534n1). The musical reference would have worked to extend the context of the tale's principal hypotext (Franz Liszt's oratorio *Die Legende von der heiligen Elisabeth* [1865]) and to establish the space as one defined by vertigo – that ingredient through which the acrobat becomes him/herself and another, and that force that is, according to Roger Caillois, "linked to the desire of disorder and destruction" (qtd. in Carmeli 206). If Laforgue eliminated the word "cirque" and the reference to the music accompanying the tightrope walker in the final version, he found a more efficient means for creating the tale's vertiginous spaces in which the heroine, Ruth, perceives the manifestation of miracles, the first occurring at a bullfighting ring in Biarritz, the second during the procession of the Holy Sacrament in the spa town.

In Biarritz, the word "cirque" describes the bullfighting ring at which Ruth sits in the governor's box, the spectator of a particularly gory *corrida* near the end of which several horses lie disemboweled (Laforgue, *Moralités* 101). This ring is most certainly that of a modern circus, a popular entertainment space in which, in this instance, an animal acts in a way contrary to its nature.[9] At the circus, a spectator can expect to witness unexpected animal behavior: "a horse makes a fool of his trainer; a tiger rides an elephant (supposedly incompatible animals, predators and prey, or irreconcilable enemies are presented in immediate conjunction); an elephant uses the telephone, plays music or, like man, eats dinner at a table" (Bouissac 8). Laforgue's reference to a "cirque" here is not a metaphor. He marks this space as that of the circus, and accordingly, the fearsome bull, visibly communicating with the spectators, points its neck toward Ruth to identify her as the true cause of the carnage, a gesture at which she faints.

Vertigo emerges on two levels in this scene, first, literally in Ruth's fainting spell and, second, in the semantic confusion that results from the bull's action, which is misinterpreted by Ruth as having overarching meaning. The signifying instability created by the bull's unexpected behavior – the truly extraordinary event – permits for the transformation of Ruth into Lady Macbeth and of her fainting spell mutterings into Lady Macbeth's sleepwalking revelations.

The subsequent and titular "miracle" takes place in the spa town during the procession of the Holy Sacrament. Figuring in the pathetic band following the procession, marchers are "clarinettes de Jocrisse à la foire" (Laforgue, *Moralités* 104). Jocrisse, a spiritual cousin of Pierrot, works here not merely as a metaphor to denigrate the procession and its participants, but also to prepare the vertiginous space ushered in by the farce character. Through the presence of Jocrisse, the procession also becomes a *parade de foire*, the circus parade's poorer fairground cousin. With this seemingly descriptive appraisal, the conditions for a second fainting spell are in place as well as for a loosening of constraints on the heroine's identity. Ruth returns as the Lady Macbeth of Shakespeare's sleepwalking scene, but the gap that opens up in this space also permits for the perception of Ruth as another Félicité, a reference to Gustave Flaubert's *Un coeur simple* (1877). Félicité passes away while listening to the celebration of the Holy Sacrament, the apotheosis of which is her vision of a giant parrot taking her up to heaven. Ruth does not die following her hallucination, but her melodramatic perception of a miracle is just as ridiculous. While Ruth's hallucination points to the tragic in the Shakespearean manner, the spirit of tragedy is seriously undermined by her equally palpable comic presence as another Félicité.

Lohengrin and Écuyer de cirque

While the third tale, "Lohengrin, fils de Parsifal," contains no initial circus references, it is in the context established by the other tales that the reader can infer that this Knight of the Swan, unlike his medieval counterpart who travels by a swan-drawn boat, is an aerialist whose "true kingdom [is] the sky" (Hannoosh 129). Lohengrin recalls, as did Hamlet, Laforgue's Pierrot in *Pierrot fumiste* in his refusal on his wedding night to consummate his marriage with his very willing wife. As with the preceding tales, the space necessary for the emergence of narrative incompatibilities occurs specifically, however, through circus-related vocabulary. In "Lohengrin, fils de Parsifal," this happens in the second part, which takes place at the Villa-Nuptiale where the newly wedded couple, Lohengrin and Elsa, is to spend a week. Lohengrin notes that the hedges lining the pathways leading to the villa are "féeriques," and the narrator equally draws the reader's attention to the conditions of the atmosphere by describing the entrance as possessing an "enchantement polaire" (Laforgue, *Moralités* 121).[10] The hedges form the border of a space that is not merely descriptively magical or otherworldly; it is the space of a *féerie*, an entertainment like the one characterized by Baudelaire in "De l'essence du rire" as appearing with the wave of a fairy wand and existing "sur la frontière du merveilleux" (377).[11] As in "Le Miracle des roses," "cirque" performs a double service, indicating both a geological and a particular kind of entertainement space:

> Mais, c'était, en effet, des cascades qu'ils entendaient, un *cirque* d'éternelles cascades autour d'un bassin dont l'eau, profonde d'un pied à peine et translucide, livrait aux *féeries* lunaires les scintillants micas de son fond de sable pur. (122, emphasis mine)

On a semantic level, the enchanted space eliminates the normal constraints on meaning in the humorous *mots-valise* that Elsa employs in her attempt to coax Lohengrin into lovemaking: "pompes voluptiales" (*volupté* and *nuptiales*), "pubéreuses" (*puberté* and *tubéreuses*), "ennuiverselles" (*ennui* and *universelles*), "expériences nervicides" (*nerfs* and -cide, a suffix indicating the killing of something), "nuits martyriséennes" (*martyrisées* and *élyséennes*), and "massacrilège-moi" (*massacrer* and *sacrilège*) (126–27).[12] These *mots-valise* function as graphic echoes of the union, but not fusion, of disparate persons or elements in the same space and time of the tales. As Yvan Leclerc remarks regarding Laforgue's use of *mots-valise* in his verse, "Il importe à Laforgue que les deux mots accouplés restent distincts dans la lettre et le son" (34). However much conjoined, their meanings never fuse, leaving their dual nature intact.

The Elsa who pairs incompatible words undergoes a *dédoublement* triggered by her swanlike neck, the trait that had recommended her to Lohengrin from the opening section (Laforgue, *Moralités* 118). The suggestion that Elsa differs from the swan of myth is made when Lohengrin caresses her neck and stops a moment at her Adam's apple, asking what it is. As Hannoosh, Grojnowski, and Scepi have noted, Elsa's Adam's apple leads to a play on words that suggests that Elsa is a temptress Eve and as such poses a threat to Lohengrin's purity. But that Adam's apple also suggests a reversal of gender roles, with the swanlike Elsa as a defiling water bird from another myth: Leda. Elsa's incompatibly double nature is that of woman, destined by her body to "l'esclavage des parturitions," *and* that of Zeus/swan as seducer from whom a feminized Lohengrin must flee (127).[13]

Like the other heroines of the tales, Elsa's physical appearance is androgynous: she is "maigre, toutes en lignes dures et gauches"; she has "le buste droit sans honte de ses deux seins si peu joufflus qu'elle pourrait les cacher sous des soucoupes" (Laforgue, *Moralités* 122). With the reference to her Adam's apple, these features shift her gender toward the masculine, a transition reminiscent of des Esseintes's appreciation of Miss Urania, the trapezist in J. K. Huysmans's *À rebours*. By virtue of the degree of Miss Urania's strength and dexterity and the distance relative to the spectator, des Esseintes has difficulty determining her gender since the markers change constantly. Through her initial gestures, she is visibly female, but as she continues her number, the female trapezist glides through a momentary androgynous middle stage on her way to becoming "complètement un homme" (Huysmans 134).

To help Lohengrin escape the threat to his immaculacy, his fluffy white pillow metamorphoses into his trusty swan/steed. The moment of *vertige*, however, is not this transformation, but rather the ensuing impossibly double nature with which Laforgue endows the pair of Lohengrin and swan/steed. In Wagner's opera (the tale's hypotext), a dove eventually replaces the pure swan. In the *moralité*, the swan is both innocent companion *and* Zeus/the eagle as abductor of Ganymede in Greek mythology. Indeed, the virginal Lohengrin incongruously begs his swan not to help him escape but rather to kidnap him according to the myth ("ravis-moi, pauvre Ganymède") (Laforgue, *Moralités* 128). If his stated objective is to return to his father, Parsifal, and to a "liberté méditative" unsullied by a woman's presence (the "gouffre d'en haut"), the myth of Ganymede also dictates that he go to the equivalent of Mount Olympus to become the object of the immortals' erotic desire (129). That he finds himself in conditions under which he is *à la fois* himself and another is stressed by the narrator's reference to the smashing of the window by a "cyclone de féerie lunaire," an allusion to the magical space that makes such incongruous pairings possible (129).

Hannoosh has suggested that Lohengrin's ascent into the skies identifies this aerialist with Saint Julien l'Hospitalier of Flaubert's novella, a hypotext that supports Laforgue's parodic re-creation (*Moralités* 131). But if, as Laforgue's narrator claims, poets celebrate the ascent of Lohengrin as a "petite fête de l'Assomption," the text explicitly equates the bodily ascension of Lohengrin with that of the Virgin Mary into Heaven. As such, the reference reactivates the earlier reversal of gender roles initiated with the image of Elsa as Zeus/the seducing swan and Lohengrin as Leda (129).[14] With the designation of Lohengrin's ascent as an Assumption, the *clownesque* objective (a pairing of incompatibles) is realized: Lohengrin is Ganymede *and* the Virgin Mary. As a virgin, he is the object of veneration of poets and is destined for the "gouffre d'en haut," but as Ganymede, he is also the object of their erotic desire and therefore dragged into the "gouffre d'en bas."[15]

Salomé and Tightrope Walker

In "Salomé," a state of vertigo announces itself in the second section when the Tetrarch and the Princes du Nord arrive at the aquarium on their tour of the palace. The narrator offers a description as detailed and exotic as that by Flaubert in his *Hérodias*, one of the primary hypotexts of the tale, but he also identifies that space as one in which animals act in ways incompatible with accepted notions of their capabilities: "des cirques de gradins basaltiques où des crabes d'une obtuse et tâtonnante bonne humeur d'après-dîner s'empêtrent en couples avec de petits yeux rigoleurs de pince-sans-rire" (Laforgue, *Moralités* 140). Here, once again, "cirque" is both corrie *and* circus. In its capacity as circus arena, the Aquarium's crabs not only comport themselves in an uncustomarily humanlike fashion, they also possess what a deadpan look never has: laughing eyes.

The tale's next circus space appears at the banquet in the third section. As Hannoosh notes, in describing the venue as "un bariolé vélarium," Laforgue transforms "the palatial hall of all the Salomé representations into a [circus] tent" (*Moralités* 144, 161). This circus tent is not just that from Antiquity, as is confirmed when the narrator refers to the space as "une scène d'Alcazar" (144). Like the Folies Bergère and the Olympia in the *fin de siècle*, the Alcazar was a music-hall that featured among other entertainments circus acts from aerialists to tightrope dancers and clowns. In the hall of Laforgue's tale, the guests are treated to a circus variety show beginning with a contortionist ("la jeune fille serpent"), then clown-musicians, followed by a clown pantomime, the flying trapeze, a figure skater who ends his routine by skating off the ice upside-down on his fingernails (a reference to Flaubert's Salomé who ends her dance in *Hérodias* by walking on her hands), a *tableau vivant* act, and ending with Salomé's long, incomprehensible speech.[16] Should one question why Salomé figures on the same bill as circus performers, Hannoosh reminds us that the portal of the Rouen cathedral depicts her as an "acrobat, dancing on her hands" (162).

The space has opened a breach in which Salomé becomes multiple, both herself and another. As Hannoosh notes, to deliver her speech, she adopts the pose of Salomé in Gustave Moreau's *L'Apparition* (1876) and *Salomé tatouée* (1871): "she balances on her toes and holds her arms outstretched" (163). She is also Flaubert's Salammbô in her dress, accessories, and actions. Laforgue counterbalances the solemn and sublime Flaubertian heroines, however, with Salomé – the floor acrobat (*acrobate au tapis*) and tightrope walker (*funambule*). She is a floor acrobat through the tumbling image of her on the tympanum of the Rouen cathedral and through the depiction of her dancing on her hands in Flaubert's *Hérodias*. She is a tightrope walker through Moreau's Salomé paintings: one can interpret her pose – standing on her toes and extending her arms – as the balancing stance of the *funambule*. Her double identity – she is both herself and acrobat – dooms her chant to the nonsensical, an echo of Hamlet's incomprehensible monologue in the cemetery.

Later, in her private chambers, Salomé's status remains double, invoking the Herodias of Heinrich Heine's epic poem *Atta Troll* (1847). Repeating the historical conflation of Herodias and her daughter in his own version of a parodic *moralité légendaire*, Heine mingles the Greek goddess Diana, the Celtic fairy Abunda, and the biblical Herodias in a ghoulishly comical hunt, in which the latter is damned to ride like an *écuyère de panneau*, juggling and kissing the head of John the Baptist.[17] The dichotomy between the "gouffre d'en haut" and the "gouffre d'en bas" re-emerges with Salomé, who aspires to the "gouffre d'en haut" like Banville's artist-clown (she is the "soeur de lait de la Voie Lactée" and wears a gown that is like the night, studded with diamonds that resemble the stars in the night sky) but falls like Laforgue's Hamlet – and like an unfortunate tightrope walker – into the "gouffre d'en bas" when she loses her balance and plummets as she tosses the Baptist's head over the railing into the sea far below (151).

Persée and *Écuyère de haute école;* Andromède and *Écuyère de panneau*

In "Persée et Andromède, ou le plus heureux des trois," the island on which Andromède lives with her guardian, the Dragon, is identified as a circus space in the second section when the heroine gambols in the ocean. As she lies on the sand, the waves unfolding on her, one in particular, "une volute cabrée," introduces a literal unharnessing of semantic registers (Laforgue, *Moralités* 163). Andromède runs into the water and executes acrobatic "sauts de carpe" in waves that take on the form, agency, and locomotion of horses. Andromède is transformed into an *écuyère de panneau* attempting to catch some of the liberty horses-waves by the mane-crest and mount them.

When, in accordance with the myth, Persée arrives on a hippogriff to rescue Andromède, he is an equestrian of classical dressage (*écuyer de haute école*). Composed of the body of a horse and the wings and head of an eagle, the hippogriff visually mirrors Laforgue's practice of impossible pairings with each body part joined but not combining with the others. Directing in masterful fashion his composite steed, Persée moves around in oval patterns, "passant et repassant devant elle," as if performing in a circus ring. Later, when he sets to slaying the sea monster, he encircles it "par des voltiges éblouissantes," narcissistically displaying his acrobatic skill in the ring (Laforgue, *Moralités* 170, 172). Persée mounts, however, like a woman, "en amazone" or sidesaddle, an incongruity that indicates that the vertiginous atmosphere associated with circus space is controverting expectations about behavior, and perhaps even about the outcome of the tale (170).[18] That the space is "sur la frontière du merveilleux" is evident in the narrator's references to "l'enchantement du lever de lune" and to "l'horizon magique" (173). It is a space in which Persée aspires to the heroic, but cuts simultaneously a comic figure as an *écuyer en travesti*.

Andromède, too, undergoes a doubling in this magical atmosphere, anxiously anticipated in an act of contemplation: the appreciation of the beauty of her own eyes reflected in the water of a shallow pond. The narrator relates her desire to look back into her own eyes as narcissistic ("que n'est-elle un autre, pour passer sa vie à les épier"), but her longing to realize the destiny of her *moralité* anticipates an ending in which she will become both herself and another, an aspiration that exceeds her patent narcissism ("on voit qu'elle ne sait pas où prendre son être, pour l'exorciser") (Laforgue, *Moralités* 162, 164).[19] She imagines herself in the tragic mode of her myth, tied to a rock, exposed to a devouring beast. But the atmosphere embraces as well the *féerie* (and fairy tales) and its happy endings. Hannoosh has rightly argued that the hypotext of his *féerie* is Mme Leprince de Beaumont's "La Belle et la Bête," in which Andromède is Belle and her sea monster guardian la Bête. In accordance with the fairy tale narrative, upon receiving his ward's loving kiss, the latter is magically resuscitated and transformed into a charming Prince. She is simultaneously Andromède *and* Belle, and the sea monster Cetus *and* la Bête.

Syrinx and Acrobat; Pan and Clown

The last tale, "Pan et la Syrinx, ou l'invention de la flûte à sept tuyaux," as Hannoosh and Grojnowski note, dramatizes an act of creation within the context of a dialogue about art and the Ideal (Hannoosh 195; Grojnowski 462). Although Hamlet writes a play and although, as Hannoosh contends, "Many of the characters of the *Moralités* are creators, notably poets," "Pan et la Syrinx" is the only tale that leads from the expression of an aesthetic ideal to its realization and is, in many respects, the narrative staging of Laforgue's creative practice throughout the collection (225n21). Laforgue, like Pan, who refers to himself as an "artiste," is able to create art that is new and original when two conditions are present: his language/flute will express "une miraculeuse gamme d'ère nouvelle" at the moment that his characters/Syrinx undergo(es) a *dédoublement* (Laforgue, *Moralités* 191, 199). In this light, its position as the last tale is justified.[20]

If "Pan et Syrinx" possesses few overt circus references, it is nevertheless made clear from one circus word – "funambules" – that appears near the end that Syrinx is an acrobat, that Arcadia is a circus space, and that this is the space of Laforguian artistic creation. Syrinx has a perfect body and, like her cousin Narcissus, possesses a self-sufficient corporeal beauty. Unlike her cousin who contemplates "son image immobile," her narcissism, as Starobinski notes regarding the lady acrobat, is that of her body in motion (44). According to the myth, hers is a body in flight from

Pan. Like Diane the goddess of the hunt whom she follows faithfully and the deity that Pan calls "un homme," she is androgynous (Laforgue, *Moralités* 201). So, too, is the lady acrobat. Like the lady acrobat, Syrinx appears delicate, a perception enhanced by the lightness and ease of her movements. This appearance is deceptive, however, as she possesses strong muscles, the result of her "habitude de la gymnastique" (190). By virtue of her physical and moral strength, she easily resists all efforts to subjugate her. This imperative comes not only from her association with the chaste Diane, but also from the acrobat's ethic of chastity in the pursuit of "sa propre perfection à travers la réussite de l'acte prodigieux qui met en valeur toutes les ressources de son corps" (Starobinski 44). In harmony with her constant cultivation of physical perfection, she asks Pan to compose a musical piece devoted to her beauty ("eh bien, chantez-moi d'abord ma beauté"), something that he will have difficulty doing until he invents the flute with seven reeds, the creative act defining the tale (Laforgue, *Moralités* 191). Her beauty, however, is first and foremost that of her entire body in motion, not simply that of her face.

The highlight of the chase occurs when Syrinx arrives at the river Ladon, a sort of border separating life and death, and leaps "dans le léger rideau des roseaux et se laisse aller dans les eaux" (Laforgue, *Moralités* 198). The seemingly metaphorical curtain is similar to that through which acrobats emerge into a circus ring. Starobinski notes that "Tout vrai clown surgit d'un autre espace, d'un autre univers" (139). Syrinx is the acrobat that passes back into that other space. Her leap is the same one identified by Starobinski as provoking a signifying "vide" and by Baudelaire as "le vertige" (Starobinski 141; Baudelaire 377).

Pan, like Persée's hippogriff, is a composite figure – half man, half goat – whose various parts retain their distinctiveness. Like Syrinx, he undergoes a doubling. He describes himself throughout the tale as a Caliban, the lustful beast-man from Shakespeare's *The Tempest*. After Syrinx's transformation, which results in the invention of his flute, Pan wonders "N'est-ce que l'histoire d'un soir d'été?" (Laforgue, *Moralités* 201). This question is most often understood as a reference to Stéphane Mallarmé's "L'Après-midi d'un faune" in which Pan muses, "Aimai-je un rêve?" (63). There is another intertext, however, with as strong an influence on Laforgue's text and on Pan's own *dédoublement*: Shakespeare's *A Midsummer Night's Dream*, in which Nick Bottom is the victim of a prank by the fairy Puck who transforms his head into that of a donkey, making him a beast-man like Pan.[21] Bottom's return to a wakeful state will result in a creative work, a silly ballet called "Bottomes Dreame." While Pan had chosen Caliban as his literary twin, it is clear that his narrative follows more closely that of Bottom.

The first notes of Pan's new flute are "des trilles funambules," identifying Syrinx's spirit (which becomes part of the flute) as that of an acrobat and the space as that of the circus ring's contradictions, incompatibilities, and incongruities (Laforgue, *Moralités* 200). Pan's first musical efforts are songs and invocations associated with the ceremony of the Eucharist ("introïts," "kyries," "offertoires") that become prayers ("oraisons"), then litanies, finally becoming songs to the Virgin Mary ("magnificats," "miserere," and "Stabat autour d'une crèche") (200). These pieces provoke Pan to wonder, "Est-ce l'Annonciation?," likening his creation to an Immaculate Conception (201). The position of the question "N'est-ce que l'histoire d'un soir d'été?" directly after "Est-ce l'Annonciation?" represents the two incompatible narratives that now characterize Pan (201). His invention possesses both the solemnity of the Annunciation *and* the levity of Bottom's play. The tale's vertiginous moment places Pan impossibly in both the "gouffre d'en haut" (the Annunciation) and the "gouffre d'en bas," the latter humorously and graphically implied by the word "bottom."

*

In the oft-quoted passage from an 1882 letter to Mme Mültzer, Laforgue wrote:

> Adorez-vous le cirque? Je viens d'y passer cinq soirées consécutives. Les clowns me paraissent arrivés à la vraie sagesse. Je devrais être clown, j'ai manqué ma destinée; c'est irrévocablement fini. (*Œuvres* I: 753)

Russell King cites this passage as evidence that the "modern circus clown quite probably provided the initial stimulus" in his subsequent literary-poetic identification with Pierrot (248). King sees Pierrot as the source of what he calls Laforgue's "ambivalent aesthetics" in both poetry (*Les Complaintes*) and prose (*Moralités légendaires*), a succinct expression for the poet's "curious fusion and juxtaposition of the serious and the esoteric" (248). King's term, however, suggests indecision or, at the very least, oscillation between two poles on Laforgue's part. Yet there is little hesitation in the letter to his sister from 1883, in which he claimed to have appropriated the clown's methods in his formulation of an innovative aesthetic style and approach.

The clown had not disappeared in a perceived progression leading to Pierrot as the dominant clown figure in his work. Indeed, in *Moralités légendaires*, something greater than a poetic association with a figure or a mask emerges: a *clownesque* poetics and practice. Each tale's characters experience a moment of existential limbo in which they are both themselves and another. This impossibly delicate balance occurs in a space designated as circus-like and at a moment that is the circus equivalent of being outside of time. The tales' characters are legendary, as the title claims, but their timelessness is also of another order. Hamlet, Ruth

(Saint Elizabeth of Thuringia), Lohengrin, Salomé, Persée, Andromède, Syrinx, and Pan cannot possibly be both tragic-heroic figures and clowns-acrobats in the same instant. The reader and the characters stumble into a real obstacle to continued narrative movement in the unthinkable image of that which cannot be and yet is. At the very moment of their unimaginable doubling, Laforgue's characters become suspended in a narrative non-time. No temporality from ordinary experience permits, for example, the simultaneous ascent of Lohengrin toward transcendent purity *and* his descent into carnal defilement. As at the circus where the emblematic wave of the acrobat's hand or the waving of the fairy's wand brings about the "seeing of that which does not and cannot take place, [the] bearing witness to that which is otherwise not witnessed, playfully touching the ontological foundations of the public's everyday life," Laforgue offers to his reader characters with paradoxical identities that can be sustained only within the magical space and time of the text (Carmeli 215).

Notes

1 May 14, 1883.
2 A good example of Pierrot's preference for victuals over lovemaking is Flaubert's 1847 *Pierrot au sérail* where, given the choice between enjoying the favors of a bevy of harem beauties and enjoying a copious buffet, Pierrot selects the delectable repast.
3 Pierrot evolves into an unrequited, not a lucky lover of Columbine in the middle of the nineteenth century.
4 Roger Pearson, "Poetry and the Sixth Sense," Society of Dix-Neuvièmistes conference, Limerick, Ireland, March 30, 2012.
5 In "Les Deux Pigeons," Juliette calls Gaspard "Vil clown," and in Laforgue's summary of "Corinne au Cap Misène," Lord Nelvil wears "bottes à l'écuyère" (*Moralités* 212; *Œuvres* II: 490, 505).
6 King offers "Pierrots, I" as an example of Laforgue's violation of conventional literary divisions in the fusing of genres and devices such as "wit, humour, irony, satire and parody" (249).
7 Carmeli sees the ambiguous status of the acrobat as the culmination of a series of ambiguous conditions, the one immediately preceding the entrance of the acrobat being the interior of the circus tent itself where the "boundaries of everyday reality, in which the labor of staging circus is carried out, and the realm staged in a circus show" are blurred (197). The blurring effect of the labor of staging the circus performance can occur on the stage as well. For example, in Huysmans's "Les Folies-Bergère en 1879", the mounting of the trapeze and net are integral to the shift in semantic register that transports him sensorially to the port of Antwerp.
8 As Albert Sonnenfeld notes, one of the earliest instances of Laforgue donning the Hamlet mask was in 1880 with "Excuse macabre" (92). The "obsession" continued until his death in 1887.
9 It is also a Roman circus arena in which spectators seek a sign from an official, ostensibly either a thumb up or down, to put an end to a brutal entertainment. And since there are threads linking the tales together, the "cirque" is also an echo of other rings, notably Hamlet and the echo of Pierrot, both of whom "[font] des ronds" in pools of water.

10 One must not confuse the state of enchantment produced by circus-related vocabulary with the one typically associated with Lohengrin who owes his power to a magic spell. Indeed, as scholars have noted, the latter spell has already been broken since Lohengrin reveals his name and origins from the outset of Laforgue's tale, contrary to the legend and opera in which he must keep this information secret. In Laforgue's tale, he is therefore receptive to an enchantment of another order.

11 Whether staged in a circus or in a boulevard theater, the *féerie* generally featured acrobatics and pantomime.

12 "Nuits martyriséennes" may be a play on Jean-Antoine Gleïzès's *Les Nuits elyséennes* (1800).

13 In "Complainte de Lord Pierrot" from *Les Complaintes*, Pierrot, dressed in white, plays the role of the swan to Léda ("En costume blanc, je ferai le cygne/Après nous le déluge, ô ma Léda!") (Laforgue, *Œuvres* I: 584). In this poem, Pierrot remarks: "Tiens! L'univers/Est à l'envers ..." (584). This is an upside-down world in which all conventional categories are blurred, where even gender identity is uncertain: "Brouillez les cartes, les dictionnaires, les sexes" and "Jonglons avec les entités" (585).

14 The visual association of Mary with swans would be justified by the myriad depictions of this holy event featuring angels with voluminous swanlike wings accompanying her upwards into the skies, a notable example being Peter Paul Rubens's *The Assumption of the Virgin Mary* (1626).

15 The Grand-Prêtre of the first section of the tale refers to the revered full moon as "L'Immaculée-Conception (la seule!)" and then proceeds to recite a parodied version of the "Hail Mary" prayer (Laforgue, *Moralités* 112). That the moon goddess is the only Immaculate Conception is belied by the knowledge that there are at least two others at the end of the tale: the Virgin Mary *and* Lohengrin.

16 The narrator describes the trapeze artists as having "ellipses presques sidérales," a quality that identifies them with the "gouffre d'en haut," an important contrast to Salomé's vertiginous fall at the end into the "gouffre d'en bas" (Laforgue, *Moralités* 145).

17 The *écuyère de panneau* performed acrobatics on horseback, for example, jumping through a series of paper hoops.

18 In an echo of the description of Persée, Laforgue anticipated dressing his Lord Nelvil of "Corinne au Cap Misène" in "bottes à l'écuyère," namely in the boots of an equestrienne, not in those of a male rider (*Œuvres* II: 490, 505).

19 In the "le" of "l'exorciser," it is generally assumed that she is referring to her "bobo" (Laforgue, *Moralités* 164). Existing in an independent sentence and paragraph, however, one might interpret the sentence as indicating that she seeks her own *dédoublement*, since it anticipates Syrinx in the final tale who defers temporarily her own dual destiny: "la jeune femme tient toujours et se jure d'escalader la colline prochaine, si peu que cela doive retarder la scission de sa vie en deux" (196). Existential doubling is that toward which Syrinx flies.

20 Édouard Dujardin had made "Persée et Andromède" the final tale of the collection. All recent editions, however, follow the order of composition established by Grojnowski.

21 The fairy queen, Titania, who has been enchanted by a potion that will make her fall in love with a vile creature upon awakening, sees Bottom with his ass's head and has a romantic interlude with him. In contrast, Syrinx is in full possession of her senses and powers and denies Pan the sensual encounter that he ardently seeks.

Works Cited

Banville, Théodore de. *Odes funambulesques, Occidentales, Idylles prussiennes.* Paris: Bibliothèque-Charpentier, 1905.
Baudelaire, Charles. *Œuvres complètes.* Ed. Marcel A. Ruff. Paris: Editions du Seuil, 1968.
Boileau-Despréaux, Nicolas, and Claude Brossette. *Correspondance entre Boileau Despréaux et Brossette, avocat au Parlement de Lyon.* Paris: Techener, 1858.
Bouissac, Paul. *Circus and Culture: A Semiotic Approach.* Bloomington & London: Indiana UP, 1976.
Carmeli, Yoram. "Performing the 'Real' and 'Impossible' in the British Traveling Circus." *Semiotica* 3.4 (1990): 193–220.
Cocteau, Jean. *Journal d'un inconnu.* Paris: Grasset, 1953.
Dousteyssier-Khose, Catherine. "Fumisme: le rire jaune du Chat Noir." *(Ab) normalities.* Eds. Catherine Dousteyssier-Khoze and Paul Durham Scott. Durham: Durham Modern Languages Series, 2001. 151–61.
Forrest, Jennifer. "Théodore de Banville and *Funambulesque* Aesthetics." *Dalhousie French Studies* 72 (2005): 17–31
Grojnowski, Daniel, and Henri Scepi. Présentation. *Œuvres complètes.* By Jules Laforgue. Eds. Daniel Grojnowski and Henri Scepi. Paris: Flammarion, 2000. 5–51.
Hannoosh, Michele. *Parody and Decadence. Laforgue's* Moralités légendaires. Columbus: Ohio State University Press, 1989.
Huysmans, Joris-Karl. *À rebours.* Paris: Bibliothèque de l'Académie Goncourt, 1922.
Jones, Louisa E. *Pierrot-Watteau: A Nineteenth Century Myth.* Tübingen: Verlag; Paris: Editions Place, 1984.
King, Russell. "The Poet as Clown: Variations on a Theme in Nineteenth-Century French Poetry." *Orbis Litterarum* 33 (1978): 238–52.
Kunzle, David. "The Voices of Silence: Willette, Steinlen, and the Introduction of the Silent Strip in the Chat Noir, with a German Coda." *The Language of Comics: Word and Image.* Eds. Robin Varnum and Christian T. Gibbons. Jackson: UP of Mississippi, 2001. 3–18.
Laforgue, Jules. *Œuvres complètes. Tome Deuxième, 1883–1887.* Eds. Maryke de Courten, Jean-Louis Debauve, Pierre-Olivier Walzer, and David Arkell. 3 vols. Lausanne: L'Âge d'homme, 1995.
———. *Œuvres complètes. Tome Premier, 1860–1883.* Eds. Jean-Louis Debauve, Daniel Grojnowski, Pascal Pia and Pierre-Olivier Walzer. 3 vols. Lausanne: L'Age d'Homme, 1986.
———. *Moralités légendaires.* Eds. Daniel Grojnowski and Henri Scepi. Paris: Flammarion, 2000.
Leclerc, Yvan. "'X en soi' Laforgue et l'identité." *Romantisme: Revue du dix-neuvième siècle* 64 (1989): 29–38.
Mallarmé, Stéphane. *Vers et prose. Morceaux choisis.* Paris: Perrin, 1893.
Starobinski, Jean. *Portrait de l'artiste en saltimbanque.* Geneva: Albert Skira, 1970.

Storey, Robert. *Pierrots on the Stage of Desire: Nineteenth-Century French Literary Artists and the Comic Pantomime*. Princeton, NJ: Princeton University Press, 1985.

Vapereau, Gustave. *Dictionnaire universel des littératures*. 2nd edition. Paris: Librairie Hachette, 1884.

7 The Poetics of Pantomime and Circus, Part II

Octave Mirbeau

Unlike Laforgue, references to Octave Mirbeau do not immediately elicit a mental association with the *funambule*. However, with Laforgue, he is perhaps one of the most important fin-de-siècle writers to absorb the *funambulesque* into the aesthetic practice of the second half of his literary career. Known for the unflinching eye of reproval he cast on his society, his early references to circus acrobats served to contrast their moral rigor with the hypocrisy of representatives of systems of power. His *chronique* on the aerialist Miss Xaeo for the series *Paris déshabillé* (1880) served as the inspiration for *L'Écuyère* (1882), written under the pseudonym Alain Bauquenne. In the former, Miss Xaeo represents a true aristocracy grounded in virtue as a personal and professional ethic. Through her exemplary actions and indisputable talent, the noble aerialist reflects a harsh and unforgiving light on the insincerity and imposture of the members of high society. In *L'Écuyère*, Mirbeau goes even further, literally and symbolically exposing his Julia Forsell to the ruthless and craven machinations of a class that believes that its unmerited prestige and titles give it carte blanche to prey on the vulnerable. If he does not devote another novel to circus acrobats, Mirbeau does not relegate them to the ever-expanding list of victims of the rapacity and depravity of representatives of high society, the state, the church, the military, and education. Increasingly, *funambulesque* desemantization as an aesthetic device replaces the metaphorical acrobats, as Mirbeau's verbal fustigations cede to a more insidious design. Instead of railing against the injustices that he perceives in all limbs of the social body, he becomes himself the acrobat, manipulating the codes of power systems, a manipulation that begins in language and narrative form and whose repercussions are far-reaching. Along the way, he also discovers within himself art liberated from stifling convention.

*

Mirbeau's *Le Jardin des supplices* (1899) initiates the second and last phase of the author's body of work. The novel presents irresolvable contradictions and incongruities that often lead to a suspension of meaning and it possesses, particularly in the last section, a fragmented structure that often suspends narrative progression. These qualities, however, are not limited to *Le Jardin des supplices*, but prevail in all of Mirbeau's subsequent novels. Edmund Wilson faults these features in an article from 1949: "at their soundest, these novels arrive through distortion at satire; at their worst, they are artistically meaningless, a mere procession of obsessive grotesques" (qtd. in McCaffrey 14n22). What Wilson perceived as flaws, however, are evidence on the contrary of a rich, complex, and very modern aesthetic practice, one that informs the later novels as well.

For Lawrence Schehr, *Le Jardin des supplices* offers simultaneous dual readings, the first a political one "inscribed within the parameters of standard decadent writing" in which there are identifiable abusers and victims, and the second an aesthetic of "supplice" in which the only logic is that of an arbitrary torture system where innocence or guilt does not matter (109). Perhaps emblematic of this narrative dualism is the novel's heroine Clara, who would like to be "appreciative subject" *and* "achieve an ecstatic emancipation from the self," to be both herself and other (Ziegler, *Octave* 108). These quite dissimilar narratives found within the same novel are inseparable in the production of an experience that is at the "edges of the representation of the possible" and not simply because of the nature of the tortures that the narrator describes (Schehr 111). The extreme acts that occur in Mirbeau's torture garden are technically "unaccomplishable" and require, as Schehr asserts, a double framework with one providing a certain grounding in an "available structure on which the author and reader can peg the text, a safe paradigm and hermeneutic that permit an interpretation to occur within acceptable norms" (111, 107). But the aesthetic component needs the political/reality-based narrative for another reason, one related to what Wilson identified as distortion. Distortion undermines the very form and epistemological legitimacy of the political/reality-based reading. One finds at work in Mirbeau's subsequent novels the same devices found in *Le Jardin des supplices* – dual semantic categories that create a sense of vertigo in the "fluidity of meaning" and the fragmentation that suspends narrative progression – leading me to wonder if Mirbeau found in the dual semantic model an effective means for fulfilling his political *and* aesthetic objectives within the same work (Ziegler, *Octave* 106).

Contemporaneous with the writing of *Le Jardin des supplices* was the Dreyfus Affair. This monumental injustice corresponded with a radical reconfiguration of his methods in his relentless fight against the corruption and evil of social institutions (the justice system, the army, schools, the church). As well, Mirbeau's aesthetic grounding underwent significant reformulation. With *Le Jardin des supplices*, as Pierre Michel states, Mirbeau seriously challenges the narrative conventions "du roman balzacien et du roman naturaliste" (135). Mirbeau initiates not only the "disintegration of a political apparatus" but that of an aesthetic one as well (Ziegler, *The Nothing Machine* 118).

In *Le Jardin des supplices*, Mirbeau began to encourage contradictions within and between political and aesthetic narratives found in one and the same work in such a way as to dismantle systems of power (political, social, and aesthetic), however temporarily, with each system's own components, indeed, to strip them of their logic and their claim to naturalness. Schehr's comments regarding Mirbellian "supplice" applies to his general literary practice beginning with *Le Jardin des supplices*: what he does in each novel "goes beyond a logic of representation, [...] beyond a logic of logic itself" (117). Mirbeau exceeds the reader's ability to mentally grasp the incongruous pairings of images, words, contexts, and narratives that are the fruit of exploiting the porous interstices of two or more dissimilar cultural codes. After the torture garden, Mirbeau will use a chambermaid, a sanitarium, an automobile, and a dog as "instrument[s] of epistemological destabilization," through which "[t]axonomies, conventions, accepted judgments are overturned" (Ziegler, *Octave* 151, 163).

Mirbeau found the devices of semantic destablization through ambiguous dualisms in the related arts of pantomime and circus clowning and acrobatics, as his frequent references to them attest. These are arts whose performances are permeated with double meanings focalized in the performers' bodies on the stage or in the ring. Arnaud Rykner identifies a dualism in the pantomimist whose body is both "matériau et son outil principal" (34).

Bouissac describes circus performance as a "metacultural code" that plays with the accepted rules governing all cultural systems (7). The spectator may experience either disquieting or delicious freedom in the momentary invalidation of the presumed truth and naturalness of the rules of those systems. In adapting this practice of "being at the same time both 'within' and 'outside of culture,'" Mirbeau moved outside of political and aesthetic systems toward an original poetics (Bouissac 7).

Pantomime Clowning and Epistemological Destabilization

A pantomime performance, as Baudelaire noted in his essay "De l'essence du rire," creates a space permeated by destabilizing vertigo, a state in which events occur that defy all logic. A pantomimist is decapitated and yet is able to retrieve his head and put it into his pocket, the same pocket into which he had earlier stuffed a continual stream of items, with each object becoming increasingly cumbersome or incongruous than the last: "Pierrot passe devant une femme qui lave le carreau de sa porte: après lui avoir dévalisé les poches, il veut faire passer dans les siennes l'éponge, le balai, le baquet et l'eau elle-même" (Baudelaire 376). To bring about an experience of the vertigo of pantomime, it is not enough to put into position the familiar components that one associates with the medium: stock characters like those from the *commedia dell'arte* (Harlequin, Columbine, Pantaloon, etc., to whom we can add Pierrot) and behavior traditionally linked to those masks (Harlequin is witty and resourceful; Columbine is flirtatious and impudent; Pantaloon is exceedingly miserly and an easy mark for pranks; and Pierrot is all appetite, sloth, and navieté). While the vertigo that Baudelaire describes does require the presence of these elements, a vertiginous atmosphere can be generated only through a performative gesture. For Baudelaire, it is the waving of the fairy's wand that issues in the destablizing state of pantomime.[1]

The state of vertigo permits, among other things, unrelated objects or states to occupy momentarily the same space. Accordingly, in Octave Mirbeau's short story "Le Pantalon," Jean des Lombes's death is both comic and tragic; the narrator experiences both remorse and laughter; Jean's frenetic last movements are burlesque and piteous; and even the church decor at the one-year memorial of Jean's death juggles a tone of solemnity with that of joyous celebration in the wedding scheduled to follow.[2] At the moment that the narrator and his accomplice decide to "faire à Jean une farce énorme," the metaphorical equivalent of a wave of a fairy wand pushes the tale over "la frontière du merveilleux," transforming the tale from a conventional short story into a textual pantomime by adopting the format's paradoxical semantic confusion (Baudelaire 377; Mirbeau "Le Pantalon").

Paul Bouissac offers an example of the disorienting pairing of unrelated semantic categories in an act featuring the great English clown Joseph Grimaldi. Impressed by the pomp of a passing hussar, the clown set to making himself a comparable suit: "His hat: a lady's muff, a watch-pocket pinned to the side of it, a table brush stuck out of the crown; his cords and tassels are contrived with a bellrope; boots: a pair of coal scuttles (handles like spurs); the sword: a poker" (170).[3] "The accessories selected by Grimaldi," notes Bouissac,

> were very similar in shape and material to the uniform of a real hussar but as different as possible with respect to the existing cultural system. The trappings of a woman and a hearth were transformed into the paraphernalia of a warrior (one who is defined as virile and remote from the hearth). (170)

The humor of the "imitation" springs from the costume's disquieting yet magical reference to items associated with two dissimilar cultural spaces.

In "Pantomime départementale" and "Le Pantalon," Mirbeau also expands the field of semantic play to each tale's story.[4] In the case of "Pantomime départementale," he opens the semantic floodgates by making a conventional narrative account of a policeman's attempt to arrest a beggar serve simultaneously as a pantomime sketch. Here, the title pairing of "départementale" (referring to the law and its codes) with "pantomime" (a medium in which clowns manipulate social-cultural codes) along with the narrator's characterization of the tale that he is about to tell as both "sombre et funambulesque" (i.e., as belonging to two different semantic registers, the first to a grim law and order story, the second to clowning) work like the waving of the fairy wand to magically place in suspension conventional narrative progression and whatever message the original journalistic account (and ostensibly the re-telling by the narrator) intended to relay. In addition, the title of "Le Pantalon" refers not only to Jean des Lombes's altered pair of pants but also identifies him as Pantaloon. While the incorporation of clowning tactics should technically unfold visually without recourse to language, Mirbeau's two short stories approximate them textually by holding meaning in abeyance in the pairing of incompatible elements, thereby impeding language from conveying a stable, unambiguous message.

As mentioned, the state of vertigo owes everything to the presence of clowns in the two stories. In the ring or on the stage, acrobats and clowns function as real performers and as playing their own bodies, a paradoxical and irresolvable doubling that disturbs the spectator with an existential quandary: on the one hand, there is physical and psychic distance between spectator and performer (she is presenting a rehearsed number, which resembles in that sense that of an actor), and on the other hand, there is a physical and psychic connection between them (the performer addresses the spectator directly as her "real" self).[5] Mirbeau's two short stories reproduce the paradox of differing modalities. The law and order story is recounted by a reliable narrator who offers the reader, to quote Schehr again, a "safe paradigm and hermeneutic that permit an interpretation to occur within acceptable norms" (107). On the other hand, the pantomime recontextualizes the law and order narrative, unraveling the latter's weave in its progression. In the presence of two contradictory codes (one conventional, linked with writing and linear narrative development, the other non-narrative linked to clown performance and the absence of story), the reader undergoes a moment of dizzying liberation from conventions that she took to be true, natural, and real.[6]

In the conventional narratives of "Pantomime départementale" and "Le Pantalon," one finds Mirbeau's familiar moral positions: in the former against the abuse of power by local law enforcement and in the second against church hypocrisy, an approach reminiscent of his earlier novels in which he attacks all forms of social injustice. In those novels, he uses language as a vehicle for the building and communicating of a rational argument and the unmasking of corruption and injustice. In the non-narrative component of the two tales, however, Mirbeau adapts the dynamics of clowning to his literary poetics (the vagabond's unique mode of resistance in "Pantomime départementale" and the pantomime prank in "Le Pantalon"). It is as if Mirbeau's distrust of social systems brought him to a distrust of language, especially traditional modes for the expression of social critique and moral outrage (e.g., the language/voice of reason, sarcasm, satire that uses a person's words/actions against them, parody). He abandoned recourse to them, embracing a more productive and liberating approach directed against language itself, which he reveals in "Pantomime départementale" to be an authoritarian system complicit with other institutions of power like the state, the church, the military, and education, and as equally destructive to the individual.

"Pantomime départementale"[7]

As noted earlier, in his transition from cudgel-wielder to magician of disorder, Mirbeau caused to co-exist in the same tale the semantic registers of two unrelated cultural contexts. It is as if he realized that revealing the hypocrisy and injustice of social institutions within language itself was futile for the righting of wrongs. Indeed, it is as if he rethought his approach entirely, which in turn gave way to new objectives. "Pantomime départementale" is the story of the attempt by a proverbial representative of authority (a policeman) to enforce regulations against vagrancy and mendicity, and thereby restore law and order. Rather than have the narrator rail against or simply ridicule the authorities involved, Mirbeau turns to the vagrant's clowning, a mode existing outside language, for the way to evasion, and for achieving the impossible.[8]

"Pantomime départementale" begins with the image of a vagrant standing longingly before a bakery window. The tattered state of his clothing (his pants are held together beneath his knees "par une triple ligature de ficelle"), his scruffy beard, the holes in his muddy felt slippers, and his empty bindle betray an extreme state of homelessness ("Pantomime"). In an act of Christian charity, the shop employee offers him some bread. A policeman stops him as he leaves and poses a series of questions to which the vagrant fails to respond. The latter's silence leads the policeman to decide to take the vagabond, who is "en état de mendicité," to the police station ("Pantomime").

The vagrant's silence, however, is double, since, in harmony with the story's title, it belongs as well to pantomime. When the officer attempts to arrest the tramp, the latter initiates *funambulesque* methods that remove him entirely from the complicity/refusal dynamic associated with the system that seeks to incarcerate him. He does not attempt to show the policeman the flaw in his reasoning, nor does he cry out against the injustice of the situation, nor does he meekly go along in resignation, accustomed as he must certainly be to imprisonment for vagrancy or mendicity. On the contrary, the tramp uses the street and its features as his apparatus, falling limply to the ground, his slack musculature seeming to merge with the very material of the sidewalk. The policeman tries in vain to get a grip on this suddenly fluid body. Another policeman arrives, and while the two of them succeed in lifting the tramp to an upright position, they are unable to get him to walk, since his body has abandoned itself completely to its own weight: like a rag doll, his knees give way underneath him and his feet will not "prendre contact avec le sol" ("Pantomime"). When they come near a traffic stump, the tramp uses it to slip his arms out of those of his persecutors and falls again like a boneless blob onto the ground, becoming "incrusté, cimenté dans le trottoir" ("Pantomime"). He brings down the second policeman as well, with the latter's boots comically in the air as in a scene in a Keystone Cops film. The tramp's body seems to magically possess two contradictory properties: on the one hand, it is flaccid as it slips through the policemen's grasp, and on the other hand, it is hard and solid like the cement with which it comes into contact.

Three passing soldiers are commandeered "au nom de la loi afin que force restât à l'autorité" ("Pantomime"). After more than a quarter hour of effort, the ten arms finally succeed in getting the tramp on his feet. If they are able to take him off to the station, however, it is because, as the narrator points out, the tramp finally goes along with them "de bonne grâce" ("Pantomime"). If he eventually submits to them, it is as well because the particular freedom that he exercises is by nature short-lived. One cannot maintain true freedom over time because the system (language, law, etc.) will make adjustments and succeed in incorporating the unknown element into its body of knowledge.

While the narrator of the event does describe the tramp's clothing, he does not offer one for the policeman. We do not really require those physical details, he claims, since we can "suppléer à ce manque d'information par des évocations traditionnelles et des iconographies variées qui sont dans toutes les mains": the policeman's uniform clearly communicates law and order (Mirbeau "Pantomime"). It will continue to communicate law and order even when the semantic breach occurs, but now the vagrant will turn the tables as he confers on the policeman a new role as clown. In this new role, the uniform will lose its claim to naturalness and its ability to command. Indeed, the crowd/audience will perceive his authority along the lines of the unmotivated bullying of "*le clown autoritaire*" Lucien Godard at the Cirque Médrano when he would greet the "lower" clowns "comme un fonctionnaire [...] à son guichet," a scene, Régis Gignoux tells us, that "nous jouons chaque jour sans amuser personne" (Disher 199; qtd in Disher 200). In the circus atmosphere, however, an ordinary activity becomes highly amusing, especially when it concerns an abuse of authority that usually produces fear and loathing in its victims. Godard would ask questions reminiscent of Mirbeau's policeman, incurring the spectators' hisses:

> Qu'est-ce que vous voulez? C'est impossible ... Ah! vous avez l'autorisation? Vos papiers? ... Bien ... Parfait ... Passez par ici ... Non, par là ... Défendu de vous asseoir ... Dépêchez-vous. (Disher 200)

While there is no doubt a degree of vicarious revenge in witnessing the comeuppance of a figure of authority by one of his usual victims, the hisses also betray the realization on the part of the audience that Godard's authority is arbitrary: they are, after all, at the circus, not at the tax office. Correspondingly, the policeman's uniform becomes an object of ridicule for the crowd/audience in the new (pantomime) code.

The second half of the tale plays out in the gesture and silence of the clown/pantomimist with the tramp serving as a comic foil to the policemen. The tramp's role as foil is in part facilitated by the description of his appearance recalling a particular clown that appeared in the circus around 1870, the *auguste*. The *auguste* is "ill shaven, ill combed, ill behaved, a slovenly tatterdemalion, sloppy, inarticulate," and when he has a red nose, it is most likely a reference to an inebriated state (Bouissac 164). With the engagement of the semantic shifters of pantomime, we can now understand the journalist's conclusion that the tramp was drunk: his nose was red.[9]

The *auguste* was usually paired with the white-faced clown, but he could also play against the ringmaster. Both the white-faced clown and the ringmaster speak with authority and are the guarantors of social order. When Mirbeau's tale's semantic shift occurs, the policeman unwittingly and unwillingly (since he is a figure turned to ridicule and his uniform temporarily loses its prestige) assumes the role of the straight man to the *auguste*. The policeman is an appropriate stand-in for the white-faced clown and the ringmaster in his proper use of language and of objects in his surroundings. Bouissac notes that the white-faced clown's relation to objects is conventional, that of the *auguste* transgressive: "The system of objects, in all cultures, is governed by rules of shape and proportion, collocation, use and function. The white-faced clown knows and practices these rules, whereas the other clown light-heartedly violates them" (166). The *auguste* does not violate these rules, however, for if he did, it would once again imply the validity of those rules by their very negation: the tramp would be a simple transgressor who can be controlled, that is, someone on whom one can exercise authority, and the object would be used in the manner for which it was intended. What the *auguste* does is reveal the arbitrariness of those uses. Like the *auguste*, the tramp transforms objects into something entirely new, endowing them with uses and functions wholly unrelated to their original ones. He "redesigns" objects to become the precise apparatus of his actions. For example, Disher quotes from the memoirs of the famous Pantaloon (James Barnes) from the early nineteenth century where he describes the objects that he and his troupe were taking with them as they passed through customs in France: "There was a sofa that changed to a fire-grate; a pot of porter with cotton-wool froth, which would transform to a nosegay; a twelfth-cake that turned into a rat-trap; and a long string of sausages, which in an instant became a 'suit of darbies'" (126).

Barnes notes that these objects were "detained" because the "custom-house authorities could not possibly describe them" (Disher 126). There was no word for each of the items, a situation that caused the customs officials to temporarily hold onto them until they figured out a way to log them in a record book. Language as a system of order and knowledge eventually finds a way of categorizing phenomena that seem to escape classification. Roland Barthes notes that power is "perpetual in historical time. Exhausted, defeated here, it reappears there; it never disappears. Make a revolution to destroy it, power will immediately revive and flourish again in the new state of affairs" (4). But until that moment occurs, the tramp makes objects display unstable, continuously shifting properties. His very ordinary props are the pavement, the traffic post, and his own body, which is described as both solid ("une pierre de taille") and soft ("un paquet de chiffons insaisissable," "inébranlable chiffe" (Mirbeau, "Pantomime"). The ordinary environment becomes magical as it is transformed by contact with the man who is perhaps "enchanté" (Mirbeau, "Pantomime").

"Le Pantalon"

On the eve of a hunting party, the narrator and Jacques Cercleux launch a prank in which they have the gamekeeper's wife take in the seams of Jean des Lombes's pants while he sleeps. When they awaken him in the morning, Jacques comments to Jean that his face is black and swollen. Jean looks in a mirror and sees nothing out of the ordinary, so his friends urge him to get dressed. Nevertheless, anxious about his friends' comments regarding his health, he furiously attempts to get his legs into trousers that no longer fit him. His face turns deathly pale and his eyes grow wild as he moves around the bedroom in a panic, knocking himself aimlessly against the walls, offering an exceedingly humorous spectacle. Believing that he is going to die, he cries out for a doctor, then for a priest, making his friends laugh even harder. Then he falls motionless to the floor, spits up streams of red foam, and dies.[10] In the conventional narrative, Jean's hypochondria prevents him from trusting his mirror in which he sees no change in his appearance. In the conventional reading of the tale, Jean dies from an aneurism caused by his extreme state of agitation. In the pantomime reading, he dies from a prank that placed him in existential limbo: his mirror reflects health (his mirror other is in the pink) but his pants communicate illness (he is pathologically bloated), presenting him with a disturbing quandary.

On the surface, Octave Mirbeau's "Le Pantalon" is a tale about an inoffensive prank that goes horribly wrong, ending in the death of its hapless victim. We learn in the first paragraph, however, that Jean des Lombes "n'a jamais eu de chance," a facile explanation for a lifetime of unfortunate events that molded his life and character and determined how that life would end. Like "Pantomime départementale," the tale's title and the narrator's pantomime references signal the presence of a double state, contradicting the narrator's own claim that Jean was the casualty of simple bad luck. On the contrary, the powerful semantic forces of pantomime determine Jean's fate as well, particularly those associated with stock characters: Pantaloon, whose signature long pants stand in ironic contrast to the ones that are altered in the execution of the story's prank and who is the traditional object of pranks[11]; Harlequin, whose bat metaphorically delivers blows to the narrator[12]; and Pierrot, whose white face Jean assumes in his last moments. In traditional pantomime, Pantaloon would not die, since farce characters generally recover miraculously from whatever bodily harm others inflict upon them. Here, however, Jean as Pierrot follows fin-de-siècle pierrotic scenarios in which he can die. In both the prank and pantomime versions of Mirbeau's tale, Jean dies, but the two deaths are not the same. The one in the conventional story is tragic, that in the pantomime is comic.[13]

Like "Pantomime départementale," "Le Pantalon" is a double tale whose pantomimic elements work to suspend the linear progression of the conventional bad luck story. Mirbeau is able to do in the latter what he was unable to do in the former: sustain the suspension of systems of meaning. In the latter tale, the policemen eventually succeed in getting the tramp to the precinct, whereas in "Le Pantalon" the narrator never determines if the circumstances surrounding Jean's death are decidedly comic or tragic, even after the one-year memorial of his death: "Oui, c'est raide! ... mais c'est tordant aussi! ... Il n'y a pas à dire ... C'est tordant! ... Faut-il rire? ... Faut-il pleurer? ..." ("Le Pantalon"). The tale ends in a state of vertigo, caught between two mutually exclusive responses (remorse and hilarity) before the classifying power of language can intervene.

The tale's implementation of two different notions of time works as well to prevent the narrator (and by extension the reader) from arriving at a conclusion. The order of events is on the surface innocuously arranged, starting with the end (the commemoration a year later) and proceeding to the period of Jean's death (the morning of the hunting party). The chronological time of the linear narrative that the reader is able to reconstruct is countered, however, by a pantomime time characterized by cycles, epitomized in the *cercle* of Jacques Cercleux's name.[14] Additionally, the irresolvable pairing of cultural contexts at the church (a death anniversary *and* a wedding) signals that the state of farce has completed its cycle and is beginning afresh, suspending forward motion. The pitiful slipping of Jean into oblivion (none of his friends attend the ceremony) is countered by the comedy of church hypocrisy and venality in its catering to the wealthy and powerful, offering a scene worthy of a Buster Keaton film. The organ player skips notes in his rush to move on to happier wedding melodies; the church omits flowers altogether; the priests race through the commemorative mass and hasten to take down the funerary decor: "Et les enfants de choeur, et les chants de la maîtrise, et les diacres, et l'encens, et l'aspersoir, tout semblait dire: Allons! Dépêchons-nous! ... Et rendons tout de suite ce gêneur à l'éternité!" ("Le Pantalon"). With the cyclical temporality at play in the parallel narrative, not only does the church not have done with Jean once and for all, the pantomime medium menaces it with the annual return of his memory. Rather than resort to a mere satire of the church, Mirbeau ambushes and hog-ties it as an institution, rendering meaningless its services through an ambivalent dual state.

The Aesthetic/Acrobatic Leap into the Abyss from Below and Above

Beginning June 12, 1880, Octave Mirbeau wrote a series of sociological articles in *Le Gaulois*, collected under the rubric *Paris déshabillé*. Among the Parisian social types subjected to his analysis (pseudo-anemics, morphinomaniacs, neurotics, etc., mostly women) was Miss Zaeo, circus trapezist. The true target of his critical eye in this article, however, was less this aerialist than the vogue for the circus acrobat, in particular, the fashionable elite fueling the circus craze. Like his friend, Jules Barbey d'Aurevilly, whom he would sometimes accompany to the circus, Mirbeau admired Miss Zaeo, the tight-rope dancer Miss Oceana, and the *écuyères de haute école* Elisa Petzhold and Émilie Loisset for their skill and their professional and personal ethic, qualities that contrasted with those whose only effort, to borrow from Beaumarchais's *Le Mariage de Figaro* (1778), was that of being born into privilege. This admiration and this opposition inform Mirbeau's 1882 novel *L'Écuyère*, written under the pseudonym Alain Bauquenne.

If he did not devote another novel to the circus acrobat, Mirbeau's references to this figure and the space within which she performed surfaced frequently in other novels. If he did not cultivate a pronounced aesthetic association with the figure of the circus acrobat, he was affected by the entertainment's "perform[ance of] the 'real' and 'impossible,'" the "real" and the "impossible" being terms that are relevant to Mirbeau's incorporation and celebration of a particular facet of circus experience in the novels of his last phase (Carmeli 193). Unlike other fin-de-siècle writers, he did not adopt the acrobat as an allegory of the condition of the artist. Nor did he merely reproduce circus performance as part of the *varia* of the cultural landscape, in which it was a preferred entertainment of men of letters, *Tout Paris*, and the bourgeoisie. Rather, as with his appropriation of the doubling mechanisms in pantomime, he tapped the circus's manipulation of cultural codes and semantic registers, particularly beginning with *Le Jardin des supplices*. Mirbeau stands out among many of his contemporaries in his sensitive understanding and manipulation of the poetics of circus performance, a perception reminiscent not only of the Jules Laforgue of *Moralités légendaires* but of that author's location of the space of the acrobat as one equally capable of producing a liberating creativity.

Even the deceptively casual references that acknowledge the reality of the circus as a contemporary entertainment possess unexpected depth and anticipate his embracing of its aesthetic in the later novels. In *Le Calvaire* (1886), Jean Mintié's wanton mistress Juliette proposes to take riding lessons at the Cirque d'Été with the intention of becoming an *écuyère*, a reference that echoes Mirbeau's *Paris déshabillé* article on Miss Zaeo from six years earlier. This is not an instance in which the circus could be interchangeable with the theater, with Juliette considering becoming an actress. Mirbeau intended a striking ironic image, drawing on the chastity and self-restraint for which circus equestriennes were celebrated – Mirbeau's own Julia Forsell from *L'Écuyère* being an example – and contrasting those qualities with the depravity that characterizes Juliette. He also invariably emphasizes, like the Goncourt brothers, the high level of skill involved in circus acrobatics, a skill that comes from years of a training begun best in one's childhood. Juliette's idea for getting employment, therefore, is ludicrous because it is not even remotely attainable for her. Her lofty plans to contribute financially to the well-being of the couple will unfold ironically, not in a circus ring, but in a brothel, a site irreconcilable with aspirations to moral and physical purity and self-discipline.

A similar use of the consummate skill of the acrobat is made in *Sébastien Roch* (1890). During the period in which Père de Marel gives music lessons to young Sébastien, he comes to the conclusion that the boy is too passionate and sensitive, and ultimately ill-suited to a discipline requiring application and self-control. He comments to the boy that "J'aimerais mieux vous apprendre la gymnastique … le trapèze vous vaudrait mieux" (138). Père de Marel's exclamation establishes acrobatic arts like the flying trapeze as requiring an impossibly high degree of mastery and precision, and comically a skill far outside those possessed by the reverend father. Père de Marel is just one of the many smotherers of imagination and creativity in Mirbeau's early semi-autobiographical novels, and in this instance, he erects an abyss between Sébastien and music, one of the things that the boy truly loves.

The narrator does not conceptualize Père de Marel's stifling action in terms of an abyss, but he could easily have, given how often the image emerges at critical moments in all of Mirbeau's novels. The abyss evolves over the course of the novels, however, taking the form in the first three of a looming chasm at the edge of which characters teeter precariously and becoming in *Dans le ciel* (1892–93) an abyss from "en haut" as well as from "en bas" (Baudelaire, *Œuvres complètes* 88). The abyss from below in the early novels is oppressive. In *Octave Mirbeau's Fictions of the Transcendental*, Ziegler refers to the spiritual aspirations of these early protagonists as being defined by the death drive; they possess a will to return to the insentience of the womb, and this often takes the form of feeling the pull of the abyss from below. But, beginning with *Le Jardin des supplices* (1899), the double abyss is transformed into something positive, something that Ziegler describes as the author's arrival at the conceptualization of a secular transcendental, at an acknowledgment and acceptance of the unknown and unknowable that characterizes the experience of the vertigo in the abyss, and an embracing of it as a life and creative force. *Le vertige* is primarily a source of distress in the early novels; in the later novels, it is a source of exhilaration.

The abyss becomes a powerful symbol as early as Mibeau's *L'Écuyère*, and it is in line with the death drive identified by Ziegler. Julia Forsell, whose sense of honor never recovers after she is violently raped, desires ardently for the Undine, or water nymph, to spirit her deep into the watery abyss. Mirbeau did not describe the abyss from above as such in this novel, but the opposition materializes in Julia's desire to ascend during the practice and performance of her equestrian act. Recalling almost verbatim the strivings of the acrobatic clown of Banville's poem "Le Saut du tremplin", Julia aspires to go "Plus haut! toujours plus haut bondir" to that pure, transcendent realm above that defines her personal and professional ethic (*L'Écuyère* 70).[15]

Nor does the image of mirroring abysses emerge in *L'Abbé Jules* (1888), when the narrator relates the stunned experience of the parishioners at Jules's first mass. He describes the effect of Jules's confession to a series of shocking sins as comparable to "la sensation qui vous saisit à regarder un gymnaste, évoluant dans le vide, sur un trapèze, au-dessus d'un abîme ... Quelque chose comme le choc en retour du vertige de la mort" (52). The image equates, of course, the parishoners' suspended, but very powerful, reaction to the heightened tension one feels at the sight of an acrobat's life in the balance. The faithful are seated in the pews of a holy refuge that they expect to protect them from the impurities of the world and even absolve them of their own immoral behavior. The incongruity of the flood and the magnitude of Jules's unholy revelations in such a pious place shock them dumb. Jules is a trapezist poised precariously over the abyss and the vertigo that the parishioners feel is defined by an existential uncertainty: is Jules a colossal sinner or a saint? Their own salvation hangs in the balance as well. Jules raises his arms just at the moment that a ray of sun filters through the rose window and illuminates his face in "une étrange lueur d'arc-en-ciel" (52). Just when the heavens seem to designate him as a resplendent soul, however, "un nuage passa, voilant le soleil, et l'auréole disparut," plunging the congregation back into uncertainty and moral torment (52).

On the surface, one would say that, swinging between two moral poles, Jules is at cross-purposes with himself – one side is good, the other malicious. It is true that to every good deed that he might carry out, he cannot stop himself from letting his pleasure in torturing others take over. True emotion and generosity generally succumb to their counterpart in cynicism and malevolence. This polarity between the conception of a just action and its ultimate execution features a gap, however, a "trou" that Jules "franchissait d'une grotesque culbute, comme un clown," an image that adds a third component to the seeming binary relation (72). This "trou" is yet another abyss. In describing Jules's metaphorical leap over it, the narrator offers the portrait of the abbot as clown, with Jules executing a somersault.

In light of Mirbeau's association of Jules with an acrobat, we can define the latter's state, not by the terms of a binary opposition with the malevolent side being more firmly engrained in Jules's character than the benevolent one, but rather by a triangulated model, with the third component emerging in the passage through the "trou" or the "vide." In his passage through the abyss, Jules experiences the co-presence in the same space and time of "la cohérence massive de l'ordre établi" *and* of its absolute invalidation (Starobinski 143–44). In *L'Abbé Jules*, we are not always the privileged witnesses as we were in Jules's scandalous mass to how others deal with this existential quandary, this *mise en question* of those social conventions that we accept as real and natural. We do know from this scene that the congregation did not experience exhilarating freedom. If Jules does not evince childlike joy, he does relish the sense of play – which assumes, of course, malicious dimensions – and the liberating power that comes from the dismantling of accepted notions of what is usual and correct, a power that he abuses relentlessly.

It is interesting to note that his nephew Albert interprets Jules's power precisely in terms of circus and sideshow arts and their peculiar ability to place the spectator in a state of existential limbo. In anticipation of his uncle's arrival, Albert as narrator states that he experienced the same "peur attractive" that would grip him when the fair was in town (18). Drawn to *and* frightened of fairground performers, he both dreads *and* desires intensely meeting his uncle, who threatens to be "un personnage prodigieux, incompréhensible, doué de facultés diaboliques, plus hallucinant mille fois que ce paillasse à perruque rouge, qui avalait des sabres et de l'étoupe enflammée" (18).

While the majority of Mirbeau's characters from the early novels feel anguish in moments of vertigo, the sickly, malformed boy Georges Robin from *L'Abbé Jules* does not. Traumatized by the sight of his parents engaging in sex, he confides in Albert that he plans to run away with traveling acrobats the next time a circus caravan rolls through town. Georges's desire to join the circus is not a stereotypical option for children who are merely fascinated by the entertainment's dizzying movement, its colors, smells, and sounds. In line with Mirbeau's use of images of the acrobat and the abyss, Georges's project takes on richer signification. He seeks the medium's non-sense, its ability to negate what he finds too emotionally unbearable about his parents.

Sébastien Roch does not expressly desire to run away with the circus like young Georges Robin, but he does attempt to run away from the Jesuit school, and the description of his flight is toward a circus abyss: the space through which he moves is both cirque as geological ring *and* circus ring in its production of that abyss. Sébastien makes a beeline for the trees, keeping his eyes fixed forward on "l'espace vide, dont on ne savait pas si le fond était de la terre solide, ou de l'eau remuante, et que le cirque noir des sapins emplissait d'un mystère d'abîme" (*Sébastien Roch* 24). The mystery of the abyss induces in him a feeling of weightlessness that in adults would be accompanied by disquieting vertigo. It is significant here that Sébastien is a child like Georges Robin: for both boys, the abyss possesses attractive qualities. Consequently, as Sébastien moves through the ring of trees, "il ne percevait plus la résistance de la terre, sous ses pieds. Il marchait comme en rêve, si léger qu'il se croyait soutenu, emporté par deux grandes ailes au-dessus du sol" (24).

In *Dans le ciel*, the narrator describes young Georges's recovery from meningitis in similar terms. For a short period during his illness, he is in a state of limbo that he calls "le néant," which he associates with the sensations of death and which for him are strangely pleasant. He shares the acrobat's weightlessness when she is in mid-flight: "Je vécus dans le vide, suspendu et bercé dans l'infini, sans aucun point de contact avec la terre" (42). As a young man, however, the "vide" becomes a troubling abyss, particularly the one from above. Living in a ruined abbey on a mountain peak, Georges feels tormented by the endless sky. All who visit him are similarly oppressed. They succumb, he says, to vertigo because there is "[r]ien que du ciel, rien que du vide autour de soi … Jamais la terre, jamais quelque chose de ferme et de connu où poser sa vue!" (*Dans le ciel* 26). But he does not need to be physically on a mountaintop to encounter the sense of vertigo. Earlier, during his friend Lucien's absence from Paris, Georges's painful struggle to write, to create art, provokes a death-like state that takes the form of an upside-down sky: "C'était en moi et autour de moi, comme un immense abîme blanchâtre, comme un grand ciel immobile, que traversaient, de temps en temps, des vols d'oiseaux chimériques, des fuites de bêtes éperdues, métamorphoses de mes pensées en déroute" (90).

It is in *Dans le ciel* that the crisis of creativity and imagination becomes associated with the two abysses. Here, however, the abyss from below is troubling, not for the vertigo that it instills in one, but from one's inability to access its beauty. On one of their evening strolls, Lucien and Georges watch reflections on the water of the Seine. While Lucien prods Georges to concur in his vague, unimaginative assessment of the nature of the beauty of the scene before them ("C'est beau, ça, hein?"), the narrator provides the missing details that anticipate the use to which the narrators in Mirbeau's later novels put the image of the mirroring abysses (87). What seemingly begins as a faithful and relatively untroubling rendering of the reflections of bridge lights in the Seine's waters through the metaphor of its "reflets changeants comme une robe de bal," soon threatens to unhinge the two men with the descriptors losing their reassuring definition as the lights on the sturdy bridges up above become moving, truncated zigzags in the undulating river below or sink improbably both into "incandescent" colonnades of light and into "des profondeurs infinies" of darkness, both described as "ciels renversés" and as an upside-down "pâle firmament" peopled with indistinct, violent silhouettes (87). The violence of the silhouettes comes partially from a contrast of images against the water, but it also comes from the negation that occurs over the "trou" over which Jules leaps, the negation that makes firmaments of the body of a river and abysses of the sky.

Georges cannot express what he sees because he is as yet unformed aesthetically and is too much under the sway of Lucien's dominating influence. As for Lucien, he is incapable of conveying in words the beauty of this scene in the same way that he finds himself inadequate to the task of interpreting what he sees in a manure pile: "une féerie de flores, de faunes, de chevelures, un éclatement de vie splendide" (88). Without offering Lucien an escape from his creative impasse, his perceptions of the teeming life in a manure pile as a "féerie" anticipate Mirbeau's own aesthetic evolution in his relation to the abyss. As in the earlier river scene, if Lucien recognizes the experience of the "ciels renversés" as a rich source for creation, he is powerless to translate it into words, much less a work of art.

References to the atmosphere of the "féerie" return repeatedly in *Le Jardin des supplices*, particularly in chapters 7 and 8 as the narrator and Clara visit the garden's series of torture stations. The "enchantement perpétuel" that permeates their exploration of the grounds assumes vertiginous qualities. The torture garden's climate ushers in a magical air of vertigo in its unsettling reversals, in the irresolvable co-presence of dissimilar cultural codes, and ultimately, in the opening of the floodgates of semantic registers. There is a basic inversion in the identification of Clara with the male and the narrator with the female. Reminiscent of the indeterminate tenor of "Le Pantalon" ("Faut-il rire? ... Faut-il pleurer? ..."), Clara's pout is both "comique et tragique, tout ensemble" (284). One torturer's face expresses a "cruauté comique" (286). At one moment Clara is both "gaie et sérieuse, souriante et le front barré de plis d'ombre qu'elle avait, dans la colère comme dans la volupté" (296). At another, the narrator is helpless to say if Clara's tone is that of "l'émotion ou de l'ironie," but the reader should understand that in this space it is both emotional *and* ironic (297).

Clara embodies and embraces semantic indeterminateness, and accordingly she does not hesitate to take a "heedless plunge into the unknown," something Georges and Lucien of *Dans le ciel* were unable to do (Ziegler, *Octave* 95). Gleefully, she applauds the torturer's creations that resemble the transformation props described by the Pantaloon James Barnes. In the garden's topsy-turvy world, an altogether new aesthetic emerges. The torturer's skill likened to that of a tailor, he presents a coolie whose peeled skin resembles uncannily an Inverness cape; a male prisoner's body that is mutilated and then magically transformed into that of a woman. More difficult to execute but considered a thrilling challenge, the torturer looks forward to the opportunity to turn a woman's body into that of a man (287). These tortures and others are not simply "unaccomplishable," they are impossible (Schehr 111). Like Barnes's pantomime troupe's dual-purpose transformation props, these creations in flesh defy apprehension and categorization, and make the right kind of reader laugh, and not just when examined out of context as Roland Villeneuve suggests.[16]

The narrator identifies the upside-down world of the garden as a circus space the closer he and Clara get to the bell torture. Not far from it, a Buddhist monk, who may be the warden of the garden, trains mongooses to do acrobatic somersaults. And in an echo of the scene in which Sébastien Roch attempts to flee the Jesuit school, Mirbeau again makes the word "circus" serve double duty: it is both corrie and the space of circus performance. The word is emblematic of the garden's vertiginous atmosphere where dissimilar codes occupy the same space. At the center of the geographical formation that is also a circus ring is the bell which the narrator describes as a "gouffre en l'air, un abîme suspendu qui semblait monter de la terre au ciel, et dont on ne voyait pas le fond" (309). The upside-down abyss makes its return not as a source of anxiety but as a positive site of creation – however, creation of another, unstable order, one in which the separation between material and semantic registers falls away, allowing for impossibly beautiful imagery. The variously colored pheasants that circle "au-dessus du cirque blanc, brodaient d'éclatantes soies, de décors sveltes et changeants, le lumineux profond du ciel" (312). And as Clara and the narrator leave the garden, they contemplate once again the strangely beautiful flowers displaying the color of blood in its many states. In one sense, they take on the color of the substance that has been nourishing them. In another, they reflect the nature of a space in which there are no more semantic borders, leading to fluid movement between them. Some of the flowers resemble cabbalistic characters: the white water lilies and lotuses look like decapitated floating heads, and a carp moving below the surface of the water is just like the "pensées rouges dans le cerveau d'une femme" (317). These unexpected analogies presciently prefigure the wild and exciting pairings produced by Surrealist poets, particularly André Breton in his 1931 "L'Union libre."

Éléonore Roy-Reverzy identifies Mirbeau's aesthetic practice in this novel as going "au-delà de la ruine des catégories esthétiques" to announce "l'avènement d'une autre poétique, d'une poétique moderne" (qtd. in Mirbeau, *Œuvres* II, 1224n68). In the novels that follow *Le Jardin des supplices*, the protagonists are willing to venture into vertigo amid the ruins of known and accepted aesthetic and epistemological categories. Célestine in *Le Journal d'une femme de chambre* (1900) feels drawn to Joseph "avec la violence d'un vertige" (*Oeuvres* II, 581). In his unwillingness to travel through semantic confusion, Roger Fresselou, who points toward "le cirque des montagnes noires" that wall him in his desolate aerie – once again, a "cirque" that is both corrie and circus ring – serves as a contrast to the narrator of *Les 21 jours d'un neurasthénique* (1901). While words and ideas "n'ont pas de sens" for Fresselou (here, an echo of the abyss's and the circus ring's suspension of meaning), he is oppressed and paralyzed to the point of inaction (265). Not the narrator, however, who descends the mountain and returns to civilization.

The nature of that return for him and for the narrator of *La 628-E8* (1907) is not defined by cynical resignation. Rather, they plunge headlong like Clara into vertigo. In *La 628-E8*, the narrator praises the sensation of delirious movement in cars, hot air balloons and boats, on skates and on swings using vocabulary that echoes that of Mirbeau's equestrian Julia Forsell in her aspiration to go ever higher and higher. In this sense, Mirbeau's relationship to the abyss comes full circle. The narrator of *La 628-E8* embraces all that "m'élève et m'emporte, très vite, ailleurs, plus loin, plus haut, toujours plus haut et toujours plus loin, au-delà de moi-même" (386). He savors the disorienting moments that make him feel as if he were drunk, even as he balances precariously "au bord de l'espace" and by extension, of time (389). His protective dermal shell seems to fall away such that he becomes a small part of that space.

This modern aesthetic produces delirious images of puddles of water reflecting the blue sky, perceived as fragments of a great mirror/sky that has crashed to the ground and shattered as his car speeds along the road (450). One of many glorious scenes of semantic detachment and displacement in *La 628-E8* takes place in the Netherlands, where the narrator observes peasants unloading cheese wheels from canal boats. These peasants have

> en se renvoyant ces ballons ronds et rouges, des figures rondes et rouges, si bien que, parfois, nous pourrions croire qu'ils jouent à la balle, avec leurs propres têtes, et que nous assistons au dernier acte d'une opérette féerique, ou encore à un ballet de jongleurs au bord de l'eau. (472)

This is the air of "le merveilleux" that Baudelaire breathed when watching English pantomime. It is astonishing how often the figure of an acrobat accompanies Mirbeau's narrators' encounters with the vertigo of the abyss, from above and from below.

Bouissac identifies children and artists as the spectators most likely to understand, appreciate, and encourage the way in which the circus plays with social codes and conventions. Mirbeau was one such artist, and his localization of the medium's poetics in the ripping of signifiers from their conventional signifieds distinguishes his aesthetic as decidedly modern. His circus and pantomime metaphors in the works of his last phase possess rich layers of semantic interference, and it is through them that we can mark his aesthetic evolution. On the fragmentation that marked his later novels, Maxime Revon commented that "ils dénoncent simplement avec une singulière bouffonnerie son tempérament de violent" (qtd. in McCaffrey 3). It would perhaps be more pertinent to say that, renouncing conventional denunciation of all knowledge systems, including language, Mirbeau's later novels dismantle them in a singular fashion by means of the metacultural manipulations – the transformation props – of buffoonery and acrobatics.

Notes

1 Carmeli identifies an equally performative gesture at the circus in the waving of the acrobat's hand (210).

2 The short story was published on June 25, 1899, in *Le Journal*, the same publication year of *Le Jardin des supplices*.

3 Bouissac technically "quotes" Disher, but the citation is far from faithful. We can attribute this error possibly to the translator who may have translated into English Bouissac's own translation of Disher's text from English into French. The quoting is further complicated in that Disher himself was citing a newspaper review for which he provided no information. The paraphrase that is Bouissac's "quote," however, captures the spirit of Grimaldi's improvisation of a hussar's uniform. One finds a reproduction of Grimaldi in this costume in Disher's book: "GRIMALDI, Bold Dragoon in the Popular Pantomime of the Red Dwarf" (104–05).

4 "Pantomime départementale" was published on March 1, 1896, in *Le Journal*.

5 Disher introduces his chapter on Pantaloon with a quote from James M. Barrie that illustrates the perplexing identity of a clown performer:

> As he was on the stage, so he was off it, clothes, powder, and all; he was not acting a part in the harlequinade, he was merely being himself. It was undoubtedly this strange discovery that set us writing a play about him.
>
> Of course bitter controversy may come of this, for not every one will agree that we are right. It is well known among the *cognoscenti* that actors in general are not the same off the stage as on; that they dress for their parts, speak words written for them which they do not necessarily believe, and afterwards wash the whole thing off and then go to clubs and cross their legs. I accept this to be so (though I think it is a pity), but Pantaloon was never an actor in that sense; he would have scorned to speak words written for him by any whippersnapper; what he said and did before the footlights were the result of mature conviction and represented his philosophy of life. (119)

6 A circus performance is generally one without a story. As Bouissac notes, "a narrator is never more at ease in describing a circus performance than when

an accident occurs, i.e., when the characteristic structure of an acrobatic act breaks down and becomes a story" (43). There is technically little chance for an accident in a clown performance, especially since, when a clown engages an additional competing but incompatible cultural code during a number, all potential for a story breaks down completely.

7 Circus clowning and pantomime often shared the same spaces and the lines separating them were often blurred. In Philip Astley's circus (late eighteenth and early nineteenth centuries), "comic relief was supplied by pantomime folk" (Disher 187). While pantomimes often took place in circuses in the last half of the nineteenth century (as they did at Astley's in the early part), both clowning (of the circus variety) and pantomime appeared on music-hall stages. Mirbeau's narrator in "Pantomime départementale" refers specifically to the pantomimes of Paul Margueritte: the scene "pourrait se passer à Paris, sur un théâtre d'art, en pantomime réglée par monsieur Paul Margueritte qui [...] excella dans ce genre dramatique délicieux, et malheureusement, presque délaissé aujourd'hui" ("Pantomime"). Margueritte, however, was not a trained pantomimist and certainly not of the acrobatic variety. Given the physical nature of the beggar's evasive tactics in the tale, it is likely that Margueritte (who actively worked to revive classic pantomime with his own scenarios and with the creation of the Cercle funambulesque in 1888) functioned more as a familiar reference for the reader. Mirbeau's tramp recalls more pliable clown representatives, from the comic strip Pierrot of Willette to more professional acrobatic pantomimists like the Hanlon-Lees or the Martinetti brothers who entertained Paris with their antics in the late 1870s and 1880s.

8 Mirbeau was the champion of "les déshérités, ces errants, pauvres condamnés à l'errance, victimes expiatoire du système capitaliste" (Wagniart 306).

9 Mirbeau quotes the journalist's description: "La mendicité fut d'autant plus facile à constater que le mendiant était ivre" ("Pantomime").

10 This description could come from Paul Margueritte's pantomime *Pierrot assassin de sa femme* (1882), in which Pierrot's frantic movements preceding his death from tickling resemble those of Jean des Lombes: "Pierrot [...] tord son corps pris de folie. Il tourne sur lui-même, trois fois: ses bras errent, ses doigts griffent dans le vide" (Bonnet 70). Jean's death from extreme fear for his health is also strangely reminiscent of the equally comical death of a train traveler in *Le Jardin des supplices*. In the "Frontispiece," a young man recounts his own experience of the murder impulse. While a train passenger was sleeping, he approached him with extended hands, ready to strangle him. The passenger awoke to this frightening vision, without however uttering words other than astonishment at his compartment mate's actions ("Quoi? ... quoi? ... quoi? ..."): "À chaque minute, l'épouvante grandissait dans le regard de l'homme qui, peu à peu, se révulsa, et je vis son visage se tacher de rouge, puis se violacer, puis se raidir" (175). If the man's fixed stare remained unchanged, it is because he had died of a "cerebral congestion" (175). Rykner describes the Pierrot of fin-de-siècle pantomime as being defined by the epileptic spasm, possessing movements evocative of Charcot's hysterics in the teaching theater and in photographs. For his part, Charcot had earlier turned to pantomime for the staging of his patients, designating the wild twisting of their faces and bodies as "clownisme" (Rykner 43).

11 The association of Jean with Pantaloon is equally overdetermined by his last name, which refers to the lumbar or loin region with which Pantaloon is associated.

12 The narrator spent the night on the town before the commemoration of Jean's death and has "le cerveau meurtri par les coups de matraque des boissons américaines" ("Le Pantalon").

13 Mirbeau's reference to Paul Margueritte in "Pantomime départementale" would perhaps have been better suited to "Le Pantalon," since Pierrot dies in Margueritte's first pantomime, *Pierrot assassin de sa femme* (1882).

14 The narrator even refers to natural cycles in the opening section: "la terre tourne, les saisons se succèdent, les fleurs éclosent et se fanent" ("Le Pantalon").

15 Banville's acrobat cries out: "Plus haut encor, jusqu'au ciel pur!" and "Plus haut! plus loin! de l'air! du bleu!/Des ailes! des ailes! des ailes!" (243).

16 "Roland Villeneuve écrit, à propos du discours du bourreau: "Séparé du contexte, ce passage paraît cocasse. On rirait presque de bon coeur" (qtd. in Mirbeau, *Le Jardin* 1223n28).

Works Cited

Baudelaire, Charles. *Œuvres complètes*. Ed. Marcel A. Ruff. Paris: Editions du Seuil, 1968.

Banville, Théodore de. *Œuvres poétiques complètes*. Ed. Peter J. Edwards. Vol. 3. Paris: Honoré Champion, 1995.

Bonnet, Gilles, ed. *Pantomimes fin de siècle*. Paris: Éditions Kimé, 2008.

Bouissac, Paul. *Circus and Culture. A Semiotic Approach*. Bloomington and London: Indiana UP, 1976.

Carmeli, Yoram. "Performing the 'Real' and 'Impossible' in the British Traveling Circus." *Semiotica* 80.3 (August 1990): 193–220.

Disher, M. Willson. *Clowns and Pantomimes*. London: Constable, 1925.

McCaffrey, Enda. *Octave Mirbeau's Literary and Intellectual Evolution as a French Writer, 1880–1914*. Lewiston, NY: E. Mellen P, 2000.

Michel, Pierre. Introduction [to *Le Jardin des supplices*]. *Œuvre romanesque*. By Octave Mirbeau. Ed. Pierre Michel. Vol. 2. Paris: Buchet/Chastel, 2001. 133–54.

Mirbeau, Octave. *Le Jardin des supplices. Œuvre romanesque*. Vol. 2. Ed. Pierre Michel. Paris: Buchet/Chastel, 2001.

———. "Le Pantalon." La collection électronique de la Bibliothèque Municipale de Lisieux. 24 February 2019 <http://www.bmlisieux.com/litterature/mirbeau/pantalon.htm>.

———. "Pantomime départementale." La collection électronique de la Bibliothèque Municipale de Lisieux. 24 February 2019 <http://www.bmlisieux.com/litterature/mirbeau/pantomim.htm>.

———. *Paris déshabillé*. Eds. Jean-François Nivet and Pierre Michel. Paris: L'Echoppe, 1991.

Rykner, Arnaud. *Corps obscènes: pantomime, tableau vivant, et autres images pas sages, suivi de Note sur le dispositif*. Paris: Orizons, 2014.

Schehr, Lawrence. "Mirbeau's Ultraviolence." *SubStance* 27.2 (1998): 106–27.

Wagniart, Jean-François. "Les Représentations de l'errance et des vagabonds dans *l'œuvre* d'Octave Mirbeau." *Cahiers Octave Mirbeau* 8 (2001): 306–15.

Ziegler, Robert. *The Nothing Machine: The Fiction of Octave Mirbeau*. Amsterdam and New York: Rodopi, 2007.

———. *Octave Mirbeau's Fictions of the Transcendental*. Newark: U of Delaware P, 2015.

Epilogue

In the last two decades of the nineteenth century, pantomime and urban stationary circus began a steady decline, with both being displaced by the arrival of moving pictures in 1895. Pantomime provided cinema with narrative and performance templates, but cinema did not return the favor by prolonging pantomime's stage life.[1] While the circus did not contribute anything more than gymnastic numbers as one attraction among the many to which the new medium turned for feeding exhibition needs in its first five years, stationary circus structures gave the cinema some of its earliest movie theaters.[2] French pantomime would have died earlier, particularly in the capital, had it not been for the short-lived boost that it received from a circle of writers and artists who renewed interest in the medium in the last decade of the century: the Cercle funambulesque (1888–98). This group was behind the creation and production of some critically successful but rarely popular pantomimes. As for acrobats, they joined traveling companies, never again to capture the attention of elegant Parisians as they rode their horses proudly in the Bois de Boulogne like Mirbeau's Julia Forsell or to have *Tout Paris* at their feet like Banville's Hébé Caristi (91).[3]

Artists and writers continued to champion the acrobat in the twentieth century. Pablo Picasso spent evenings with clowns in the bar at the Cirque Médrano. He made acrobats the center of a series of paintings from his blue period. Georges Rouault painted portraits of himself as a clown. Henri de Toulouse-Lautrec made 39 circus paintings in colored pencil that liberated him literally and figuratively from the sanitorium to which his family had had him committed. Poets like Guillaume Apollinaire, Pierre Réverdy, Max Jacob, and Tristan Tzara devoted poems to acrobats. Apollinaire first used the word "surrealism" to describe the circus-inspired ballet *Parade* (1917), co-created by Jean Cocteau (text), Pablo Picasso (curtain and costumes), Léonide Massine (choreography), and Érik Satie (music), identifying the performance space of the acrobat as fundamentally modern. *Parade*'s artists embraced an aesthetic of blurred boundaries with Satie's music, for example, achieving a dimension allowing the audience to listen simultaneously to the outdoor *parade* and the interior spectacle. As for Cocteau, he aspired to eliminate the barriers between spectator and performer, and real and make-believe. The crossing of thresholds had become a core practice of the twentieth-century avant-garde.

In *Fonctions de la peinture*, Fernand Léger encourages artists to go to the circus: "Vous quittez vos rectangles, vos fenêtres géométriques, et vous allez au pays des cercles en action" (153). The spectator-acrobat relation that appears in the circus ring breaks barriers so that one can "pousser vers la liberté" (153). For Léger, the site for flashes of liberty, however, has the potential to extend well beyond the circus ring to encompass the world.

It is hard to imagine a flash of freedom like Paul Éluard's opening line in "La Terre est bleue comme une orange" (*L'Amour la poésie*, 1929), in which the signifier of color becomes attached to the semantic category of shape without the earlier example of bizarre analogies of the sort that Huysmans experienced at the Folies Bergère, and of which the source was the desemantization produced by attendance at a trapeze act. It was at that moment that acrobats could disappear back into the nebulous fog, the same one into which Villiers had the Hanlon-Lees disappear and from which Chéret had his lady aerialists emerge. *Funambulesque* freedom had been absorbed into the creative imaginary of the twentieth century.

Note

1 While it is clear that silent film was essentially a pantomimic medium, this did not translate into cinema plundering stage pantomime for scenarios. There is at least one instance of which I am aware, however, in which a Hanlon-Lees pantomime was adapted to the screen in France: *Do mi sol do*. Georges Méliès's *Le Maestro Do-Mi-Sol-Do* (1906) offers a modified version of the piece with the story taking place in a musician's practice room where the instruments themselves, not flying and careening musicians, attack him. Clearly, Méliès did not possess the acrobatic skill of the Hanlon-Lees, whose pantomimes he most certainly saw as a teenager in his native Paris during the troupe's 1878–79 season at the Folies Bergère. The father of trick cinematography did have the ability, however, to use time-lapse technique and substitution splicing to approximate the acrobats' production of the impossible performance of the real.

2 For example, Gaumont opened its first Paris cinema, the Cinéma-Palace, in the former Hippodrome in 1908.

3 The celebrated nineteenth-century tightrope walker Mme Saqui was the inspiration for Banville's Hébé Caristi from his short story "Une vieille funambule" (*Les Parisiennes de Paris*, 1866).

Works Cited

Banville, Théodore de. *Les Parisiennes de Paris*. Paris: Michel Lévy Frères, 1866.

Léger, Fernand. *Fonctions de la peinture*. Paris: Éditions Gonthier, 1963.

Index

Note: Page numbers followed by "n" denote endnotes.